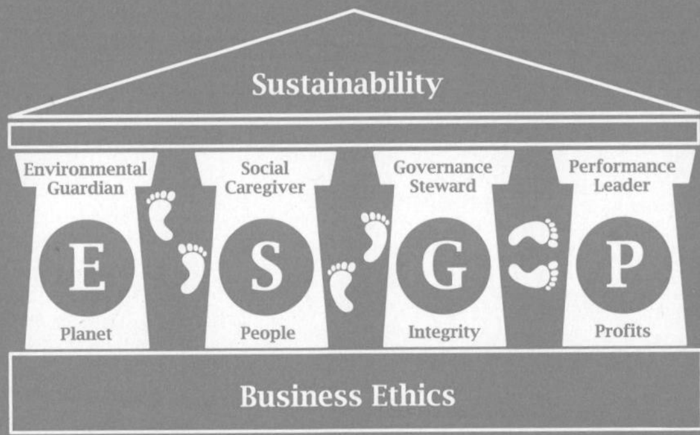

The Practice of ESG Management

The Practice of
ESG Management

Prologue

Respected Leaders of the Beloved Companies

Representatives of the company and top management involved in the business shall appear as such. Of course, if you are humble and not arrogant towards human society, the natural environment and all your stakeholders, love and respect will follow you like a shadow. The goal of carbon neutral and ESG management, which recently emerged during the global pandemic, is also to receive constant love and respect from inside and outside social groups.

Apple, Amazon, Microsoft, Walt Disney, Starbucks, Berkshire Hathaway, Alphabet (Google), JP Morgan, Netflix, and Costco were ranked as the 10 most admired companies in the world for 2021 according to Fortune magazine. These companies also had strong stock values.

	amazon	Microsoft	Walt Disney	
Steve Jobs Tim Cook	Jeff Bezos	Bill Gates Steve Ballmer Satya Nadella	Walt Disney Bob Chapek	Howard Schultz Kevin Johnson Sarya Nadella(BOD)
Berkshire Hathaway Inc.	Alphabet Google	JPMorgan Chase & Co.	NETFLIX	Costco Wholesale
Warren Buffett	Larry Page Sundar Pichai	John P. Morgan Jamie Dimon	Reed Hastings Ted Sarandos	James Sinegal Craing Jelnek

For the aviation industry, for example, Delta Air Lines has been named the Most Admired and Successful Company for the past 11 years in a row. On the other hand, United Airlines' customer service is relatively poor but growing. Midwest Airlines had a reputation for providing the best service to its customers, but it failed to survive the global financial crisis that began in 2008 and went bankrupt in 2010. Meanwhile, Texas Airlines' Frank Lorenzo, known as the master of airline mergers and acquisitions, succeeded, but eventually disappeared from the business due to financial difficulties and labor disputes.

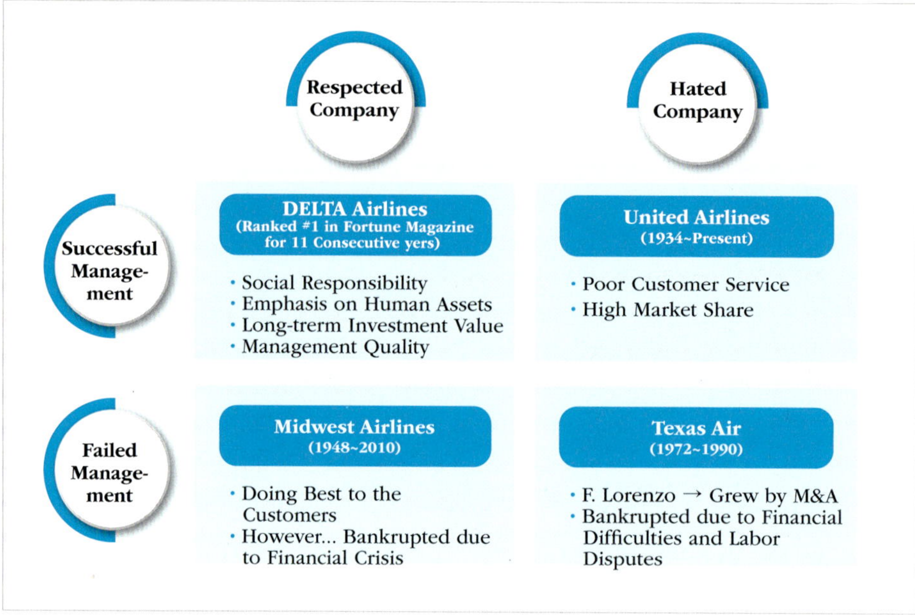

The business model of ESG management should also not disappear suddenly like Midwest Airlines or Texas Air, so that the results of ESG management based on [ESG practice → Corporate performance], that is, business model on integrity management, lead to the higher performance linking directly to the long-term sustainability.[1)]

Among the recent ESG performance indicators, eco-friendly issues such as carbon neutrality related to the global climate changes are emerging as the core of international trade and socially responsible management. Meanwhile, Patagonia and Nestlé, recognized as global examples of ESG management, immediately switched to a strategy that respects the environment and health when they were branded respectively as 'environmental villains' and 'obesity products', and as a result, each year sales growth rate of 30% and sustainable revenue generation. As such, environmental, health and eco-friendly issues to save the earth and mankind are being treated as long-term investment activities that companies must strategically pursue in line with global standards and support from the government.

Therefore, environmental issues such as carbon neutrality are 'survival tasks' that the government must initiate to lead the industry and corporate management in a global and eco-friendly way. Meanwhile, corporate social and governance issues are being led by companies as 'strategic tasks' to pursue sustainable growth according to the circumstances of individual companies in each country.

This includes efforts to lay the groundwork for ethical compliance management projects promoted by the Korean companies such as Samsung, LG, SK, CJ, Kyobo, and Yuhan Corp. and utilizing the 'measurable' index rather than just to show plausibility on corporate social responsibility. In addition, the sustainability management report or ESG management report including the contents of improvement by year must be published transparently.

Then, *"Are managers sufficiently motivated to promote carbon neutrality and ESG management?"*, and *"Which of the ESG factors do we pay the most attention and concentration?"* Without doubt, the CEO's will for achievement would be the most important in the strategic practice of ESG management.

Comparing Alderfer's ERG Motivational Model to the CEO's ESG Management Performance Types, environmental indicators will be a key mandate essential for compliance with global standards and government policies. Social indicators are related to the social impact of a company as an obligation to make strategic choices to fulfill its responsibilities. In addition, governance indicators can be divided into voluntary participation obligations for transparent management practice.[2)]

Duty / Motivation	Compulsory	Strategic	Voluntary
ESG: Responsible Investment	Environmental	Social	Governance
ERG: Motivational Needs	Existence	Relatedness	Growth

International studies have shown that ESG practices in companies have resulted in long-term growth and performance (Eccles et al., 2014; 2020). However, even Warren Buffett of Berkshire Hathaway, who emphasized CSR saying that *"Even*

2) According to Clayton Alderfer (1972), human motivation comes from three things: existence needs, relatedness needs, and growth needs. The need for existence (E) refers to the physiological and physical needs necessary for survival, the relationship need (R) refers to the desire to maintain relationships with others in society, and the growth need (G) refers to the inner growth desire to complete the self. Needs depend on how well other needs are satisfied, and two or more needs can occur at the same time. Comparing Alderfer's ERG theory with ESG management can effectively determine the weight and importance of each ESG element.

20 years of achievements can be destroyed in just five minutes," recently said: *"Creating legal profits is the biggest goal of a company."* As the ESG management appears dazzling, he refused to participate voluntarily.[3] Therefore, ESG may not be the only solution for sustainable management.

	CSR	ESG
Approach	• Doing well by 'Doing good'	• Systematic application of ESG disciplines within a business
Benefit	• ROI (return on investment) for CSR is the positive impact that interest in stakeholders can have on retention, loyalty and recruitment of employees and customers, due to the 'reputation effect'	• ESG relates to its impact on accessibility to capital and the cost of capital
Audiences	• Consumers • Employees • Communities • NGOs	• Primarily targeting investors, potential investors, influencers (financial media), benchmarks and indices (MSCI, DJSI, IFRS, SASB, FTSE4Good, etc)
Long-term	• Reputation	• Risk mitigation • Financial stability

Companies are even more familiar with CSR, *i.e.* the concept of corporate social responsibility rather than ESG, but in line with the recent trend of responsible ESG management which divides CSR into three areas of separation of issues, Korean government also declared *"2030 Nationally Determined Contribution (NDC)"*, and *"2050 Long-term low greenhouse gas Emission Development Strategies (LEDS)"* participating in *'Green Growth'* and emission trading schemes that target innovatively reduce greenhouse gases (GHG).

As the contents and goals pursued by the three main areas of ESG are quite different, it is also necessary to reflect the role of major actors who animate each of the ESG area: Environmental preservation has been emphasized by the government with support and regulation, but it is given as an essential duty for companies to take the lead. Social responsibility was seen as a corporate promotional event, but it is reshaping as a strategic investment target for sustainable growth. Governance has been led by the public opinion with the spirit of time,

3) WSJ (May 6, 2021), BlackRock at Odds with Warren Buffett's Berkshire Hathaway over Disclosures.

but now voluntary compliance is strongly required. In fact, companies, as their **mission**, must play the role of **environmental** guardians, social caregivers, and ethics stewards for more transparent **governance**.

In this book, the following concerns motivated us to address sustainability:

1. *ESG is a new burden or a new opportunity for companies?*
2. *Why ESG management is important and how to practice it?*
3. *Why ESG should be practiced based on ethics and integrity?*
4. *How efforts on ESG and ESG assessment been made in Korea?*
5. *What are some of the world's best ESG management practices?*

In summary, the indicators for each area of ESG for corporate sustainability contain the wisdom of 'The Art of War' saying that, *"It is not the strong who survive, but the survivors are the strong."* In the era of digital transformation, ESG management performed and evaluated by humans as a 'thinking reed (*roseau pensant*)' is now measured and analyzed with a 'thinking network (*reseau pensant*)' the artificial intelligence. A forthcoming book will cover state-of-the-art ESG assessments and evaluation methods. We look forward to continuing to send in ideas and critiques like co-authors from academia and industry.

January 2023

Kichan PARK (kichan@inha.ac.kr)
Jeongchul CHOI (215213@inha.ac.kr)
Françoise CHEVALIER (chevalier@hec.fr)

Essential Questions on ESG Management

Triple Bottom Line

1. What are the main sources of happiness by generation (Baby Boomer to MZ)?
2. What is the definition and content of each of SBL, DBL, TBL, and QBL?
3. Explain the 'Three Zeros (Carbon-Corruption-Abuse)' of ESG management.
4. Explain the 'Three Zeros (Poverty-Unemployment-Carbon)' of M. Yunus.
5. What is the 'Golden Circle (Why-How-What)' of Simon Sinek?

Social Value

1. Which is the example of a 'respected CEO of a beloved company'?
2. What are the similarities and differences between CSR and ESG?
3. How should ESG's non-financial performance be measured?
4. Can good deeds offset bad deeds in business management?
5. Why creating corporate social value became important?

Corporate Sustainability

1. Is more disclosure of ESG-related information desirable?
2. Does ESG management guarantee corporate sustainability?
3. What are the development changes of SR→CSR→CSV→ESG?
4. Why organizational culture is important in ESG management?
5. What are the 6 Principles of ESG management performance reporting?

Spirit of the Times

1. How has Western Zeitgeist changed historically?
2. Are stock market investors customers of corporations?
3. What are P. Drucker's 'The 5 Most Important Questions'?
4. Why is the social aspect of a company perceived negatively?
5. What is P. Drucker's 'Rational, Integrity, and Creative Management'?

Exemplary Companies

1. How to remove of the illusion of 'Good company Syndrome'?
2. Explain CSR by comparing the morals and ethics of business.
3. Explain the employment, industrial, customer and stakeholder relations.
4. What is the representative ESG example in Korean corporate history?
5. Why governance issues are more important among ESG in Korea?

ESG Management

1. Describe ESG as SRI, SI, ROI, and RM (Risk Management).
2. Compare HERI's ESG evaluation index with the K-ESG index.
3. Describe the universality and specificity of the UN PRI standards.
4. Explain the relationship between ESG and performance by Eccles et al.
5. What is the role of environmental keeper, social caregiver, ethical steward?

Global Standards

1. What are the problems with the K-ESG announced in December 2021?
2. Compare and explain the GRI and SASB criteria as ESG indicators.
3. Compare and explain W. Visser's five steps in CSR practice.
4. Compare negative screening with positive screening.
5. Describe the 7 core themes of ISO26000.

Practice of ESG Management

1. What is the development process of the GRI guidelines launched in 1997?
2. Compare and explain the broad-consensual content of TBL.
3. Compare the 17 SDGs with the 7 Principles of ISO26000.
4. Describe 'Fiduciary Duties in the 21st Century'.
5. Describe the 36 reporting standards of the GRI.

Case Studies

1. Will ESG develop into a sustainable management model?
2. Will the global ESG evaluation model be unified into one?

Contents

The Practice of
ESG Management

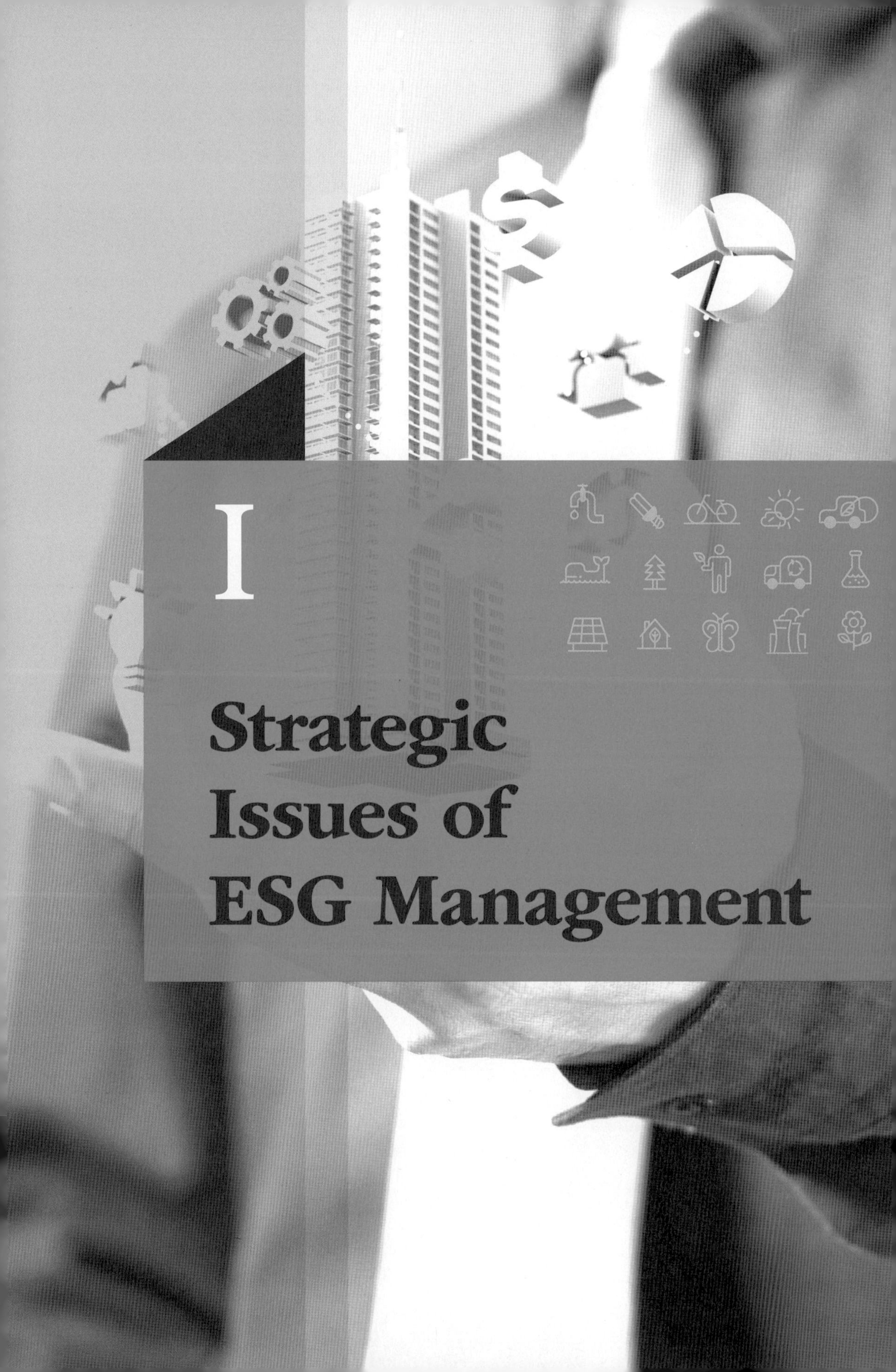

I

Strategic Issues of ESG Management

I

Strategic Issues of ESG Management

1. ESG and Economic Performance
2. ESG and Quantitative Measurement
3. ESG and Responsible Investment
4. ESG and Sustainability Management
5. ESG and Information Disclosure
6. ESG and Future Development

Capitalism, in which the role of corporations is emphasized, has undergone historical changes, as major economists have argued: After the mercantilism of the 15th to the 18th century, the capitalism born with the Industrial Revolution in the 18th century led to *industrial capitalism* and *financial capitalism* in the 19th century. Then, during the Great Depression of 1929 in the United States, a revised capitalism emerged with a planned economy run by the government. After the neoclassical economics of the 1980s, the Chicago school of Neoliberal economics, which insisted that government intervention be minimized again, is now turns to *stakeholder capitalism*, with ESG being of global concern.

1. Classical Economics

- A. Smith: Theory of Moral Sentiments (1759), The Wealth of Nations (1776)
  → The Invisible Hand
- D. Ricardo: Introduction to Political Economy and Taxation (1817)
  → Free Trade and Comparative Advantage

2. Marxist Economics

- Communist Manifesto (1848), Capital (1867)
  → "The invisible hand of the market is maintained by the visible fist of the government"

3. Max Weber's Economics

- Protestant ethics and the spirit of capitalism (1905)
  → Market and exchange rather than production are the essence of capitalism, bureaucracy and corporations contribute to the development of capitalism

4. The German Historical School and the Austrian School

- Historical School: Financial system that pursues profit through money and credit
- Austrian School (Schumpeter): Changing Markets with Creative Destruction

5. Keynesian Economics

- 《The General Theory of Employment, Interest and Money (1937)》
  → Partial socialization of investment, government-led deficit-financing expenditures during recessions

6. The Chicago School of Neoclassical Economics

- M. Friedman: Labor market flexibility, corporate governance by major shareholders, capital market-based fund management rather than government finance, etc.
- Advocacy of free market and monetarism
  → Rejecting the labor theory of value, practicing it as a neoliberal political economy

1 ESG and Economic Performance

In the case of Korea, the ESG indicators have been widely used since the Hankyoreh Newspaper's HERI (Hankyoreh Economy and Society Research Institute) team started research on corporate social responsibility (CSR) by introducing an ESG evaluation method in early 2008. Keywords for CSR and sustainable management were presented. Accordingly, the HERI team formed the ESG index to evaluate the level of CSR practice based on the following ESG-related criteria.

> First, CSR (corporate social responsibility) includes the sustainability management of the company.
> Second, sustainability management includes both financial and non-financial business matters for stakeholders.
> Third, the CSR assessment covers the three ESG dimensions: Environmental (E), Social (S) and Governance (G).
> Fourth, companies with higher ESG performance are assessed based on recent research results that show greater sustainability.
> Fifth, ESG performance is evaluated according to global SRI (socially responsible investing) standards, and evaluation indicators are reestablished in stages according to Asian values.

Therefore, the concept of ESG covered in this book came from CSR, *i.e.*, the pursuit of corporate sustainability contained in CSR activities, and the three areas to assess from overall the level of sustainability of the company, namely, ESG such as environmental, social and governance.

Issue 1 Isn't ESG relevant to a company's financial performance in terms of profit generation?

In the case of measuring, analyzing, and evaluating ESG management activities, the process of evaluating both the non-financial performance of a company in creating social value and ultimately the economic or financial performance of creating long-term profits, *i.e.*, [ESG management practice → social value creation → long-term profit creation], each should be treated as [input variable →

parameter/control variable → output variable], and it is necessary to handle it according to the mechanism of virtuous or vicious cycle. The claim that the social value creation effect of a company leads to long-term profits as a mediator or moderator is proven by various research results.[4)]

Now, every single country is calling for companies to create sustainable outcomes through responsible ESG impact investing as a major policy. However, since there are research results showing significantly different causal relationships according to the characteristics of countries, industries, and companies, there is a 'compromise' between the 'value creation' and 'profit creation' effects of each factor of ESG.

ESG management (input) → Social value creation (parameter) → Long-term profit creation (output / outcome) process

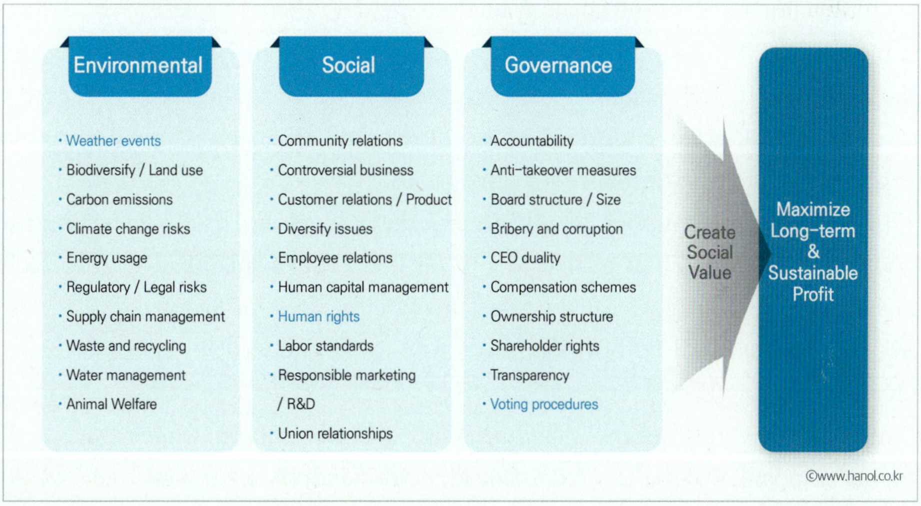

2 ESG and Quantitative Measurement

In the early 21st century, when ESG indicators began to appear, fewer companies were writing sustainability reports, and the means to analyze non-financial

4) Jensen, 2002; Porter & Kramer, 2011; Eccles et al., 2011/2014/2019; Dent et al., 2019; Fairchild, 2020; Kong, 2020; Sinha, 2021; Baue, 2021; Hinton, 2021.

information was far less important than it is today. Even an accurate analysis of each company was difficult to compare internationally.

Recently, as the use of artificial intelligence (AI) and big data has become common and the disclosure of related information by companies has spread, the accuracy and reliability of statistics have greatly increased. As a result of this huge investment in high-tech companies, increasing interest in ESG, and investment and regulatory trends in ESG, the importance of statistical explanatory power and corporate ESG information disclosure is also rapidly increasing.

Issue 2 How to measure the non-financial performance related qualitative indicators covered by the ESG?

For example, the explanatory power of GEMLT, MSCI-Morgan Stanley Capital International's ESG information analysis model, almost tripled in 2018-2020 compared to 2007-2018. Thanks to the GEMLT-ESG risk analysis model, the predictive power of ESG statistics grows to the same level as the predictive power of current stock price, and MSCI is also developing an analysis model to assess ESG management performance for universities.

In addition, the number of institutions that assess and provide qualitative non-financial information related to ESG in the form of quantitative data, such as Bloomberg, Corporate Knights, Sustainanalytics, Oekom Research, CDP (Carbon Disclosure Project), Forbes Magazine, Arabesque, and FTSE, also increasing rapidly.[5)]

ESG analysis institutions, including MSCI and Bloomberg, target more than 10,000 companies globally: ① Classification and analysis of strengths and weaknesses by ESG indicator[6)] ② Alcohol, gambling, weapons, military, nuclear power, tobacco, drugs, etc.[7)] Classification and analysis of business are being carried out. As an example, the results of MSCI's ESG ranking of the 5 best companies in 2020 are as follows:

5) Confer MSCI-ESG Fund Ratings Methodology and MSCI-ESG Ratings Methodology. "Introducing MSCI FaCS: A New Factor Classification Standard for Equity Portfolios" (Bonne G., Roisenberg L., Subramanian R., and Melas D., 2018), *MSCI Research Insight*.

6) Positive screening method.

7) Negative screening method.

2020 MSCI ESG Sustainability Assessment Rankings

TOP 5 Companies	1. Edwards Lifescience	2. Equinix	3. Prologis	4. Emcor Group	5. Cadence Design System
Industry	Medical Supplies	Finance, Real Estate, Trust		Building Management	S/W Design
ESG Evaluation	AA	AA	AA	AA	AA
Comprehensive Evaluation	99	99	99	99	98
Strength Evaluation	95	95	94	87	92
EPS (earnings per share)	92	94	85	96	97
SMR[8)] Evaluation	A	C	A	B	A
3year's EPS Growth	25	79	12	24	23
ROE (return on equity)	32	5	8	16	46
Sales Change Rate (%)	15	10	38	19	12
EPS Rate of Change (%)	11	99	18	21	27
Dividend Income	NA	1.72	2.38	0.37	NA

Source: Investor's Business Daily (Dec 2, 2019).

Data on carbon emission, particularly important among environmental indicators, can be provided by CDP.[9)] Here, the company's direct emissions are relatively accurate. However, how to accurately measure the amount of indirect carbon emitted from the supply chain remains an important challenge.

---

8) SMR (Superior Sales Growth, Profit Margins, Return on Equity Ratio): IBD (Investor's Business Daily) is an index that comprehensively looks at a company's total sales, net profit, and ROE.

9) Carbon Disclosure Project (CDP): A global climate change project to build a low-carbon society and a sustainable social foundation, started in 2000 by CDP, a British non-profit organization of the same name.

3 ESG and Responsible Investment

ESG-related indicators are presented in the UNGC (*"Who Cares Wins"*, 2004) Report, arousing the role of companies as 'Environment Guardian (E)', 'Social Caregiver (S)', and 'Ethical Governance Steward (G)'. It can be introduced as a strategic guide to improve the long-term corporate sustainability, breaking away from the traditional notion of generating short-term revenue.

On the other hand, the recently emerging theory of responsible ESG investing emphasizes only the specific activities of asset management institutions and institutional investors from the point of view of narrow-minded investors. Nevertheless, it also shows a positive effect that the ESG performance evaluation index has been confirmed as a global standard for selecting '*excellent (exemplary) companies*' in our society. Emphasizing the role of ESG management in each ESG disciplines can be clearly illustrated as shown in the following figure:

The practice of ESG management and the role of company

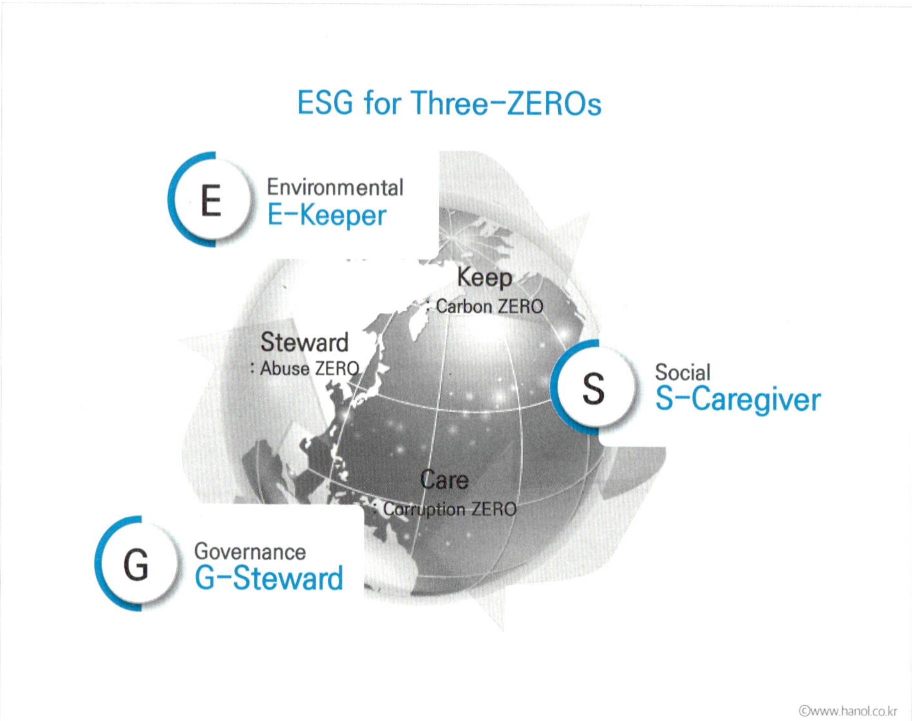

Issue 3 How does the responsible ESG investing work in practice?

Artificial intelligence and big data facilitate the analysis and evaluation of responsible ESG investments. On the other hand, there is a limit to focusing more on financial analysis, rather than the basic philosophy of ESG management, which evaluates the qualitative performance of a company.

Of course, evaluation activities centered on responsible investing that emerged as an early stage in ESG management are meaningful in that they remind investors of the importance of ESG. Four fundamental principles apply to this responsible ESG investment evaluation:

[Assessment Principle 1: *Exclusion criteria*] Socially undesirable industries and businesses such as tobacco, alcoholic beverages, gambling, and narcotics are excluded from the responsible investing assessment.
[Assessment Principle 2: *Selection criteria*] The responsible ESG investing assessment focuses on a positive screening, which selects the best ESG-related companies (good company, exemplary company, and excellent company) and encourages the investment.
[Assessment Principle 3: *Role criteria*] Asset owners and institutional investors intervene directly in target companies as shareholders. An important aspect of the assessment is how they are involved in strategic issues such as the appointment of officers and outside directors, including the CEO, and large-scale investment decisions etc.
[Assessment Principle 4: *Aggregation criteria*] Examine the strengths and weaknesses of ESG management activities for a certain period. If a business causes a social scandal such as a court lawsuit or a 'Gapjil' (abuse of positional power) incident, negative screening is applied to exclude or deduct points based on proportion.

For example, the Expert Committee for the selection of 'EA30-CSR Excellent Companies' by HERI in Korea strongly applied a negative screening method of excluding the company based on the principle that *"Good Karma cannot make up for the bad Karma"*. On the other hand, the MSCI-ESG assessments in the United States are applying a point-deduction method such that *"Bad Karma can be compensated for by good Karma"*.

As such, one of the biggest issues in assessing responsible ESG investing is to determine the standard for overall judgment whether to exclude companies that have caused 'bad karma (corrupt management)', or whether to treat bad karma as a deduction issue by the level of incident. Although the global standards recommend a combination of good and bad deeds (karma), Korea still has a strong national sentiment for the exclusionary method applying the negative screenings.

4 ESG and Sustainability Management

The background to the emergence of ESG movement is the incident on March 24, 1989, when an oil tanker named *Exxon Valdez* was stranded in Prince Williams Strait, Alaska, and a huge amount of oil sank and escaped, killing the animals and plants in the sea. In Korea too, there was a crude oil spill off the coast of 'Taean' on December 7, 2007, it reminded us of the terrible environmental damage caused by just such a corporate incident.

Issue 4 How can ESG management ensure corporate sustainability?

In December 2004, the UN Global Compact (UNGC), released a report titled "*Who Cares Wins*" emphasizing corporate social responsibility and concern for sustainability for the coexistence of the global environment and business. As such, the conceptual basis of ESG is laid on CSR, and the common goal pursued is set on sustainability. In 2011, Porter and Kramer highlighted 'Creating Shared Value (CSV)'[10] as win-win management for corporate TBL-*Triple Bottom Line* (Environmental, Social, Economic) issues, meanwhile Nadja Guenster et al. (2011)[11] suggested 'Creating Economic Value through Eco-friendly Approach' that aims to improve the corporate sustainability.

Bob Eccles et al. (2014) analyzed 90 companies with high ESG performance and 90 companies with low ESG performance from 1992 to 2010 and found that the financial performance of companies with high ESG performance obviously increased year by year. In other words, a model of virtuous cycle mechanism, [ESG management → Financial performance → Sustainability], has been demonstrated. Thus, active investment (*input*) in ESG appears as financial performance (*parameter*) such as reducing risks and increasing profits of a company. It also showed that when financial performance is improved (*output and outcome*), the brand image and sustainability are also enhanced.[12]

As such, ESG activities are emerging as a necessity rather than an option by standardizing corporate ESG indicators globally or nationally and making it mandatory to disclose relevant corporate information. It is the mechanism of [Corporate capacity and strategy (*input variable*) → ESG practice (*parameter*) → Improved sustainability (*output and outcome variable*)], emphasizing the mediating roles of the ESG management. Simply put, it is clearly demonstrated by the research findings that "*there is no sustainability without the strategic practice of ESG management*".

10) Michael E. Porter and Mark R. Kramer (2011), "Creating Shared Value", *HBR*. Jan-Feb 2011.

11) Guenster N, Derwall J, Bauer. R, and Koedijk K. (2011), "The Economic Value of Corporate Eco-Efficiency", *European Financial Management* (Vol.17, Issue 4, pp.679-704).

12) Bob Eccles, Ioannis Ioannou, and Georges Serafeim (2014), "The impact of corporate sustainability on organizational processes and performance", *Management Science* (60, no.11, pp.2835-2857).

Corporate sustainability strengthening process through ESG

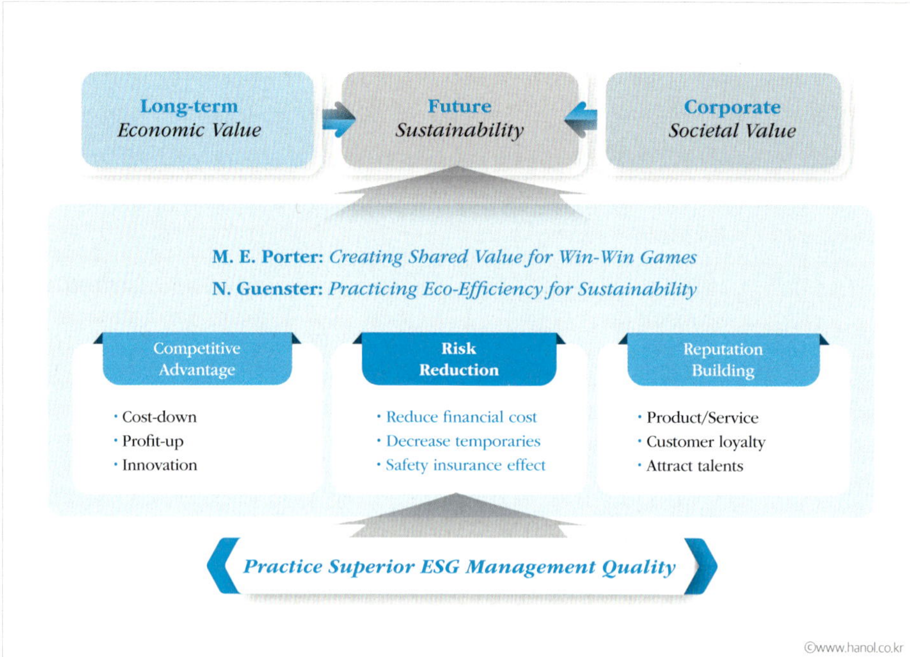

5 ESG and Information Disclosure

A company's ESG practice activities are evaluated by the input activities of the company's strategy to ESG indicators, and the level of sustainability indicated by the ESG practice activities. However, there is a problem in that the evaluation methods and contents for the level of entry and exit activities are quite different depending on the institution (asset owner, professional evaluation institution, etc.) that evaluates the ESG management performance of a company.

Disclosure of corporate information is important for accurate evaluation, but the more non-financial ESG information is disclosed, the less consistent the evaluation results for each evaluation institution.[13)]

13) Christensen, Dane M. and Serafeim, George and Sikochi, Anywhere, "Why is Corporate Virtue in the Eye of the Beholder? The Case of ESG Ratings" (February 26, 2021). *The Accounting Review*.

Issue 5 Is it more desirable for ESG-related companies to disclose more information?

Studies prior to 2017 found a consistent relationship between ESG ratings and stock market, financial performance, financial constraints, and governance characteristics.[14] On the other hand, studies from 2018 onwards highlight the inconsistency of ESG ratings, even using the same S&P 500 company information.[15] As such, it is difficult to define the ESG criteria itself in evaluating and measuring ESG performance levels, and how to guide investors to make effective investment decisions when ESG ratings vary by rating agency remains an important issue.

In other words, in the absence of a social consensus (or social contract) for the international GRI standards or the domestic K-ESG standards, the ESG ratings provided by various rating agencies may rather confuse all stakeholders, including investors.

Therefore, as investors, we need to be clear about what our chosen methodology measures and why we evaluate with these indicators and methods. Otherwise, you won't be able to understand the truth behind your ESG score. As such, non-financial information used in ESG indicators is implied from the subjective point of view of companies, and it is natural that significantly different ratings are given to each evaluation agency as the breadth and depth of information disclosure deepens.

Although corporate information disclosure is essential for ESG assessment, as the amount of information disclosure increases, and as subjective information used by evaluation agencies increases accordingly, a dilemma of presenting different results among the agencies and in addition, more diverse interpretations of social and governance related variables are expected.

In fact, in a study by Christenson et al. (2021), the assessment scores for the environmental (E) and social (S) sector among the ESG domains were more diverse than those for the governance sector (G), and each assessment agency

14) Cheng, Ioannou, Serafeim, 2014; Khan, Serafeim, Yoon, 2016; Hubbard, Christensen, Graffin, 2017.

15) Sindreu & Kent, 2018; Allen, 2018; Berg, Koelbel, Rigobon, 2020; Cookson & Niessner, 2020.

showed inconsistent results. Therefore, in order to measure ESG performance correctly, the following conditions must be met in the first step:

First, companies must disclose information for each non-financial ESG sector.
Second, information must distinguish between objectively comparable items and subjective enterprise-specific items.
Third, the input factor (disclosure of information) indicating the source of the output factor (evaluation score) should be explained.
Fourth, a positive screening target and a negative screening target should be provided separately.
Fifth, global standards and evaluation methods for ESG evaluation agencies and differentiation by country are strongly required.

6 ESG and Future Development

Since CSR (corporate social responsibility) was first emphasized by Howard R. Bowen in 1953, and Peter F. Drucker in 1954, efforts have been made to prove the new role of capitalism, company, and management in the creation of corporate social value.

The evolution from CSR to ESG: Key studies

years	Representative argument
1950's	SR (social responsibility): Bowen (1953), Drucker (1954)
1960's	SR (social responsibility): Davis (1960), Frederick (1960), McGuire (1963)
1970's	CSR (corporate social responsibility): Heald (1970), Johnson (1971), Steiner (1971)
1980's	CSR (corporate social responsibility): Jones (1980), Tuzzolino & Armandi (1981), Strand (1983)
1990's	CSR (social contribution): Carroll (1991), Elkington (1998)
2000's	CSR (social contribution): Carroll (2004), Porter & Kramer (2006)
2010's	CSV (creating shared value): Porter & Kramer (2011)
2020's	ESG (environmental-social-governance): UNGC (2004), Eccles et al. (2014, 2019), Christensen et al. (2020)

Digital transformation through technological innovation, including artificial intelligence, provides a more rational analysis of these changes in corporate roles. It is very clear that the current focus on responsible ESG investing is biased in favor of investors. Management was also well aware that ESG, which started from CSR, was refocused on three areas: separation of powers and a responsible management system, was important for corporate value and investment attraction. However, they were reluctant to implement it as it was considered an additional burden on companies

Establishment of Organizational Culture for ESG Management

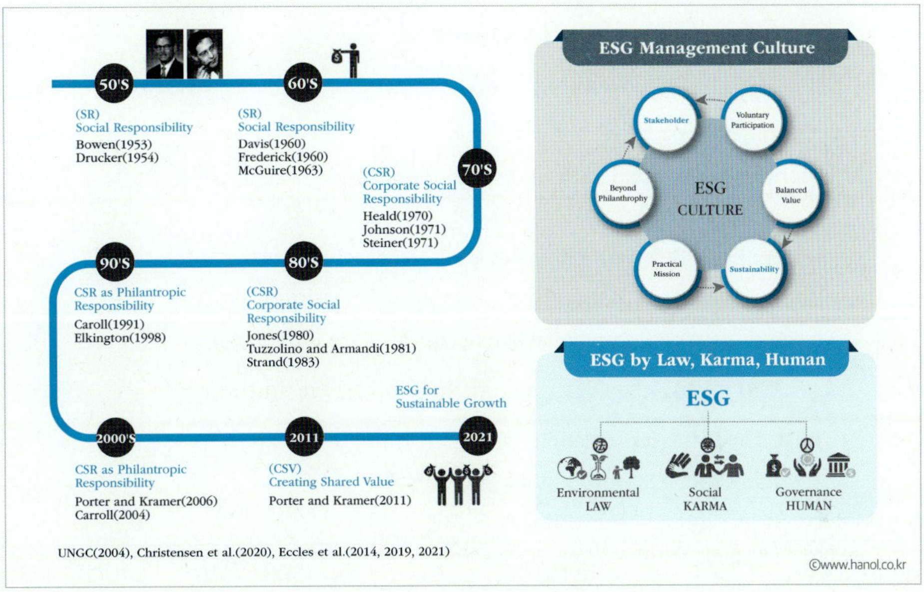

The future of ESG lies in the strategic execution of ESG management, and the success of ESG management depends on the *priorities and weights* of each action plan. This goes beyond volunteering and sponsoring, creating social and economic value, and balancing all stakeholders.

Establishing and improving corporate sustainability requires the creation of a new organizational ESG culture. As the first task for this, it is required to first prepare the ESG management report (or sustainability report) according to the following principles presented by GRI Standards or Euronext (2020): Prioritize topics; Benchmark performance; Collect accurate data; Include negative screenings with Consistent methodology and Clear reporting layout, etc.

Guidelines to Issuers for ESG Reporting (Euronext, 2020)

Summary

1. **What is ESG and Who is this Guidance for?**

2. **Why Report on ESG Considerations?**
   1) Supporting corporate reputation and strategy
   2) Addressing ESG issues as Key Component of Investor Relations
      ① Identifying and understanding investors' ESG information needs
      ② ESG A compass for risk mitigation
   3) Align your strategy with regulatory requirements

3. **Guiding Principles of Report Preparation**
   1) Responsibility and oversight of the records
   2) Relevance and materiality

4. **ESG Reporting Process**
   1) Materiality analysis: identification and prioritization
      ① Identifying stakeholders mapping their interest
      ② Identifying the relevant themes for the company (Materiality)
      ③ Prioritization
   2) Implementation and operational management
   3) Drafting and presentation
      ① Quality of the information
      ② Format of the presentation
      ③ Making your ESG information accessible
   4) Reporting as a continuous dialogue
   5) Assessing and assuring

5. **Using Capital Markets to Implement ESG**
   1) The Regulatory landscape of Green Bonds
   2) Equity financing for your transition

6. **EURONEXT and its role in sustainability**

7. **Appendix**
   1) Key ESG reporting regulations
   2) Reference to existing standards
   3) Guidance for issuers in preparing their report
   4) Objectives for reporting on ESG

Source: "*Exchange in Focus: Euronext ESG Guidelines for listed companies*", (14 January 2020, Sustainable Stock Exchanges Initiatives).

Issue 6 How the ESG management will evolve in the future?

From a narrow perspective on responsible ESG investing, companies that are unfamiliar with, such as *Edwards Lifescience, Equinix, Prologis and Emcor Group* stand out. However, from a more global perspective, companies such as *Patagonia, Nvidia, Microsoft, Accenture*, and *Siemens* emerge as global leaders.

In these companies, ESG is internalized as their management philosophy and mission statement and being practiced as a management strategy built with their own DNA. It reminds us that as Peter F. Drucker has pointed out, *"However great a strategic activity may be, it will never succeed unless it is formed with a desirable organizational culture unique to a company".*[16)]

Reinforcing corporate sustainability by creating long-term profits is a topic that has been raised as a corporate social responsibility (CSR) activity. And ESG is abbreviated with these keywords, along with a bunch of metrics for each ESG

16) Drucker underlined the importance of organizational culture stating: *"Culture eats strategy for its breakfast"*, that when considered as a weighting factor, organizational culture is 85%, and whatever the excellence of a management strategy, it is only 15%.

area to show that the goals are fairly identical.

In the early 20th century, managers who followed *'Scientific Management'* were engrossed in the division of labor and productivity, that is, improving the efficiency of work ignoring the spirit of coexistence and co-prosperity ideas of F.W. Taylor, it was resulted in numerous industrial accidents and miseries.[17)]

Therefore, if asset managers and institutional investors who evaluate a company's ESG performance and the company itself focus only on the evaluation score, the future of ESG management will eventually disappear and become a target of criticism from regulatory tools. Therefore, ESG should be used as a means of protecting the natural environment and solving important social and organizational problems, with the primary goal of enhancing corporate sustainability, although it is aimed at all organizations above all else.

These tasks include carbon neutrality, green finance, carbon trading system, carbon border tax and carbon frontiers (CBAM), over-consumption prevention, educational opportunities, health and safety, human rights, and biodiversity.

For a sustainable company, society and the planet, corporate voluntary participation is strongly required along with ESG sector indicators that suggest CSR activities in three areas. And managers need to deal more closely and broadly with ESG management activities from a strategic perspective.

By creating social value through corporate voluntary efforts and establishing a transparent governance structure, the timing of implementation will be much more flexible. However, since carbon neutrality and the emission trading system are directly related to our way of life, environmental ESG issues must be dealt with separately.

A total change in international trade, government policy and industrial structure is now necessary. Therefore, efforts towards a secure and sustainable carbon neutral society in the face of climate change should be continued as well as investment in new technological innovations as a long-term task led primarily by the government.

The final issue for the future of ESG is localization activities to increase acceptance by country, industry, business size and management philosophy of each company. As a representative example, *Uber*, which has been on the rise, lost to

---

17) Park K., Lee Y.C., Lee D.H. (2005), *Management Gurus (Readings on Management Thoughts)*, Denan Publishing, Korea.

Didi Chuxing in China and *Grab* in Southeast Asia. This is because localization efforts were insufficient, such as not being able to listen to customers.[18)]

ESG standards must also be established in a way that matches the context of each country and the actual conditions of industries and companies to ensure sustainability. This is because, if ESG standards are established as one platform, new opportunities to expand the scope of activities can be established, especially in other evaluation activities that fit the local situation or in a way that responds to the spirit of the times.

18) Uber did not fully reflect customer opinions because it had applied only the American standards, that is, customers only paid by credit card, and did not operate a call center.

The Practice of
ESG Management

Ⅱ

ESG on Corporate Social Value

II

ESG on Corporate Social Value

1. Social Aspect of the Enterprise
2. Corporate Social Performance
3. Corporate Socio-Cultural Characteristics
4. Corporate Social Responsibility
5. Social Audit and Auditor's Role
6. Corporate Social Challenges

Businesses run by companies as the protagonists of the industrial society are the sources of occupation that provide jobs and livelihoods through employment or start-ups. In addition, companies, as the main agents of the market economy, pursue '*going-concern value* (*value for a sustainable business*)', that pursues changes and development centering on the business related '*Karma*' complex.

> The '*Spirit of Karma*' is based on the retributive justice for good or bad deeds. It also implies the seriousness that "*No matter how much good Karma you do practice, you cannot compensate or erase your own bad Karma*".

Confucius (孔子) said in the 'Spring-and-Autumn (春秋)' that "*Good deeds are encouraged, and bad deeds are punished* (勸善懲惡)". In this way, the task of dealing with 'Karma (業)' and 'Law (法)' is an eternal task that will not go away if human society exists, and it is also a measure of luck for a business. The 21st century 'Spirit of Karma' is projected in the so-called 'National Sentiment Act' through the social network service (SNS) and is expressed as the *Zeitgeist* (Spirit of Time) that demands corporate social responsibility beyond the positive law.

Practice of the Spirit of Karma and the Spirit of Law (Park K.)

Karma & Stewardship \ Law & Compliance		Systerm: Positive law	Opinion: Emotional law
		Legal Order	Social Value
Consciousness: Good Karma	Positive Screening	Award	Love
Greed: Bad Karma	Negative Screening	Punish	Hate

The '*Spirit of Law*' also exists as a regulation for the achievement of an equal and fair society and the resolution of social polarization. The 'Spirit of Karma', which distinguishes good and bad deeds, enables companies to pursue sustainable management with Eastern ideology, while the 'Spirit of Law' deals with corporate social responsibility based on the philosophical context of modern Western ideologies and values. They stand out as criteria to achieve both virtues.

On the other hand, Western values can be traced historically back to the civilizations of Greece, Rome, and Egypt in BC, examining the 'Spirit of Karma' and the 'Spirit of Law (Rule of Law)', or by referring to medieval religious philosophy from AD 393 to the 15th century (1453, the fall of the Eastern Roman Empire), when Christianity was the state religion.

However, in the light of 'Karma' and 'Law' about businesses, it is necessary to look at when the wealth begins to accumulate: After Renaissance (14-16C) and Enlightenment (17C) era, the Industrial Revolution (18C) when the companies and cities were born, and as well as the birth of new wealth due to primitive capitalism and the birth of the modern state followed.

Historical change of Western Social Values (Park K., 2015)[19]

1. Greece-Rome (B.C.~A.D. 4): Animism
→ "Human being created gods for their necessity"

2. Middle(Dark) Ages (A.D. 5~13): Christianism
→ "God created human being"

3. Renaissance (A.D. 14~17): Humanism
→ "Regain the Ancient Greek-Roman"

4. Industrial Revolution (A.D. 18~20): Materialism/Capitalism
→ "Machine replaced labor force"

5. Socialism (A.D. 19~20): Humanism
→ "Toward a world for the Proletariat"

6. Neo Capitalism (20c E.): Keynesian
→ "TVA and the Grass Roots"

7. Globalization (20c L.): Post-Capitalism/Socialism
→ "American as the Global Standard & China boom"

8. 4th Industrial Revolution (21c E.): Intelligence Divide
→ "Knowledge Management and Artificial Inteligence"

19) Park K. (2015), *Professor Kichan PARK on Strategic Management*, IUP.

In the 18th century connecting the Renaissance period and the Industrial Revolution era, J.J. Rousseau emphasized the following three causes of inequality in *'Discours sur l'inégalité'* (Discourse on inequality). The first was the tyranny of private property which divided the bourgeoisie and the proletariat, the second was the subordination relationship which divided the ruler and the ruled, and the third was the tyranny of power which established the relationship between private property and subordination as an institution.

Rousseau underlined that "*Only a social contract by consensus between the members makes possible a fair governance structure*". Only then can we restore human relations equal to the original good, and he left the words '*Retour à la nature* (Back to nature)', as '*Leave nature as it is* (無爲自然)' of Lao-tseu (老子).

It is argued that everything begins to fall when the hands of selfish people who seek their own freedom rather than the happiness of a social community based on equality and brotherhood through governance are touched. To become a successful business, corporate governance must also create value for the social community where the public, customers and stakeholders are together.

Peter F. Drucker's thesis, which constantly raised questions about the nature of business and management in the capitalist system, saying: "*There are stupid answers, but no stupid questions*", has been reorganized into the key questions following by later disciples such as Jim Collins and Philip Kotler.[20)]

1. What is our mission? – *Jim Collins*
2. Who is our customer? – *Philip Kotler*
3. What does the customer value? – *Jim Kouzes*
4. What are our results? – *Judith Rodin*
5. What is our plan? – *V. Kasturi Rangan*

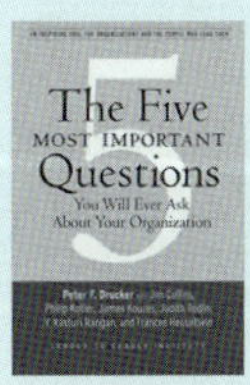

"What do You Want To Be Remembered For?"

"*Capitalism, born with private property, free competition, and the search for profit as the highest virtue, is it not destined to take the path of corporate profit rather than social responsibility under the values of freedom and growth?*"

20) Peter F. Drucker, Frances Hesselbein Leadership Institute (Editor, 2008), *The Five Most Important Questions You Will Ever Ask About Your Organization*, Jossey-Bass.

In addition, in the era of the 4th Industrial Revolution, with ESG standards, artificial intelligence, virtual reality, carbon neutrality and transparent management that impose social responsibilities on companies are now new forms of subordination and of legal regulation.

"*Would this not be another source of inequality and aggravating social stress?*" Therefore, top management should practice with the idea that "*Try not to become a man of Success, but rather try to become a man of Value*" emphasized by Albert Einstein for the environment, society, and for the sustainable corporate management.

1 Social Aspect of the Enterprise

There is a general misconception about the social image and social characteristics of a business, which are primarily determined by the CEO. In other words, the meaning of the word '*SOCIAL*' is seen as a negative element that weighs on business activities such as social inequalities, social regulation, social restrictions, social rigidity, social conflicts, and social tensions etc.

> '*The Social*', which designates the social characteristics of a company, is also interpreted by the business leaders as a property opposed to the activities of rational, successful, and continuous management of the company.

It is also seen as a phenomenon that only comes with social cost, the burden of mandatory disclosure of a company's '*Bilan Social*' (Social Balance Sheet, Social Report) like France, or a constant debate as if it is scratching and crushing even minor issues. Discussing the social characteristics of corporate management is also regarded as an irrational activity. In other words, groups that avoid irrational and non-quantitative phenomena, such as '*Machine-like*' engineers or '*Profit-seeking*' accountants, criticize the social problems of companies that promote fairness and transparency as troubling issues.

In fact, many companies live to solve unequal social problems and fulfill their social responsibilities, but on the other hand, they are avoiding social responsibility by playing hide-and-seek with civic groups such as labor unions and

NGOs and government agencies. To this extent, we focus on a *'Lame-type'* lucrative management, which only focuses on economic performance and market development activities for the business activities of companies that need to live and evolve dynamically.

So, leaders ask "*What is a business*?" Moreover, it is necessary to seek answers to the questions on the value of the existence of a company and its social responsibility: "*What must be done to permanently enrich the life of the company itself*?" In addition, for sustainable growth, it is necessary to emphasize the social role of companies and to conduct research and practice at the social level of companies. The reason for emphasizing the social aspect of a company and its social existence value as the intrinsic role of a company is as follows:

> First, management's humanistic perspective on corporate social value creation is still lacking in Korea and France, as well as around the world.

Internally, in a climate that values academic background and career path, people who have graduated from prestigious universities are recognized as elites, but there are many elites below average by human nature. Outside of the public relations dimension, they are passive in voluntary social contribution and social value activities. While these elite groups play a vicious role of putting their abilities to the fore to drive out dissent or dissent within an organization, meritocracy is often a source of injustice among all members of an organization.[21]

Back in the days when economic development was a top priority, some powers claimed to be elite groups and suppressed the opposition with the only values of the time "Live Better!" In fact, it is not an exaggeration to say that these elite dictatorships dominated the history of modern societies around the world. Furthermore, the so-called 'close relationship between politics and business' through elite networks has not yet disappeared as growing into a conglomerate has become a means of safeguarding business success.

21) Daniel Markovits (2019), *The Meritocracy Trap: How America's Foundational Myth Feeds Inequality, Dismantles the Middle Class, and Devours the Elite*, Penguin Books.

Second, the representative research interests of academia are focusing on increasing mechanical efficiency, and the industry is leading corporate management with only one wing. In other words, it focuses on maximizing profits while ignoring social responsibility.

The phenomena of social change, including change and innovation, which are difficult to solve with equations, frighten the subconscious mind of researchers. In other words, social problems are viewed as subjects of study rather than simple and neat tastes like machines, budgets, and mathematical formulas, because they are considered ugly, opaque, and contain dangerous and radical elements. For this reason, the interest and importance of the social aspect of corporate management has not been highlighted, and it has been treated as a research task that should be avoided at times.

It cannot be denied that corporate management emphasized only the economic aspect and always treated the social aspect as a secondary problem. In other words, the dominant argument was that *'growth comes first, distribution comes second'*, that a company can fulfill its social responsibilities only when economic performance is achieved. The teleological argument that "*The pursuit of profit governs all business activities as if God controls the souls of men*" has been continuously reinforced by accountability to shareholders.

Third, to facilitate all communication of business activities, it is necessary to emphasize the social aspect of the company.

Communication is not just an exchange; it is an activity of listening and understanding the other person clearly. However, communication is often understood to explain and justify one's thesis. The reason we are so obsessed with defending our own claims is that we either see the other person as ignorant or simply do not understand the essence of communication.

And the reason we want to justify our claims is that we set the bar for social success only for elite education and successful careers, and we try to claim that our view is always right. As a result, although there are so many explanations that make sense, few people ever hear and understand them.

Listening to others is the most important way to understand their authenticity and creativity. On the other hand, refuting and arguing is nothing more than quieting the other person's will. In other words, only when we listen to others can we meet opinions that are different from ours, and we can learn social rationality that evokes a new atmosphere. Therefore, communication activities are particularly important among the reasons why the social aspect of a company should be emphasized.

2 Corporate Social Performance

Financial analysis and accounting techniques are essential analytical tools, but the strength of a business is evidenced by a manager's intuition for the future. If intuition is a quality that a manager should have, economic and social data can be said to be the source of enhancing a manager's judgment.

The social aspect of management is very complex. Because economic valuation is based on 'facts and figures', results are obtained by analyzing relevant data. On the other hand, to examine the social domain of a company, it is necessary to consider the subjective opinions and differentiated characteristics of various groups of actors beyond objective quantitative information. Indeed, social performance has its own social responsibility issues that members perceive when performing their duties.

As such, the social area of corporate management is closely related to human resource management activities. In short, it is difficult to apply cutting edge algorithms using artificial intelligence, big data and cloud services, and the part that needs to be constantly corrected is the human problem. Therefore, systematic efforts are needed to specify, standardize, and generalize techniques for measuring and analyzing the social problems of companies dealing with the relationship between humans and nature.

First, the traditional concern of managers in the field of corporate society is the issue of 'job-person' compatibility: *"Is there a strong consistency between the organization's work and the skills of its members?"*

"Does the company increase the capacities of its members, or does it erode the capacities of its members?" To this end, since the 1990s, learning organizations, skilled organizations, knowledge management, and rapid learning organizations have been introduced to develop employees' competencies and secure a competitive advantage. Likewise, advanced analytics frameworks and techniques are used in the business world.

> Second, a new concern of managers in the field of corporate society is the question of 'corporate reputation': *"Do your products and services create brand value and social respect?"*

Each company pursues global competitiveness and global quality superiority throughout its business activities to earn respect from the customers as well as the quality of its products recognized in domestic and overseas markets. ESG criteria for evaluating corporate social responsibility, sustainability management, and responsible investment target companies are also important because they not only evaluate the overall quality of these business activities, but also constitute a standardized global norm.

Since the 1980s, the spirit of innovation with a focus on quality has brought a different perspective to the organization of enterprises that previously focused on efficient production. We remind you once again that the '*social value of a company*' evaluated by customers and investors is determined by the members of the company, including the management as follows:

> First, it is important to consider the needs of customers and investors first, and keep in mind that the needs of members who are internal customers of the company must also be included.
> Second, rather than looking at the main functions of the organization from a vertical perspective, it is necessary to review the horizontal responsibilities of each department and grant appropriate decision-making authority to each department.
> Third, organizational management requires fast, accurate, and '*agile management*' to openly improve the individual and group capabilities and performance of its members.

As such, the vision and mission of a company should be established based on an understanding of human values, the importance of the spirit of quality, and the importance of the spirit of challenge for social functioning and organizational learning. In fact, regardless of country or company, the vision and mission are particularly emphasized in countries and companies with high growth rates, even if their socio-economic level is lower than those of advanced countries or large corporations.

In the case of Korea, policies and slogans; '*This Year is a year of Hard-Work*', '*Creating a New Korea*', '*People's World*', '*Dynamic Korea*', '*Green Growth*', '*Creative Economy*', and '*Income-led Growth*' as spurs to promote economic and social development. Henceforth, the social and economic growth of China, which has maintained the policy of '*Growth in Stability* (穩中求進)' following the open policy, as well as of Vietnam, which implemented a digitalization policy since after '*Doi Moi* (*Renovation, Innovation*)' movement stands out.

A trend worth noting is the fact that corporate social responsibility and goals are becoming increasingly important for the balanced growth of the economy and society. From the early 1960s to the late 1980s, Korea experienced social conflict amid disproportionate growth as the government and corporations pursued economic development policies for export and import in accordance with the principle of 'Priority on economic growth'.

Now, the transition to balanced growth stocks to resolve the digital information gap, income gap, and knowledge competency gap must be facilitated by a new opportunity, namely, ESG management activities.

3 Corporate Socio-Cultural Characteristics

'*The Social*' is formed by the members of society, and '*the Social Phenomenon*' appears through the relative relationship between them. Meanwhile, the social phenomenon of the organization is "*How will the authority and the responsibility of management activities be organized and distributed?*" and "*How do members perceive the reality of management activities?*" It is expressed differently depending on the response method. Therefore, the differentiated sociality of a company plays a leading role in the formation of cultural and historical values of the company, and the result is expressed in the organizational culture that can be said to be a unique characteristic of each company.[22)]

1. View of organizational culture *as a behavioral pattern of its members*

This means that organizational culture is the behavioral manner of members linked to social practices that are dominant at a given time and place. For example, the methods of decision making, and communication seen by businesses in the Middle East are completely different from what Korean businesses see today. When conducting an audit in the Middle East, it is customary to unconditionally follow a senior manager's instruction to abruptly change the audit procedure. If the reason for the senior manager's instructions is requested or the reason for the change is questioned, this can be interpreted as a lack of trust and the auditing activity itself will be completely interrupted.

On the other hand, companies in Eastern Europe have a very difficult climate for group discussions: It is believed that a person must be at least 35 years old if she or he has long service or a lot of experience, so that they can give a word of wisdom or information to others. This climate also occurs in Asian countries, including of course Korea, and is often interpreted as a Confucian tradition or historical custom. South American companies have a strong Native American culture. In other words, social customs based on internal solidarity and trust among members based on racial roots are still ingrained in the company.[23)]

2. Perspective to understand organizational culture *as a matter of corporate behavior and interrelationship*

This implies that the long history and management methods of the company are accumulated to form a corporate culture. The corporate culture is differentiated again according to the following criteria: First, *the social vision expected by members* (competitive, cooperative, or individualistic characteristics); second, *the source of power* (level of training, charismatic leadership, credibility, legitimacy); third, *the behavioral vision* (implementation of explicit or implicit codes of conduct, voluntary or compulsive behaviors, bottom-up or top-down strategies).

22) Park K. (1997), *Team Performance Appraisal*, KMA (Korea Management Association).

23) Park K. (1999), *Social Audit*, KMA (Korea Management Association).

Academia sees the opportunity to become interested in corporate culture and social issues in the early 1980s, when interest in Japanese-style management increased despite the two oil shocks in the 1970s. The rapidly changing business environment and desirable climate creation in the world bestseller '*In Search of Excellence (1982)*' by Thomas Peters and Robert Waterman received great attention. Accordingly, many companies are trying to come up with a strategic and practical plan that focuses on creating a social atmosphere for the organization, collecting member satisfaction by class, collecting various opinions, and managing social conflicts within the organization. However, despite these efforts, they contributed to the spread of MBO (management by objectives) but did not significantly contribute to the creation of an innovative culture of the company as a social value creator.

Michael Hammer's *Business Process Reengineering (BPR)*, which was popular around the world in the mid-1990s, also advocated an innovative increase in work efficiency through the promotion of parallel work based on information technology (IT). Michael Hammer's Business Process Reengineering (BPR), which was popular all over the world in the mid-1990s, also advocated innovative increases in work efficiency through information technology (IT)-based parallel work promotion. However, as Hammer himself asserted, "*the vehicle that runs on the wonderful highway called IT doesn't change,*" and many critics say that a solid organizational atmosphere is a chronic problem. Therefore, the role of organizational culture is important for change. Drucker also pointed out that "*Strategy accounts for only 15% of business activity and the remaining 85% is organizational culture*".

Meanwhile, in 2017, executive chairman of WEF (World Economic Forum) Klaus Schwab showcased an innovative organizational culture with foundational skills such as '*complex problem solving*', '*critical thinking*' and '*creativity*' in his book '*The Fourth Industrial Revolution (2016)*'. The social role of enterprises in training and bridging the knowledge gap and employment opportunities is becoming increasingly important. Therefore, it is more important to view the Covid-19 pandemic shock, carbon neutrality and ESG management guidelines as opportunities for innovation and social value rather than as risks and burdens. And companies must create an atmosphere of internal innovation that pursues continuous growth through creativity and challenge.

4 Corporate Social Responsibility

CSR (Corporate Social Responsibility) refers to moral obligations in all decision-making activities in corporate management. First, CSR includes moral abbreviations for norms or values to be observed daily at the individual level, and second, includes professional ethics and business ethics in specific areas of society. In particular, large corporations with great social influence strongly demand that they fulfill their duty as leaders to society; *'Noblesse Oblige'*.

> As such, CSR includes social responsibility for employees as *internal customers*, such as employment, qualifications, compensation, and working conditions, and social responsibility for all stakeholders as *external customers*, such as tax payment, environmental preservation, responsibility to shareholders, and transparent management.

In the case of CSR, the level of responsibility (legal standards, industry average, improvement, target level, etc.) is more important than the subject of responsibility itself. Therefore, companies firstly must respond to the following challenges: *"To what extent will companies take responsibility for their own employment?"*, *"How much education and training should be provided?"*, and *"How much social security should be spent for the employees?"*

As such, corporate social performance through CSR includes internal management activities related to employment, remuneration, occupational hygiene and safety (OHS), working conditions, education and training, labor-management relations, and living conditions of employees and families, as well as the performance of external social responsibility activities.

> Similar to France and Germany, in Europe, the scope of CSR has traditionally been limited to *'internal social responsibility'* for employees within the organization, and social responsibility for the external environment of the company has been relatively excluded. In other words, by focusing on the establishment and practice of a social audit system for social performance within the company, the focus is on strengthening the company's ability to fulfill its social responsibilities.

This can be traced back to the historical development process in which various internal social relations such as trade unions, employers and employee groups were emphasized rather than external social relations such as government, customers, investors, and NGOs. In particular, the *"Direct, Collective, and Participatory communication system"* within a company instituted by the 'Auroux Act (*Loi Auroux*)' in 1985 in France, is a representative example.

Meanwhile, now they strengthen communication with the external customers and care stakeholder relations by adding global responsible management indicators such as carbon neutrality with global trends in ESG-related environmental and socially responsible management based on the ethical and moral transparent management.

The Auroux Act stems from the philosophy that direct communication with the internal group of employees should take precedence over communication with the external stakeholder group, and that corporate social responsibility activities can also be justified on this basis.

The Role of Actors and their Relationships (Park K., 2015)

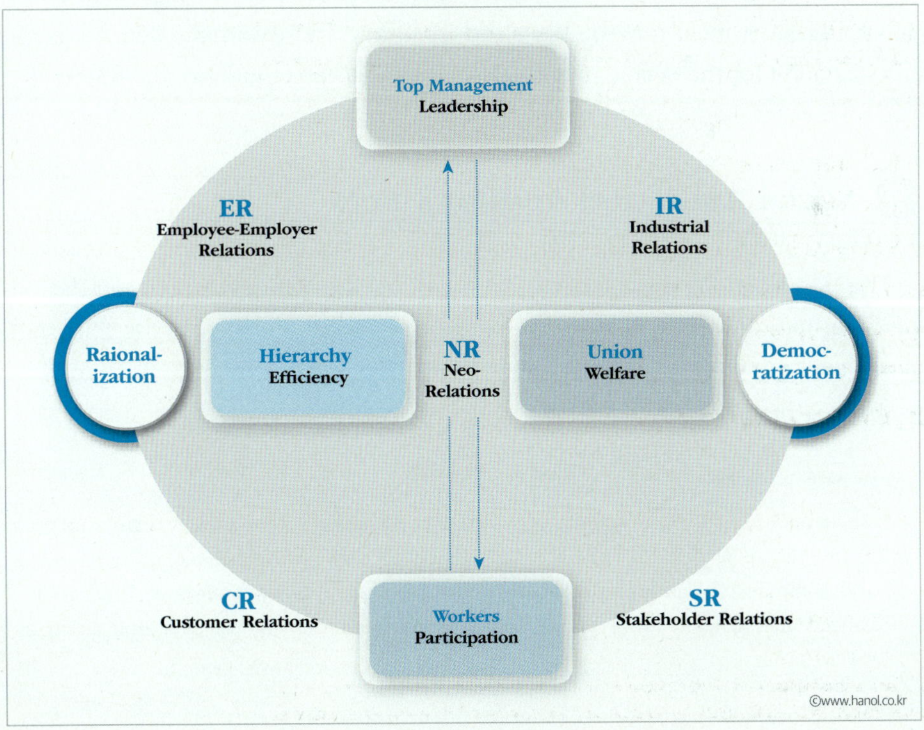

1. ER: In the individual employment contract between the employer and the employee, communication has been made to increase efficiency by rationally performing the role assigned to the position in question.
2. IR: Communication that guarantees equality by democratically performing the duties entrusted to workers in collective bargaining activities between employers and trade unions is emphasized.
3. NR: Here, the Auroux Act opened new avenues for negotiating activities in which employee representatives communicate directly with management rather than through management or unions.

Just as true relations of trust cannot be formed if you lack self-confidence no matter how much you insist on trusting others, the external social responsibility without the fulfillment of internal social responsibility would also be the same as the contempt of a company wearing the ESG mask. And it is used only as analysis data for institutional investors.

Therefore, evaluations dealing with non-financial performance such as Social Report (Bilan Social: social balance sheet), Sustainability Report, CSR, CSV, and ESG Report are conducted by the power groups (executive executives, employees, unions, and managers). It must now be disclosed internally and externally and subject to a social audit for the accuracy and transparency of the content of the report.

5 Social Audit and Auditor's Role

The '*Social Audit*' is an activity that measures the difference between the value of an indicator presented by an external organization, such as the ESG standards, and the value of a norm or standard adopted by a functional department within the organization.

Social audit is a *"control activity over the control method"*. Therefore, it is necessary to establish a pivotal role in ESG management as well as in financial, accounting, and computerized audits using various social science analysis techniques and advanced management information analysis systems such as AI, big data, and cloud services.

Some consider the concept of social auditing to be new. But we can find the appearance of auditors in ancient Egypt. At that time, the role of the auditor was to accurately verify the import and export of wheat, the yield, and the total amount of tax. Around 300 BC, even in Athens, Greece, professional accountants oversaw the accounting and treasury of state finances and property to manage public assets. The term *'audit'* derives from the Roman custom of examining the testimony of witnesses and judging the veracity of appeals in court, and the term *'auditor'* originated in England at the end of the 13th century. An *'Audit Committee'* was formed in London at the beginning of the 14th century and the first auditors were elected (Park, 1999).

In the 19th century, audit activity spread in the United States, a British investment. At the time, UK investors wanted their investment returns to be properly regulated by an independent notary. To this end, UK auditors have introduced a style of auditing methods and procedures unique to the United States.

Meanwhile, the rapid growth of the US economy after World War I strengthened guarantees for corporate capital and bank credit assets. Investors who did not believe the accounting data presented by the company were expressed in an overly optimistic or fictitious way and demanded independent external audit activities. At the same time, regular internal audits were carried out in the public sector, such as in the case of the railway industry.

After the Great Depression, in the 1930s, when the Accounting Act on the Jobs of Certified Public Accountants was passed, it was stipulated that the contents of a company's financial statements submitted to the stock exchange must be verified and certified by an external auditor. As a result, the roles of internal and external auditors began to separate.

The role of an accountant belonging to an external accounting firm was to check the relevance of the presentation of financial performance, the adequacy of accounting management rules, laws and customs, and the adequacy of the performance level in relation to the transfer. It focuses on managing the books of accounts. Meanwhile, the role of internal auditors expanded with the establishment of the *'Internal Auditors' Association* in 1941. As interest in the role of auditors increased both internally and externally, and as the scope of audit activities expanded, audit activities were separated from the "Traditional Accounting and Notarization".

> In 1971, the United States broke with the past accounting record method and defined audit activities as follows: *"Auditing activities are conducted to determine whether the process of establishment and implementation is used in an efficient and economical manner, and whether the objectives of the organization have been achieved. It is an independent assessment of the various functions of the company"*.

Despite these changes, confusion over the role of the auditor is still common. The difference between the roles of internal auditors and external auditors differs depending on the field of activity, type of activity, objective pursued and the content of the laws and regulations. In France, external auditors are guaranteed access to general management areas, including cost auditing, when they are involved in the finances and accounting of a company.

On the other hand, internal auditors deal with matters related to all business activities other than financial matters. Therefore, internal audit aims to improve the efficiency of management activities by suggesting the improvement of business and the strategic application of established policies and procedures through the audit of planning activities to be carried out by the companies.

> The nature of internal audits also differs in how they deal with negligence or fraud. In other words, while external auditors do not address trivial waste or tax evasion issues that do not materially affect their financial position, internal auditors address these issues directly through due diligence and forecasting activities.

Inadequate management such as negligence or embezzlement that occurs in a business, such as the Enron scandal, can lead to bankruptcy. Therefore, internal auditors must strictly review the effectiveness and efficiency of audited management activities, including the verification of tax evasion and errors, methods of application of the procedures, reliability of information and adequacy of regulations.

The existence of such various concepts of social audit shows what the term *'social audit'* means and the fact that it has not yet been standardized. The diversity of terminology is closely related to the diversity of audit methods. That is, some methods emphasize that auditing is linked to the activities of analysis and evaluation of the problems, while other emphasize that it should include the making of recommendations or action plans along with the effectiveness analysis in the audit implementation procedure.

The method of social auditing can be described as *"diagnosing the causes of expressed problems and assessing their significance, ultimately enabling auditors to make formal alternatives to hitherto unused recommendations and action plans"*. As such, social auditing is an activity that anticipates changes and considers all financial and non-financial risks that a company must take. (Spreckley, 1981).

1. The first stage of the audit concerns the reliability and validity of the information and the legal consistency of the performance achieved.
2. The second stage of the audit verifies whether the enforcement procedures are applied, consistency of achievement goals, the level of application, and the level of ability to induce expected results.
3. The third stage of the audit consists of activities related to strategic decision making. Here, the final performance, that is, the evaluation of effectiveness, should always be considered as a top priority.

These social audits, as in the past, go beyond financial and management audits and require scientific analysis with cutting-edge expertise in each subject: Confirmation of board of directors (BOD) composition and functions directly related to social responsibility, such as prevention of water pollution directly related to the electrification of diesel vehicles and carbon neutrality issues, prevention of leukemia and damage to humidifier disinfectants caused by industrial accidents, etc. It is difficult to identify the cause of the problem only with the given role of the audit function.

Social audit in the era of ESG management, which mainly uses a company's non-financial information, is quite different from existing financial audit activities in terms of target and scope, applied methodology, objective pursued, content of the audit activity, fact finding approach, and expertise in technical analysis, etc.

Therefore, through ESG management, it should be regarded as a timely opportunity to transform the existing role of the audit office including the method of appointing auditors.

6 Corporate Social Challenges

"Is a company an economic entity or a social entity?" Corporations are one of the three main national economic actors (households, corporations, and the government), and their influence continues to grow. Corporations are particularly key players in a market economy that provides wealth and well-being to people, among the three main elements of a state: people, territory, and sovereignty.

> Therefore, it can be said that a company is a subject that maintains the market economy system and fulfills its responsibilities to the entire human society and the people, as well as to the industrial society and its members, customers, and business-related stakeholders.

'Exemplary companies' that faithfully practice the social responsibilities to their members of the organization, customers and stakeholders can fulfill their overall social responsibilities based on ESG indicators for example.

However, there is a problem that high performance of global social responsibility for ESG indicators does not always lead to high performance of social responsibility for internal members of an organization, customers, and stakeholders. As such, ESG also has many parts to adapt to the circumstances of each company. In other words, internationally standardized and generally applied GRI, SDGs and ESG standards should be applied differently depending on the social impact, industry sector, economy and country-specific characteristics of the companies being evaluated.

As a single example, the problem with global ESG management that emphasizes *'good company' and 'good management', "Do 'good people' always succeed? Do 'good companies' always have a competitive advantage? Does a 'good President' always uphold social justice?"*

As you can see from the question, the *'good'* syndrome can rather be an obstacle to the development of people, businesses, and society. Therefore, rather than trying to *'washing ESG with a good looking'* at the global, national, and industrial level, the right aspects of corporate management, namely integrity and ethics, should be the basis.

Therefore, ESG departments are required to evaluate their activities in accordance with the law based on ethics and integrity, and to assume environmental and social responsibilities to improve sustainability. And ESG is needed as a new management strategy for companies that communicate transparently with stakeholders.

In fact, among the ESG fields, environmental issues such as greenhouse gas reduction and carbon neutrality are the most comprehensive and areas that all companies around the world should consider together, but in fact, as a Korean company, it is a more important issue as a social consensus on corporate governance for transparent management.

Recently, LG, Shinsegae, and Hanjin KAL have established separate ESG committees or sustainability management committees, and Samsung, Hyundai, Kia, and Hyosung, which previously operated transparent management committees, expanded their activities and contents mainly focusing on ESG. As such, the virtuous cycle of ESG management in Korea should appear as [recovery of corporate governance → implementation of major ESG issues → expansion of corporate information disclosure].

Corporate Social Responsibility and Creating Social Values

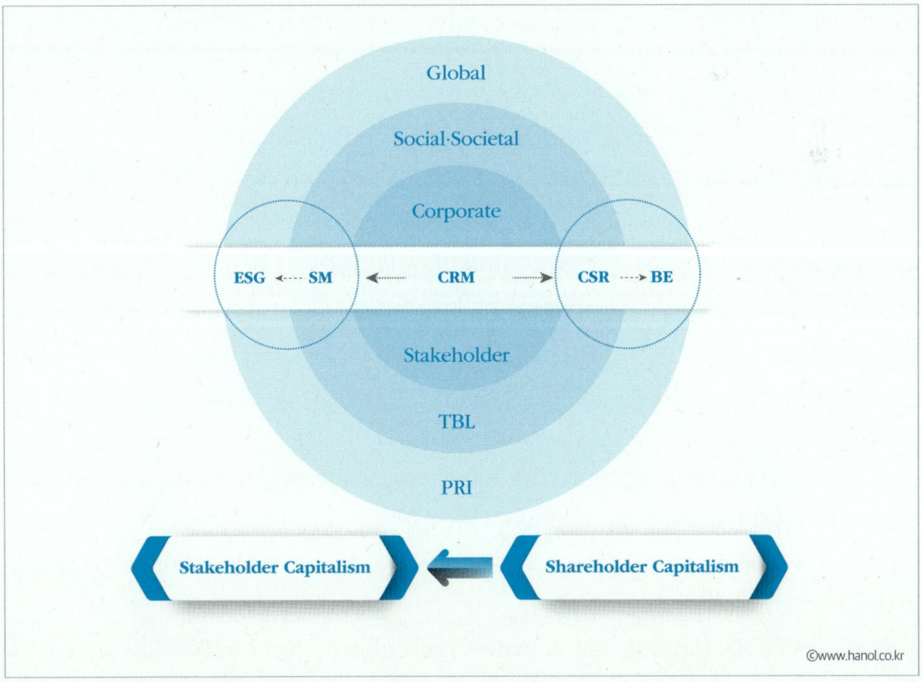

Therefore, the environmental indicator (E), which includes the principles of the natural cycle that is difficult to control in the three areas of the evaluation criteria for responsible ESG investment, can be applied as a universal criterion in all countries. However, the social index (S) including human free will must consider the specificity of each country's historical, economic, and social situation for a more humane role in the ESG standards.

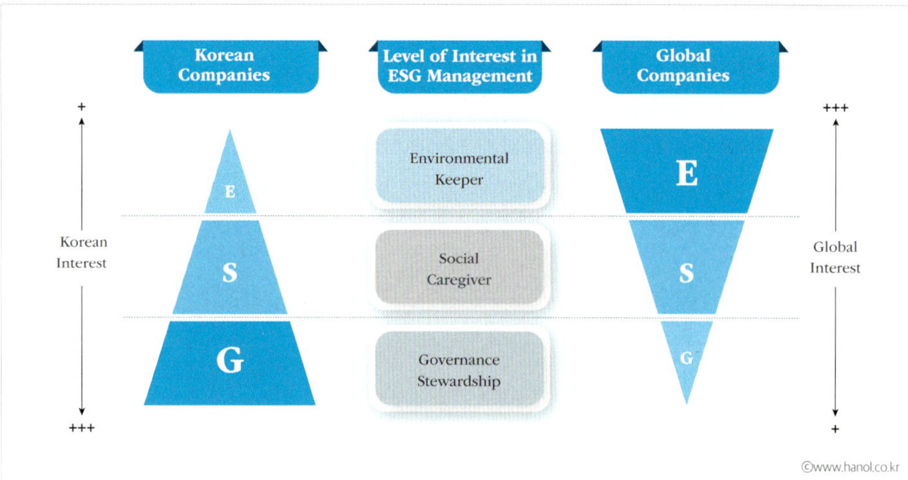

In the case of the Governance indicator (G), which contains the integrity management (正道經營) of a company, it is firstly required to apply a differentiated weight for the ESG indicators by category considering the size of company, management method, workforce, and financial situation etc.

For example, the question arises whether global ESG standards should be applied, even if a company cannot provide salaries and benefits commensurate with the qualifications and abilities of its employees. In this case, considering the initial goal of the ESG standard first established in 2004 by the UNGC, various measures should be taken to manage employees as a corporate social responsibility.

In fact, in ESG management, the members of the organization are the most important customers of the company as the subject of satisfying 'outside customer'. Now the concept of the customer itself extends to all stakeholders inside and outside the company.

Responsible ESG investment activities on a global level break with shareholder capitalism, which maximizes shareholder returns through the creation of corporate financial performance. It serves as a fast-evolving link to stakeholder capitalism, which deals with non-financial performance related to profit sharing with stakeholders and corporate social care.

Evolution of the importance of each ESG sector (Park K., 2021)[24]

content and time	Before 2000	2000~2015	After 2015
Importance and Weight	[S → G → E] → I Corporate *Image*	[G →S → E] → V Hidden *Value*	[E → S → G] → P Long-term *Profit*
CSR, ESG Evolution	CSR (Bowen, 1953) → ESG (UNGC, 2004) → PRI (UN, 2006) → CSV (Porter, 2011) → SMI (GRI, 2016) → ESG-P (BRT, 2019)		
Core Goal	CSR	CSV	ESG
Strategy & Advocate	Charity: Bowen, Drucker, Carroll	Win-Win: Vogel, Porter, Trépo	Duty: ISO, GRI, UN Global Compact

With the recent book by Bill Gates, interest in carbon zero goals and accurate measurement method to counter global warming is rising worldwide.[25] As Drucker put it, *"What's measured improves: Management is possible only when measures are possible"*.

In the U.S. BRT (Business Roundtable, 2019), which deals with corporate social issues such as CSR, CSV, ESG, and SMI (Sustainable Management Index) as strategic tasks, to generate sustainable profits, methods of analyzing and measuring corporate social phenomena, and emphasizes the importance of understanding the change process of organizational culture.

In this regard, the *Field Theory* [B = f(P·E) = f(S)] of K. Lewin, according to which *"Behavior appears as the interaction between the person (P) and the environment (E), and the condition of man and the environment appears as a situation (S)"*, and it is necessary to examine the argument that changes in human attitudes start with abandoning existing customs and stereotypes. That

24) Park K. (2021), *ESG and Sustainable Society*, Oct. 2021, https://youtu.be/mpvi_6F1c84

25) Three major proposals proposed by Bill Gates in his book "How to avoid a climate disaster (2021)": ① Make 51 billion tons of annual greenhouse gas emissions from developed countries to 'Net Zero' by 2050, ② Create a 'technology-policy-market structure' that transforms a carbon civilization into a clean energy civilization, ③ Do what the government, businesses, and each can do for a plan that is compatible with growth and the planet.

is, through the process of [Unfreezing → Changing practices → Refreezing], it is reconstructed in consideration of the 3-step change model.

Three-step Model of Change (Park K., 2021)

Learn ESG model	Create ESG culture	Evaluate ESG practice
· Understand current situation (As-Is) · Analysis of strengths and weaknesses by function · Confirmation of priority and weight	· CEO's interest and initiative · Understanding and Participation · System improvement and policy reflection	· Comparison with the target level (To-Be) · Improvement of strengths and weaknesses by function · Check priority and weight

To evaluate the social performance of a company, the social scorecard, social audit report, GRI Standards, SDGs, SRI, ISO26000 and emerging ESG standards that have been developed at different times are used to analyze the means to promote new changes, to analyze the business activities of the company (presented as an evaluation criterion). However, there will be a political and strategic game for the company in which the key groups that implement change - CEOs, managers, employees, unions, customers, and stakeholders - all participate.

As the *'Law of the Global Business Game'* of ESG becomes more prominent, managers and members in and around organization become the subject of the game: *'Environmental Keeper (E)-Social Caregiver (S)-Ethical Steward (G)'*, which is linked to the financial performance of corporate management. It is now necessary to measure, analyze, evaluate, and improve a company's social value creation activities using non-financial performance indicators.

Globally, corporate social responsibility (CSR) and socially responsible investment (SRI) in a narrow sense are emerging as important issues. As such, ESG has gone beyond the interest of asset managers and institutional investors, and governments around the world are emphasizing responsible ESG management throughout the supply chain for a sustainable society.

Obviously, it is desirable for ESG standards to spread as key indicators of corporate environmental and social responsibility and sustainability. For this, transparency, and accuracy of ESG data dealing with non-financial performance and voluntary reporting activities of companies are important, and the development and dissemination of scientific analysis methods that strictly measure and report them should be supported.

There are concerns about the amount of data manipulation and legal litigation around the world just by simply measuring greenhouse gas emissions directly related to the carbon trading system and border carbon tax. The European Union (EU) has already mandated the disclosure of non-financial information to companies with 500 or more employees, and other countries are following suit.[26)]

Transparent disclosure of ESG-related information is a prerequisite for ethical ESG management, as non-financial information of the company inevitably contains subjective views. As stated in the United Nations Sustainable Securities Exchange Initiative (SSEI), transparent disclosure of ESG information to companies is expected to have the following positive impacts on companies involved:

1. Reasonable financing is possible by demonstrating transparency and efficiency of business activities.
2. Pursuit of profit and growth through cost reduction, profit creation, risk aversion, and new opportunities.
3. Creation of corporate reputation and brand value through CSR for the environment, society and economy.
4 Establishing a trusting relationship with stakeholders by providing information related to the company's value creation capabilities.
5. Improve trust relationship with investors through transparent information provision and official reporting procedures.
6, Acquisition of excellent evaluation results on the impact of socially responsible management through ESG practice, etc.

Since companies can enjoy these various effects through transparent disclosure of information, it is necessary to view ESG as an opportunity for organizational change and sustainable growth through the accumulation and regular disclosure of data on non-financial company performance.

Just as there are various responses to a company's business activities, ESG management must seek various methods of analysis and interpretation. If there

26) In the case of EU, CSR was made mandatory in 2014 and ESG information disclosure in 2017 for companies with 500 or more employees. In March 2021, the SFDR (Sustainable Finance Disclosure Regulation) was introduced to extend this from pension funds to all financial companies. In Korea, the Financial Services Commission has announced that ESG information disclosure will be mandatory from 2025 for listed companies with assets of 2 trillion KRW or more.

is only one correct answer to the practice of ESG management, it is that transparent ethical management is essential. For example, in a company that uses eco-friendly ingredients to create food that protects our health, business ethics and philosophy are fundamental. And to become a company loved by society through transparent disclosure of ESG management information, it is necessary to provide interesting and innovative ESG management reports (sustainability reports) in response to the era of AI, big data, and metaverse.

III

The Path and Companion of ESG Management

III

The Path and Companion of ESG Management

1. What is ESG Management?
2. Birth and Development of ESG Management
3. Purpose of ESG Management
4. The Future of ESG Management

The COVID-19 pandemic that shook all our daily lives has reminded us of the importance of cutting-edge IT infrastructure. Since the online school starts, the metaverse has appeared and is expanding its scope. Businesses are also penetrating deeply into online commerce and teleworking systems.

Meanwhile, the 4th industrial revolution based on the knowledge-based industry in the 21st century, the so-called IMABCD (IoT, Mobile, Artificial intelligence, Bigdata & blockchain, Cloud service, Digital transformation technologies) era, is demanding another level of stimulating innovation.

In this regard, new knowledge gap, employment opportunity gap, and social inequality caused by strict unethical management standards are also drawing attention. In particular, the spread of AI technology goes beyond the information gap, and the inequality in advanced social technology called the 'intellectual gap' and the widening of the decent job gap go against equality of opportunity.

Traditional learning versus AI-based learning (Park K., 2020)[27]

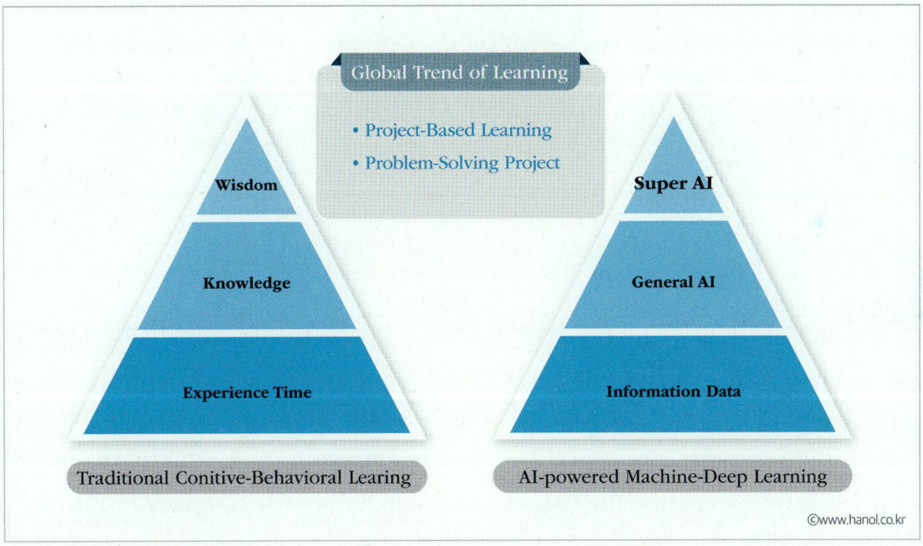

Environmental disasters due to climate warming are also occurring on various scales around the world. Therefore, it is a paradoxical paradigm that *"the best science and technology that humans should create is nature that humans*

27) Park K. (2020), *Team Activity Value Analysis Report*, Inha Vision Committee, April 2020.

should leave alone and protect through consensus!" It looks more convincing.

Governments and companies in a dominant position in the market economy create information by collecting vast amounts of data to seize opportunities, create knowledge and intelligence necessary for decision-making with practical wisdom, and create new markets. It also builds strong knowledge absorptive capacity (KAC).[28)]

As a result, MAGA (Microsoft, Amazon, Google, and Apple) are accelerating the *'intellectual gap'* that is difficult for general companies to keep up with.

Meanwhile, the global environment is increasingly suffering from climate change for example, and dysfunctional social conflicts that ignore coexistence are also increasing hidden costs.

Scholars with logic point out the market failure due to the pursuit of profit and shareholder capitalism, and the failure of the government due to ideological orientation. However, public appraisal points to unethical management activities of entrepreneurs such as corporate governance and economic cooperation that neglected corporate social responsibility and corporate mission as major causes.

Then, "*What is a business and what should it be?*"

This question is a topic that Peter F. Drucker, who is called the father of modern management, has been focusing on customer creation, MBO (management by objectives), and strategies for strengthening strengths throughout his life, starting with his 1954 book *'The Practice of Management'*. In fact, it is by no means easy for anyone to define the nature and original role of a company or business.

28) Ali M. and Park K. (2016), "The mediating role of an innovative culture in the relationship between absorptive capacity and technical and non-technical innovation", *Journal of Business Research,* vol.69, no.5, pp.1669~1675.

What is Management? (Peter F. Drucker, 1954)

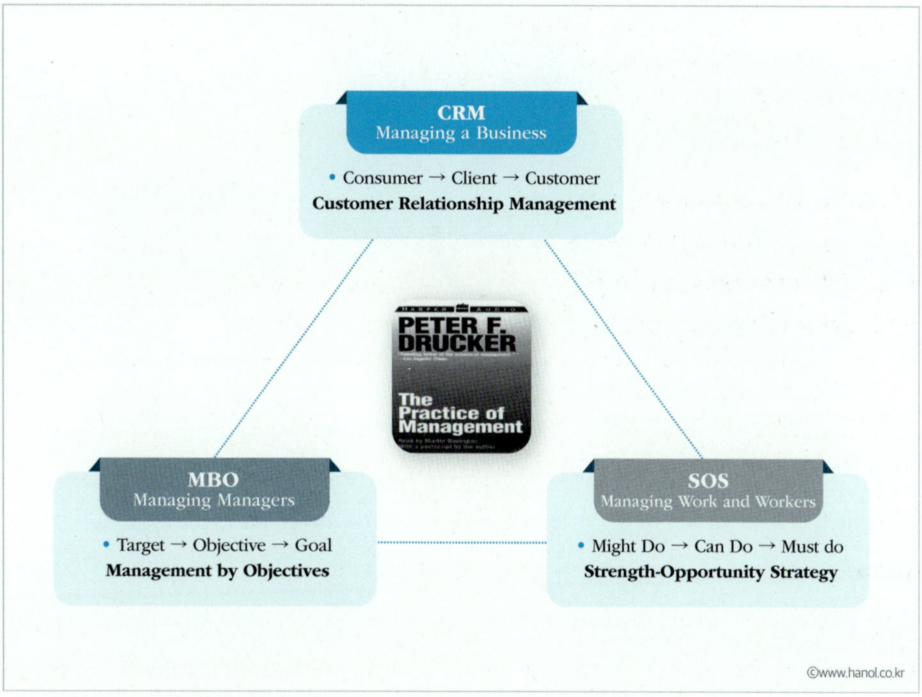

Due to the limitations in time, information, and cognitive abilities, as in Herbert Simon's theory of the 'bounded rationality', "*human decision-making activities are always limited*", companies seek the best, however often the management decisions prefer the next best solution as a kind of practical wisdom.

From a corporate social responsibility (CSR) perspective, if we do not understand the members who play on the pitch, we will eventually not be able to break free from the boundaries of *'Rationality', 'Democracy' and 'Legitimacy'*, hidden behind the mask of facts & figures in financial statements, looking only for economic performance.

Transparent management also stems from the wise decision-making activities of the members for sustainable management and is not made by the decisions of each CEO alone. If we recognize the importance of CSR, GRI, SDGs, ESG standards, sustainable development management, and stakeholder responsibilities, not only the top management but also all members of the company should be the subject of implementation.

Bounded Rationality (Herbert A. Simon, 1955)[29]

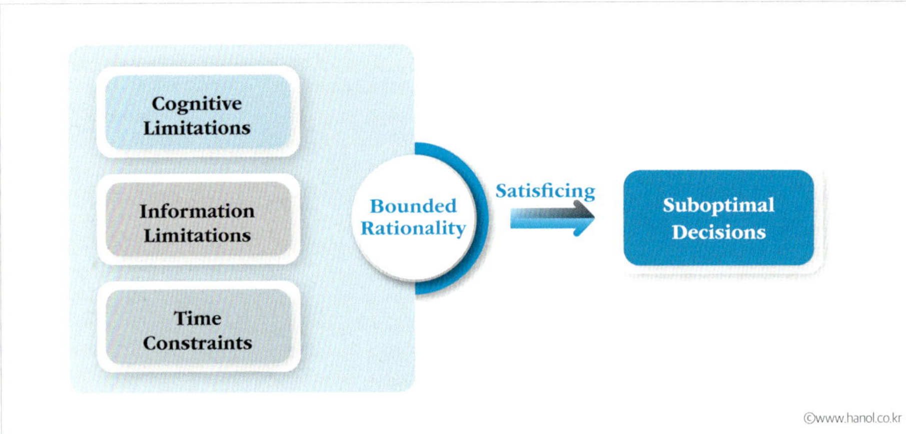

In fact, the lifespan of a person is looking forward to the age of 100, but the average lifespan of companies pursuing sustainable growth appears to be less than 30 years.[30] Even Michael Porter's competitive strategy which asserts that sales and profits made through the creation of markets and customers by generic strategy is not a sufficient condition for a long-term sustainable business.

In Korea, there are many companies that have succeeded through the efforts of outstanding entrepreneurs, but very few are loved by society. For example, Korea's Corruption Perceptions Index (CPI) evaluated by Transparency International (TI) has recently improved somewhat, but its integrity level is still low compared to Denmark and New Zealand.

As a result, a paradigm shift is required to break the wrong practices of political and economic cohesion and aristocratic trade union. However, it is not easy to find companies that practice ethical and transparent management in Korea. The situation tainted by such collusion will be an urgent task to start with responding to climate change and innovating with a focus on climate change.

29) Simon H. (1955), A Behavioral Model of Rational Choice, *The Quarterly Journal of Economics*, 69(1), pp.99-118.

30) According to McKinsey & Company, the average lifespan of a company is 90 years in the 1930s, 30 years in the 1970s, 22 years in the 1990s, and less than 15 years now in 2020s.

CPI in Korea - Transparency International (out of 100 points)

Division		2012	2013	2014	2015	2016	2017	2018	2019	2020
CPI score and ranking	score	56.0	55.0	55.0	54.0	53.0	54.0	57.0	59.0	61.0
	country	176	177	175	168	176	180	180	180	180
	ranking	45	46	44	43	52	51	45	39	33
OECD ranking	member	34	34	34	34	35	35	36	36	37
	ranking	27	27	27	28	29	29	30	27	23

Source: Corruption Perceptions Index (Transparency International, 2021).

Danish entrepreneurs and leaders say that they have no reason to meet with government officials. However, as the saying goes, *"In Korea, there are bureaucrats above the regulations"*, there are bundles of regulations, and the tyranny of bureaucratic power is not uncommon from business site to the Presidential Blue House. Therefore, Korean entrepreneurs and leaders have so many reasons to meet with government officials. If necessary, they will play their personal relationships without hesitation. It is said to be a *'network-driven'* company that needs to know what to do in order not to be hated by politics and relationships before a business is isolated from the customers and society.

If the ESG evaluation criteria of SRI also depend on index management and evaluation scores rather than the implementation of ethical management at the autonomous level of the company, it is also a question of a new regulation which hinders the capacity building of the company. Only the tyranny of another power led by an ESG rating agency can add to it.

Problems that emerge as social conflicts are resolved when the related debate itself disappears through social empathy. In other words, when the argument for fairness disappears, when the quota system for women in the composition of outside directors disappears, when the word glass ceiling disappears, and when ESG is no longer presented. In fact, without ESG standards, if all members of the company practice social responsibility and sustainable management, there is no need to make strong claims. The same goes for the discussion of each business management development process as follows:

Management Schools and the Birth of ESG management

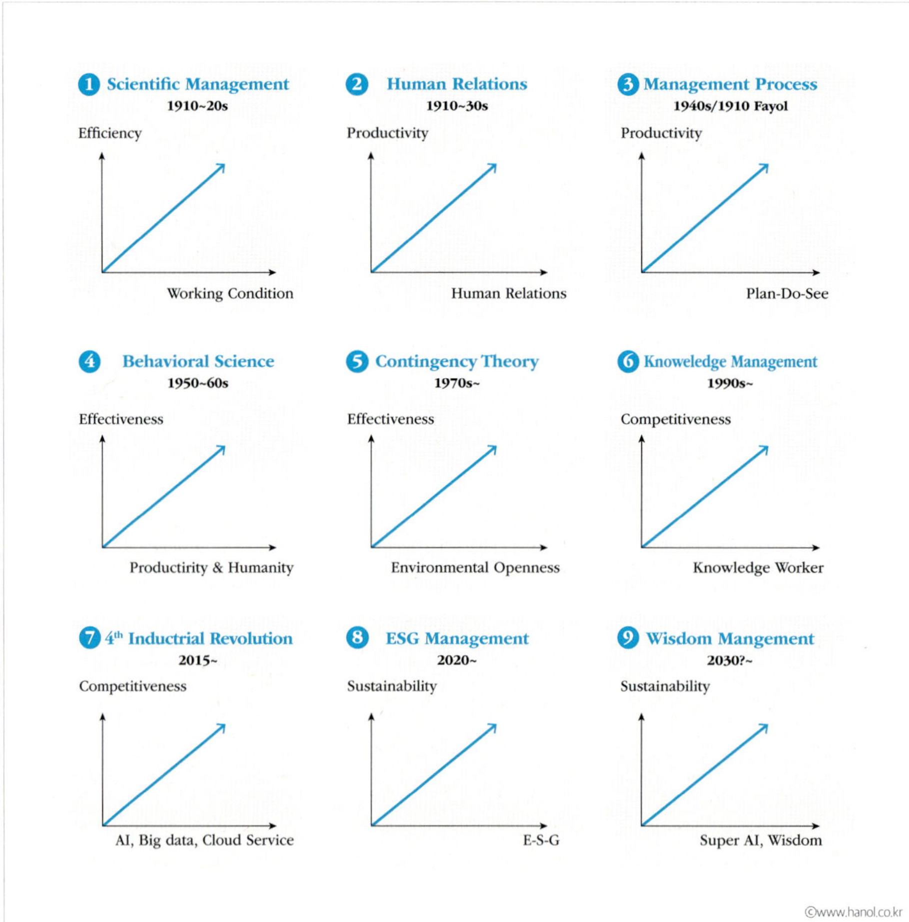

Since the advent of F.W. Taylor's scientific management method in the 1910s, various methods have been proposed as input factors for the purpose of improving organizational efficiency and productivity, improving efficiency in the marketplace, and improving competitiveness.

ESG management emphasizing the protection of the global environment and corporate sustainability in the era of the 4th industrial revolution goes beyond simple responsible investment centered on investors. In other words, it is necessary to look at the future of ESG in terms of *'strategic and humanistic management'* in parallel with the development of advanced technologies such as artificial intelligence, big data, and cloud services etc.

❶ What is ESG Management?

ESG contains the three key elements that have suggested the criteria that investors recommend using when selecting potential investment targets for SRI (socially responsible investing or sustainable-responsible-impact investing), future ROI (return on investment) and risk management linked to sustainable investment. Various historical processes are at the dawn of ESG:

Examples of ESG assessment indicators for sustainable growth

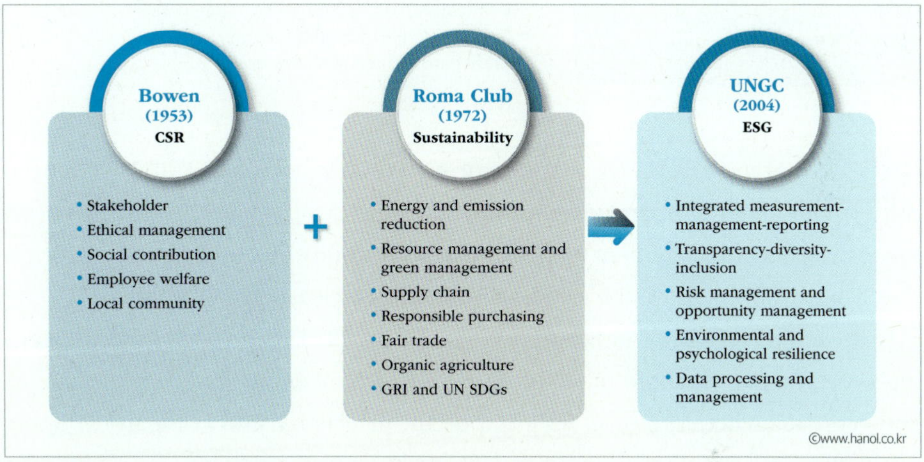

To measure and compare the corporate ESG performance, asset managers and financial institutions as investors mainly rely on ESG rating agencies. The problem is that world-renowned ESG rating agencies also measure ESG levels with their own rating indices, as the like a confirmed international ESG standards have yet to be established. Recently, artificial intelligence and big data are used for ESG performance assessment, however the strengths and the weaknesses of ESG assessment criteria are embedded here.

In other words, in the investors' decision criteria, comprehensive indicators for responsible investment assessment are employed with the advantages of using advanced analytical techniques. However, there are still drawbacks insofar as the role of investors as the decision makers for responsible investment, in lack of discussions on their ethical values and strict measurement techniques.

Examples of PRI's ESG standards for SRI

Environmental preservation management (E) : *Environmental sustainability*	· Climate change and carbon emissions · Natural resources and organic agriculture · Greening and smart growth · Environmental pollution and toxic substances · Clean technology, etc.
Social responsibility management (S) : *Social responsibility*	· Employment equality and diversity · Employee participation and local relations · Human rights protection and working environment · Consideration of health and social safety · Protection of the weak, etc.
Corporate governance (G) : *Ethical and transparent management*	· Board of directors and auditing committee · Executive remuneration and tax payment strategy · Political donations and lobbying activities · Corruption and whistleblowing · Transparent management, etc.

The ESG standards assess the extent to which a company fulfills its social responsibility and its management of sustainable development in three sectors: Environmental management (E), Social responsibility (S) and Governance (G). The UN-led PRI (Principles for Responsible Investment) clearly shows this.

However, the range of indicators suggested by PRI is very wide, and depending on the industry, there are indicators that cannot be assessed even with AI and big data. Therefore, it is very important to classify and compare to apply qualitative and quantitative indicators for each country, industry, company, and business category.

A fundamental question raised by academia as well as industry regarding ESG, is the relationship between ESG level and corporate performance:

- *Will the higher ESG level lead to higher financial performance such as future profitability and growth potential of a company?*
- *Will the higher ESG level result in higher non-financial performance such as corporate crisis response and sustainability?*

Until the 1990s this was shown to not be the case at all, but since the 2000s a mutually positive causal relationship has been clearly demonstrated.[31)]

31) Mckinsey&Company (2020), *"The ESG premium: New perspectives on value and performance"*.

Effect of the level of ESG performance on the financial performance

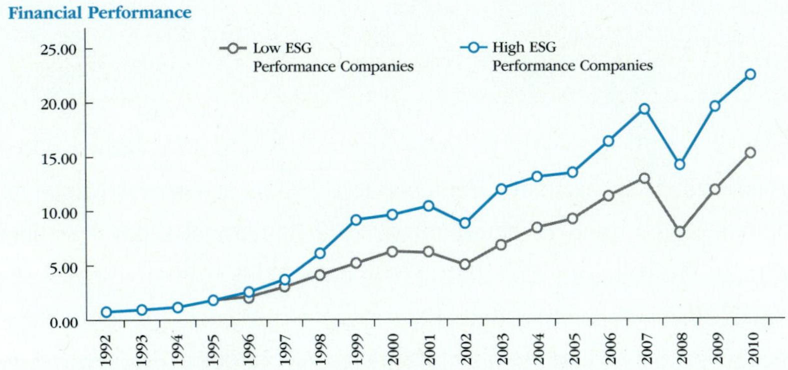

Source: Eccles G.R., Ioannou I. Serafeim G. "The Impact of a Corporate Culture of Sustainability on Corporate Behavior and Performance," *Harvard Business School*, November, 2011.

This implies that specific ESG-related indicators are suitable to measure a company's social performance, and that *"a company with high social performance exhibits high economic performance"* has an important implication.

Around the world, interest in corporate social responsibility, sustainability management, and responsible ESG management is growing. This is also reflected in the sharp increase in the proportion of investment and financial institutions that view ESG performance as an important criterion for their investment decisions, from 17% in 2016 to 36% in 2019.

Recent technological advances are strongly driven by IMABCD (IoT, Mobile, Artificial intelligence, Big data and blockchain, Cloud services, Digital transformation), and investment standards are increasingly based on ESG-related issues. As a result, you must decide how to juxtapose artificial intelligence technology with socially responsible investing (SRI) to assess the sustainability of your business.

In Korea, listed companies and public institutions publish reports related to sustainable development under various names such as sustainability reports, environment reports, carbon management reports, environmental and social reports, social responsibility management reports, UNGC implementation reports (CoP: Communication on Progress), and social contributions activity reports. From now on, it should be integrated into ESG management evaluation to select exemplary companies called good or excellent companies.

However, it is still too early to draw any conclusions. In France, Danone, well known as a dairy company, implemented ESG as a business principle, but when the company's finances deteriorated, CEO Emmanuel Faber was fired. In addition, there are still criticisms that ESG is nothing more than a business promotion, and especially cases where ESG assessment scores are rather high in companies such as steel and chemicals, which emit serious carbon emissions.

In Korea, '*K-ESG model*' was presented through more than 3,000 indicators and measurement items from major evaluation agencies such as DJSI, MSCI, EcoVadis, Sustainalytics, WEF, and GRI. However, there is a bureaucratic idea to lead ESG evaluation and control rather than promoting corporate motivation through positive screening. As such, a more fundamental debate arises, such as *"Whether there are conflicts or overlaps between the indicators, and whether the government should take the lead in ESG evaluation?"*.[32)]

Government policy, which began with a method of monitoring indicators that should be prepared according to the Korean situation as a system, is interpreted as a model of using ESG indicators mainly through regulation and negative screening, by synthesizing the real situation and the opinions expressed by the private sector and comparing them to the international ESG standards.

In the context of global competition, a strategy that differentiates one business in a different way from others is highlighted as a key success factor rather than as others do. The ESG management strategy would be no exception. The application of standardized evaluation indicators led by the government is more likely to regulate the strategic management activities of companies, which should be promoted in a flexible way according to circumstances and times.

32) After the Ministry of Trade, Industry and Energy presented the draft K-ESG model prepared with the Korea Productivity Center on April 21, 2021, the environmental indicators (14 to 17) were further strengthened and the guidelines confirmed on December 1, 2021.

Main content of Korean ESG (K-ESG) indicators -Ministry of Trade, Industry and Energy (2021.12.01)

Area	Main items (4 areas, a total of 61 diagnostic items)		
Information Disclosure (5 questions)	ESG information disclosure method	ESG information disclosure cycle	ESG information disclosure scope
	ESG Key Issues and KPIs		ESG information disclosure verification
Environmental (17 questions)	Setting environmental management goals	Environmental mgt. promotion system	Raw and subsidiary material consumption
	Ratio of recycled raw materials	Greenhouse gas emissions (Scope 1, 2)	Greenhouse gas emissions (Scope 1)
	Greenhouse gas emission verification	Energy usage	Renewable energy use rate
	Water consumption	Reuse water percentage	Waste discharge
	Waste recycling rate	Air pollutant emissions	Water pollutant emissions
	Violation of environmental laws/ regulations	Eco-friendly certified products and services	
Social (22 questions)	Goal setting and disclosure	Recruitment of new personnel	Percentage of full-time employees
	Voluntary turnover rate	Education and training expenses	Welfare expenses
	Guarantee freedom of association	Percentage of female members	Female salary ratio (relative to average salary)
	Disabled employment rate	Safety and health promotion system	Industrial accident rate
	Human rights policy establishment	Human rights risk assessment	ESG management of Partners
	ESG support for business partners	Partners ESG agreement	Strategic social contribution
Social (22 questions)	Participation of members in service	Information protection system establishment	Privacy Infringement and Remedies
	Violation of social law/ regulation		
Governance (17 questions)	ESG agenda proposal within the BOD	Outside Director Ratio	Separation of the CEO and the chairman of the BOD
	Board gender diversity	Outside Director expertise	Overall Director attendance

Area	Main items (4 areas, a total of 61 diagnostic items)		
Governance (17 questions)	In-house director attendance	Committees under the Board of Directors	Board agenda handling
	Convocation Announce of general meeting (shareholders)	General meeting of shareholders held other than concentrated days	Intensive/Electronic/ Written Voting system
	Dividend policy and implementation	Disclosure of violations of the Code of Ethics	Establishment of internal audit department
	Auditing agency expertise (accounting/ financial experts within the auditing body)		Governance law/regulations violation

Fortunately, given that responsible ESG investment and ESG management strategies are still in the early stages of adoption, the government needs to take a more cautious stance. Indeed, the diversity of ESG assessment methods can be clearly seen in the comparison of agencies provided by Deloitte Consulting:

Methods and systems of ESG assessment by Institutions (Deloitte)

Name	Methods	Scale	Evaluation Items
EcoVadis : *Supplier CSR Assessment*	Use of assessment platform: assessment based on data submitted by suppliers	100-0 Scorecard	· *5 Topics*: general (3), environment (5), labor practices and human rights policy (9), fair service practices (7), sustainable procurement (6), etc. 39 CSR questions in total
DJSI : *S&P Credit Rating*	Assess by answering topic questions: separate common assessment items from industry-specific items	0-100	· *Common assessment elements*: governance, ethical/risk/supply chain management, environmental performance, HRD, information disclosure · *Category by sector*: [*e.g.*: finance] Establishment of the ESG analysis framework, disclosure of the name and amount of the SVC/product, etc.
CDP : *Climate, Water & forest resource Assessment*	Assessment in response to subject questions: 3 areas related to the environment	A-D, F	· *Climate Change*: Greenhouse gas, governance, strategies/goals · *Forest*: Deforestation, dependence on raw materials, policy/decision · *Water*: Water importance, policy/ decision structure, water intake
MSCI : *ESG Evaluation*	Assessment based on publicly available information for 37 ESG issues	AAA-CCC (Leader - Sluggish)	· *Environment*: carbon emissions, e-waste, eco-friendly technology · *Society*: HR Development (HRD) · *Governance*: Board of Directors, Salary, Ownership Control, etc.

Name	Methods	Scale	Evaluation Items
Sustainalytics : *ESG risk Assessment*	Assessment based on public information	0-100 (Ignored - Serious)	• *Governance structure, major ESG issues by industry, special case evaluation*: 70 items for each industry
Bloomberg : *ESG public Evaluation*	Evaluate with publicly available information: only for subscribers	0-100	• Energy & Emissions, Waste, female executives, Board independence, employee accidents, transparency in ESG information disclosure
ISS : *Quality Evaluation*	Evaluation based on public info.: participates in the verification	1-10 (Risk Level)	• Around 230 assessments in 4 areas, including board structure, compensation, shareholder rights, audit, and risk management

As the saying goes, *"The devil is in the details"*. While the main indicators of Korean-style 'K-ESG' are generally acceptable, but there are concerns about new bureaucratic regulations in evaluation activities by applying them to the companies. In other words, the fact that the government, who should encourage and support transparent disclosure of information, the presented immature K-ESG indicator itself reminds us of the tyranny of power, which J.J. Rousseau pointed out to the arrogance of the government and bureaucrats.

For example, if the GRI Standards, which are used as global standards for reporting on sustainability, and the SASB (Sustainability Accounting Standards Board) Standards are compared, the subject, content, and methodology of classification of these information disclosures appear far differently: While the GRI presents standards and indicators in a broader organizational perspective rather than on specific issues, the SASB presents standards and indicators that allow a detailed examination of specific information in each area from a financial view.

Though it is announced, it is still questionable how the Korean government will institutionalize and apply these two types of standards as new versions of K-ESG in every 2-3 years as GRI is practicing. Since the GRI is already proposing an assessment framework that combines all GRI, ICRC, SDG, SASB, and now IFRS standards, it should be considered a model for the next version of K-ESG.[33]

33) The GRI standards are for the entire organization, and the SASB standards are based on financial issues, so refer to the research results that they should be used complementary (GRI and SASB reporting 'complement each other' – *GRI News Center*, 8 April 2021).

Comparison of ESG evaluation methods between GRI and SASB

Division	GRI Standards : *Organizational level*	SASB Standards : *Financial dimension*
Sustainability key Issues	Stakeholders and ESG influencing factors	Main ESG influencing factors related to finance
Form of standards	Subject-specific Standards	Industry-specific Standards
Disclosure target	For all stakeholders	For investors
Information disclosure requirements	Quantitative and qualitative indicators, guidelines, management, policies	Quantitative and qualitative indicators
GRI and SASB Standards: Concurrent use recommended	By using together, the comprehensive organizational indicators of the GRI and the detailed financial indicators of the SASB, it is possible to understand both the major issues of the company and the responsible management activities.	

On the other hand, even if the government takes the lead in the evaluation of ESG management, as argued by the French sociologist Michel Crozier, *"Society cannot be changed by the mere introduction of a new system"*. Therefore, the government should be faithful to the role of support and supervision, and the establishment and operation of ESG management-related systems should be initiated by the private sector and gradually settled as a K-ESG model suitable for Korea's industrial structure and business reality.

2 Birth and Development of ESG Management

The initial point of ESG is to focus on the prevention of global warming, the resolution of inequalities, the achievement of a fair society and the transparent management of companies.

However, a recent interest is to use it as a criterion for selecting an exemplary company with an ESG impact, that is to say a desirable investment target company, from the point of view of socially responsible investing (SRI).[34)]

Officially, the term ESG was first used in a report titled *"Who Cares*

34) Impact Investment: Investments that generate profits while also achieving environmental and social outcomes.

Wins-Connecting Financial Markets to a Changing World" by UNGC, published in early 2005 under the leadership of United Nations Secretary-General Kofi Annan (1997~2006).

Like the cover text, *"Connecting financial markets to a changing world,"* this report provides recommendations for comprehensively addressing ESG (environmental, social, and governance) related issues in corporate analysis, asset management, and stock trading.

The GRI standards presented in the UNGC report are not new ones, but rather comes from the SRI (socially responsible investing) movement of the early 90s to make decisions from an investor's perspective. Here, SRI is an investment standard that emerged from the CSR (corporate social responsibility) movement that began in the United States in the early 1950s.

- CSR movement began in 1921 as corporate donation philanthropy, when the US Internal Revenue Service made corporate social donations eligible for tax benefits if they met employee expectations. But it was hardly active under the shareholder capitalism.
- SRI movement is characterized by a focus on negative screening: First, *Ethical Investment*, which does not invest in companies such as alcohol, tobacco, and firearms, Second, *Social Investment* does not invest in companies that do not consider the protection of human rights, Third, *Eco-Investment,* which does not invest in companies that hinder the preservation of the environment, etc.
- ESG movement was officially initiated internationally by presenting the UNGC "*Who Cares Wins*" report, including environmental, social and corporate governance indicators.

Enron, which went bankrupt due to accounting fraud in 2001, showed and stressed the importance of transparent management. We can therefore say that SRI and GRI standards are indicators from the same root to assess the non-financial performance linked to the financial performance of a company.

Looking at the recent trend, while SRI focuses on *negative screening* among social screenings, GRI standards for ESG focuses more on *positive screening* that actively includes exemplary companies that fulfill their social responsibilities as investment targets. Key research findings show that ESG exemplary companies selected by positive screening have relatively low management risk and long-term stable growth.[35)]

With the ESG boom, institutional investors and financial institutions are paying more attention to the selection and investment of exemplary companies through positive screening. However, it must be clearly recognized that the 'good Karma' activities of the company derived from a positive screening can never compensate for the 'bad Karma' behaviors identified on a negative screening.

> The screening is an important criterion when interpreting ESG assessment scores for each sector of listed companies typically announced by a media.

Recently, several ESG-related rating agencies announced the sum of the ESG performance score corresponding to the good activity (or strength) and an ESG risk score corresponding to the bad activity (or weakness) by analyzing huge business news data with AI algorithms. As in Frederick Herzberg's *two-factor theory,* the satisfaction factor score, and the dissatisfaction factor score are assessed separately. This is because a model company with the highest ESG score can go bankrupt in an instant due to an evil business accounting fraud, like Enron and MCI WorldCom, which once became America's 7 largest companies.

The results of the assessment are difficult to interpret due to the limited rationality of responsible ESG investing, which favors creating value for investors rather than customers. In short, as a company, ESG management that looks into the eyes of investors is important, but it must be able to answer the more fundamental questions, *"What is a company?"* and *"What should it be?"* In other words, a company must be able to continuously generate profits through its social responsibility and innovation for customers.

1. Interest in socially responsible management

Howard Bowen's '*Social Responsibility of the Businessman*' in 1953 and Peter

35) Friede et al., 2015; Kumar et al., 2016.

The Practice of Management - Peter F. Drucker (Park K., 2015)

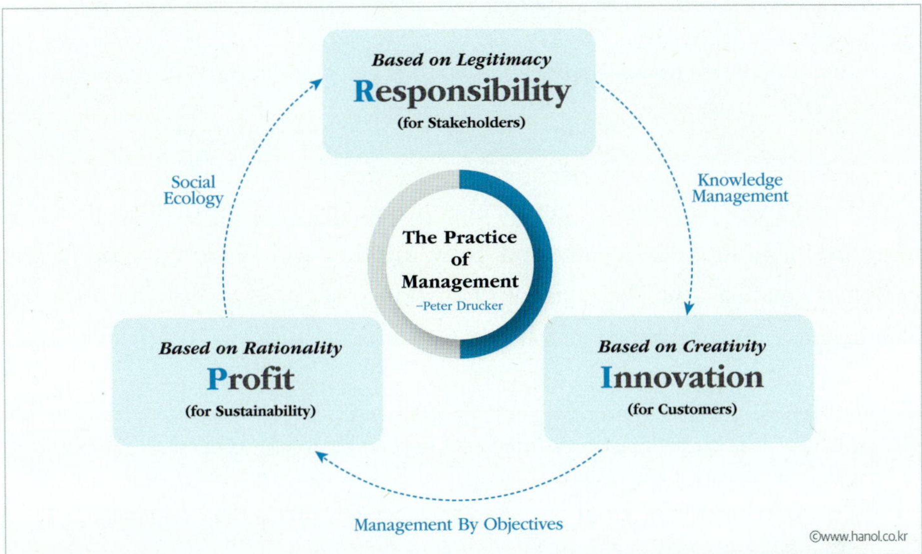

Drucker's '*The Practice of Management*' in 1954 can be regarded as the original source of the definition and necessity of corporate social responsibility.

> Along with the proposition *"What are the responsibilities society expects from entrepreneurs?"* Bowen defined social responsibility as the obligation of entrepreneurs to follow policies and decision-making that meet the goals and values of the company. In other words, entrepreneurs must have a social conscience to take responsibility for the results of their actions at a global level that goes beyond profits or financial losses.

Meanwhile, Drucker said that *"A company must seize new business opportunities and continuously practice innovative activities to create potential customers while at the same time pursuing profits and social responsibility"*: [Profit (P) · Responsibility (R) · Innovation (I)], the *'P·R·I Trinity' has been* highlighted as a true management practice.

According to Drucker, the initial task of a business is to achieve sustainable growth through the pursuit of profits and the creation of customers. However, the influence of today's businesses has grown unprecedentedly, and the greater their influence, the greater their social and environmental responsibilities.

> Drucker criticized the limits and properties of American shareholder capitalism in these terms: "*Shareholders can leave the company, but society always accompanies business. So, to the extent that corporations do not fulfill their responsibilities, society will eventually suffer.*"

Through these arguments, companies eventually came to realize that it is more desirable to enter society and grow together with society for profit and customer creation. And the concept of corporate social responsibility (CSR) has also begun to be established as follows:

- CSR is a decision-making action that goes beyond short-term economic and technological benefits (Davis, 1960).
- Companies must have social responsibilities that go beyond their economic and legal obligations (McGuire, 1963).
- The social responsibility of entrepreneurs must be realized as a business strategy (Heald, 1970).
- Managers must have the wisdom to consider the interests not only of shareholders, but also of employees, contractors, salespeople, local communities, and the country as a balanced view of the pursuit of profit (Johnson, 1971).
- Management is an 'organized body of knowledge'. Business is an 'organ of society' (Drucker, 1973).[36)]
- CSR is the set of actions taken by stakeholders to pursue it ethically in every situation, including economic, legal, ethical, and charitable responsibilities (Carroll, 1979).
- CSR is a process of making social agreements, not results (Jones, 1980).

Subsequently, as ethical management and transparent accounting standards were strengthened in the United States through CSR case studies, the Federal Sentencing Guideline in 1991 and the global standard ISO26000 for the related ISO (International Organization for Standardization) to CSR in 2010 were released. As the ISO26000 is applied as a means of regulating international trade, the ISO26000 standards affect the entire supply chain, focusing on manufacturers, not only in government and industry, but in NGOs, consumers, workers, and service areas.

36) Peter Drucker (1986), *Management: Tasks, Responsibilities*, Practices, Allied Publishers Private Limited.

7 Core Subjects of ISO26000

Subject	Indicators and Content
1. Environment	Pollution prevention, sustainable use of resources, mitigation and application of climate change, protection, and restoration of the natural environment
2. Human rights	Non-discrimination and consideration of vulnerable groups, avoidance of complicity in violations of human rights, civil rights, fundamental rights at work, political, economic, social, and cultural rights
3. Labor	Employment and labor relations, working conditions and social protection, social dialogue, human resources development, occupational health, and safety
4. Fair operation	Anti-corruption, responsible political participation, fair competition, social responsibility in the sphere of influence, respect for property rights
5. Consumer	Fair marketing, information and contract practices, consumer health and safety, consumer support, dispute resolution, consumer information and privacy, sustainable consumption, education, and awareness
6. Community	Participation, job creation, technology development, wealth and income, responsible investment, education culture, health, capacity building
7. Governance	Decision-making process and structure, delegation of authority

Meanwhile, in Europe, *Bilan Social,* promulgated in France on July 12, 1977, has been continuously strengthened thanks to the CSR guidelines. In addition, recently, the preparation of social responsibility reports and socially responsible investment (SRI) activities are also being activated.

Given the classification of Wayne Visser (2011)[37], who criticized the greedy evils of Western Capitalism, the performance level of corporate social responsibility in Korea is interpreted as the second stage (philanthropy) or the third stage (public relations) activities recognizing CSR as a tool for social contribution.

Of course, the goal of corporate social responsibility (CSR) and ESG responsible management should be established and practiced as a fourth step (strategic management) activity and afterward as a fifth step (systemic) integrated business model.

---

37) Wayne Visser (2011), *The Age of Responsibility: CSR 2.0 and the New DNA of Business.* Founder & Director, CSR International; Senior Associate, University of Cambridge Programme for Sustainability Leadership.

Current Trends of CSR (W. Visser, 2011)

Stage of CSR	Economic Age	Modus Operandi	Key Enabler	Stakeholder Target
1. Defensive	Greed	Ad hoc intervention	Investments	Shareholders, Government, Employees
2. Charitable	Philanthropy	Charitable programs	Projects	Communities
3. Promotional	Marketing	Public relations	Media	General public
4. Strategic	Management	Management systems	Codes	Shareholders, NGOs / CSOs
5. Systemic	Responsibility	Business models	Products	Regulators, Customers

2. Interest in sustainability management

The ESG standards establishes responsible investment assessment that addresses CSR and sustainable development management in an integrated manner. Sustainable management in the sense of ESG standards is a management paradigm in which sustainable growth in the global market is possible only when a company reflects not only the economic interests of shareholders but also the interests of various stakeholders and pursues environmental and social responsibilities at the same time.

The starting point for sustainability to be addressed on the global agenda was the Brundtland Commission Report *'Our Common Future'*, published by the United Nations Environment Program (UNEP) in 1987. Meanwhile, on March 24, 1989, an American tanker carrying 220,000 tons of crude oil collided with a reef on the Alaska coast, and about 40,000 tons of crude oil was spilled, causing massive environmental pollution. These environmental disasters have highlighted the importance of corporate responsibility for the environment around the world.

As a result, the GRI (Global Reporting Initiative) was launched in 1997 with UNEP led by CERES (Coalition for Environmentally Responsible Economies). The GRI, which was launched with a focus on corporate social responsibility for the environment, highlighted international interest in addressing not only environmental issues, but also economic, social, and corporate governance issues.

Mission and History of GRI

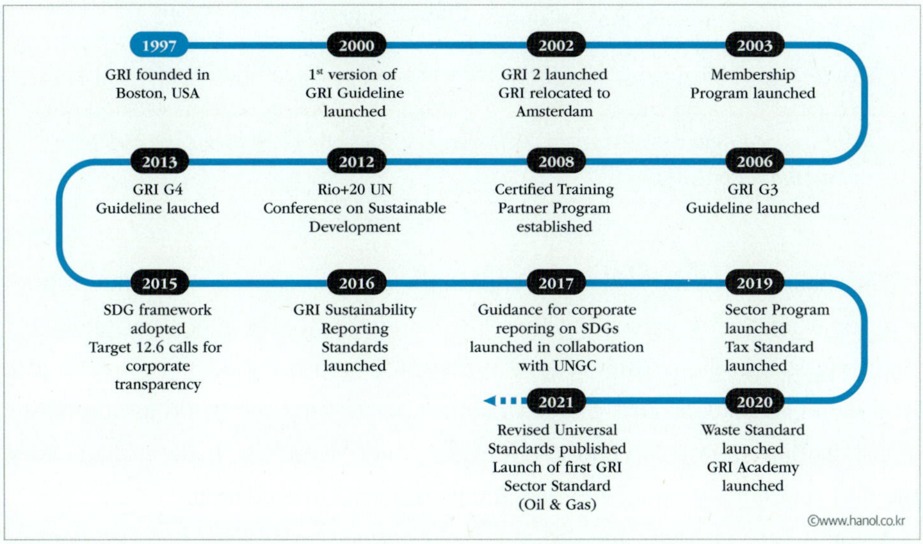

To this end, GRI continuously supplements the TBL (Triple Bottom Line) guidelines for the three core areas such as Economic, Social, and Environmental every 3-4 years as follows:

TBL for Sustainability Management (F. Spreckley, 1981)[38]

TBL	Main content of each TBL field
Environmental	Preservation of the global environment and environmental management: eco-friendly products and services, reduction of greenhouse gases and waste, etc.
Social	Human rights, safety and health, labor, product responsibility, supply chain management, community contribution, etc.
Economic	Creation of income and added value, job creation, fair trade, fair competition, etc.

The Single Bottom Line, that is, the net result of an accounting book, contains losses or gains as financial performance. The Double Bottom Line shows the social

38) Spreckley F. (1981), *Social Audit-A Management Tool for Cooperative Working*, Beechwood College.

performance of the company. And the Triple Bottom Line was first used in 1981 by Freer Spreckley in his book *'Social Audit-A Management Tool for Cooperative Working'* to mean reporting together the financial, social, and environmental performance of a company. It is emphasized that *"A company has an obligation to measure and report on Financial Performance, Social Wealth Creation, and Environmental Responsibility".*[39)]

The main role of the GRI is to prepare the guideline on sustainability reporting, for example by presenting the 'GRI standards' as the global sustainability reporting standards in 2016, after GRI first proposed the guideline in 2000 (G1). At the end of 2020, around 15,000 organizations around the world are preparing a sustainability report, and although every country tends to make it mandatory, the GRI standards is suggested essentially as a recommendation.

Among these changes, the *Brundtland Commission of the United Nations* in 1987 stressed the need for a report that comprehensively covers *Financial, Social,* and *Environmental* performance, which can be seen as laying the groundwork for guidelines for preparing sustainability reports that include both TBL and ESG.

In 1992, through UNCED (Conference on Environment and Development) and Rio Declaration, there appeared three environmental agreements: Convention on Climate Change (reduction of greenhouse gases such as CO2), Convention on Biological Diversity (conservation of ecosystems), and Convention for the Prevention of Global Desertification (prevention of desertification and resolution of water problems). In addition, environmental issues based on Kyoto Protocol in 1997, Paris Agreement and UN Framework Convention on Climate Change (UNFCCC) in 2015 emerged as the main topic of sustainable growth.

In 1997, John Elkington, recognized as an authority in Sustainable Capitalism by championing *'Green Growth', 'Green Consumer', and 'People-Planet-Profit',* has published *"Cannibals with Forks: The Triple Bottom Line of 21st Century Business".* The introduction provided a critical opportunity to prepare GRI standards for sustainable management and report based on TBL.

---

39) Spreckley's 'Theory of Social Audit' is a representative work that emphasizes that the existing shareholder capitalism should be converted to stakeholder capitalism.

History of Establishment of GRI and ESG Standards based on TBL

Year	Main Activities
1981	Spreckley's *'Social Auditory Theory'*: First use of the concept of TBL
1987	UN Bruntland Committee Report: Emphasis on writing sustainability report including Financial, Social, and Environmental performance
1992	UNED (UN Conference on Environment and Development) / Rio Declaration: Three major agreements on Climate change – Biodiversity – Prevention of global desertification
1997	Kyoto Protocol (1997) / Paris Climate Agreement (2015): Environmental issues emerge as the most important topic for sustainable growth
1997	Elkington's book *'Cannibals with Forks-The Triple Bottom Line of 21st Century Business'*: Establishing TBL-based GRI Standards
1998	The ILO announces four Principles, including the abolition of forced labor and child labor: Added as a major CSR issue
2001	UN General Assembly: MDGs (2001-2015) published and implemented followed by SDGs (2016-30) announced and implementing
2004	UNGC: Reorganization of SRI and sustainability management standards to ESG, Responsible ESG Investing (2020) is highlighted

In 1998, the International Labor Organization (ILO) announced the *'Four Principles for the Abolition of Forced Labor and Child Labor'*, and the *'Global Labor Guidelines'* were added as a matter of corporate social responsibility. Since then, GRI's socially responsible investing (SRI) and sustainable management (SM) standards have been reorganized into three broad categories of environmental, social, and governance, which have become ESG standards.

The importance of sustainability was underlined by the project promoted by the United Nations General Assembly in 2001: The Millennium Development Goals (MDGs) announced to practice by 2015, focusing on 48 indicators linked to 8 main goals and 18 detailed objectives.

The UN Sustainable Development Goals (SDGs), which are newly implemented from 2016 to 2030 after the end of the MDGs in 2015, include the universal problems of humanity (poverty, disease, education, gender equality, refugees, conflicts), global environmental problems (climate change, energy, environmental pollution, water, biodiversity), economic and social issues (technology, housing, work, employment, production and consumption, social structure, law, internal and external economy) etc.

17 common objectives that the international community must solve together

(169 detailed indicators) are implemented as follow:

17 UN Sustainable Development Goals (SDGs)

1. No Poverty: *End poverty in all its forms everywhere*
2. Zero Hunger: *End hunger, achieve food security and improved nutrition, and strengthen sustainable agriculture*
3. Good Health and Well-being: *Ensuring healthy lives and promoting the well-being of people of all ages*
4. Quality Education: *Ensure inclusive and equitable quality education and promote lifelong learning opportunities*
5. Gender Equality: *Achieving gender equality and empowering all women and girls*
6. Clean Water and Sanitation: *Ensure access to water and sanitation for all and sustainable management*
7. Affordable and Clean Energy: *Guarantee affordable, reliable, sustainable, and modern energy*
8. Decent Work and Economic Growth: *Promote sustainable, inclusive, and sustainable economic growth and full and productive employment and decent work for all*
9. Industry, Innovation, and Infrastructure: *Build resilient infrastructure, promote inclusive and sustainable industrialization, promote innovation*
10. Reducing Inequality: *Reduce inequalities within and between countries*
11. Sustainable Cities and Communities: *Create inclusive, safe, and resilient sustainable cities and settlements*
12. Responsible Consumption and Production: *Guarantee sustainable consumption and production patterns*
13. Climate Action: *Implement urgent actions to fight against climate change and its impacts*
14. Life below Water: *Conservation and sustainable use of ocean, sea, and marine resources for sustainable development*
15. Life on Land: *Protect, restore, and promote the sustainable use of terrestrial ecosystems, sustainably manage forests, fight against desertification, stop land degradation, stop biodiversity loss*
16. Peace and Justice: *Promote peaceful and inclusive societies for all levels of sustainable development, achieve justice for all and build inclusive, effective, and accountable institutions*
17. Partnership for the Goals: *Reinforcement of means of implementation and vitalization of global partnerships for sustainable development*

Responsible ESG investment evaluation criteria that has been emphasized recently is *'Consensus TBL'*, and since it was announced by the UNGC in early

2005, all organizations have reorganized indicators and weights as needed and used them in the assessment of responsible investment.

Context of ESG standards for responsible investment

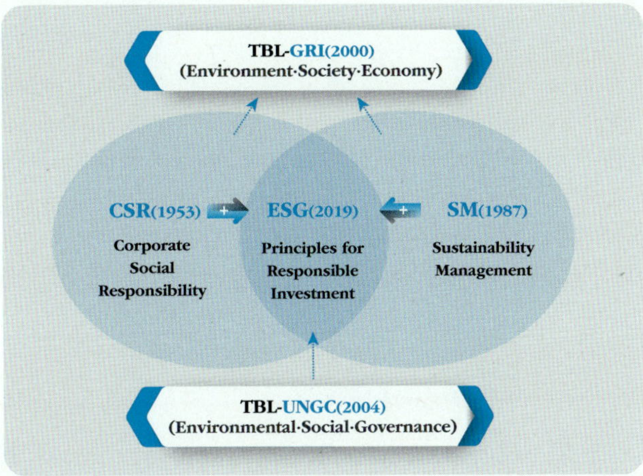

©www.hanol.co.kr

CSR, ESG, and sustainability management-related indicators should be implemented differently for each company in consideration of the industry situation, corporate competitiveness, vision, and unique organizational culture. Accordingly, it is sometimes presented as a Quadruple Bottom Line (QBL) in consideration of time variables in each ESG performance.

For example, in Amazon's Market Place Division, the SPC (Selection, Price, Convenience) is summarized based on a standard that will not change for a long time, as Jeff Bezos said, *"We have a service that will not change even after 10 years."* In other words, even 10 years from now, Amazon customers will have *'a wide range of purchasing options'*, *'lower purchase prices'* and *'quick delivery'*. Amazon will continue to grow by practicing the essence of its retail business.

Chairman Kim Beom-seok of Coupang, who was successfully listed on the New York Stock Exchange in March 2021, also said in the listing application: *"Coupang will overcome the dilemma that exists in the customer experience, including a wide range of product options, low prices, and amazing service."*

In fact, Coupang is showing the aftermath of rapid growth such as safety accidents and corporate governance problems. However, the future of Coupang is expected to be very bright, thanks to a super-fast delivery system such as *'early-morning and same-day delivery'* that Amazon cannot afford, a friendly service system for free exchanges and returns, and a membership price of less than 25% compared to Amazon.

> However, as Drucker argued, companies must simultaneously pursue creative innovation for profit, social responsibility, and customer creation. Therefore, Amazon and Coupang etc. should also implement the process [E·S·G → P]: *Environmental, Social & Governance → Performance & Profits*, to ensure that ESG management for stakeholders appear as a long-term sustainable profit generation. Thus, it is necessary to establish a sustainable growth mechanism together with ESG management, and to solve strategic tasks while clarifying the timing for achieving the goal in the QBL method.

Interest in ESG and SDGs management is growing worldwide due to the consensus on the climate crisis, but in fact, in Korea, only about 150 organizations report the performance of ESG management, and research and practice on SDGs management is not yet highlighted.

On the other hand, in the case of Japan, it explains in detail the relationship between the 7 themes of ISO26000 and the 17 principles of the UN's SDGs for ESG management led by the Ministry of Economy, Trade and Industry in one comprehensive road.

As the like, the Ministry of Trade, Industry and Energy of Korea is focusing more on establishing K-ESG standards. In contrast, Japan's Ministry of Economy, Trade, and Industry is instructing companies to understand *"What ESG management is?"*, *"What it should do, and why?"*, and then make it according to international standards and their own business characteristics.

In fact, compared to Korea, which has a strong *'Know-Whom'* organizational culture (Park, 2015), Japan shows an organizational culture that values *'Know-What'*. As such, Japan is focusing more on understanding what ESG management is, GRI Standards, ISO26000, and the 17 principles of SDGs.

Therefore, Korea, like Japan, should consider each major ESG task, highlight their strengths, and consider how to prepare a sustainability report or ESG management report. In other words, companies should be able to autonomously select various indicators in line with global standards.

ESG Matrix example by ISO26000 and SDGs (METI Japan, 2020)

ESG	ISO26000 (7 Principles)	ESG Main Tasks (Enterprise level)
E	Environment	• Climate change and air pollution • Water and waste management • Biodiversity and conservation
S	Human rights	• Human rights protect and respect • Treatment of foreign workers
	Labor practices	• Human Resources and Welfare • Employee Health and Safety • Human resource development
	Fair operating practices	• Fair Trade Compliance • Shared growth
	Consumer issues	• Product quality and safety • Health value and personal information protection
	Community involve/develop	• community service • Local environment and culture
G	Organization governance	• Ownership structure and shareholder rights • Board diversity (number of women, etc.) • Ethical management & anti-corruption compliance

SDGs 17 Goals (Matching indicators)

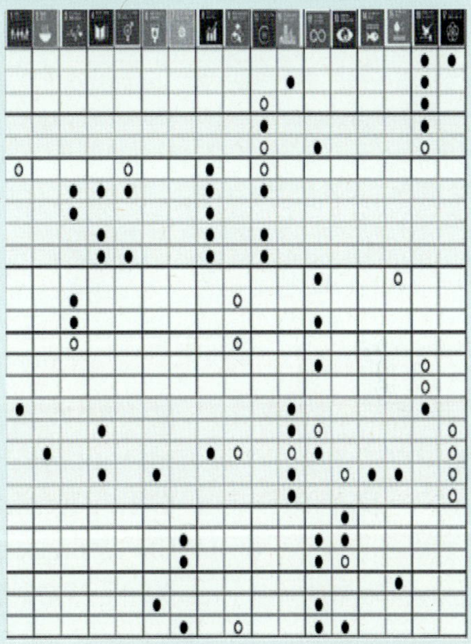

As Peter F. Drucker argued, the influence of organizational culture on performance creation is far more powerful and far more important than sophisticated business strategies. Therefore, Korea also needs to prepare detailed indicators suitable for each industry and company along with the consensus and understanding of all members of the global standards and indices that are the basis of ESG management and responsible ESG investment.

3. Interest in ESG management

It is said that there are already thousands of experts around the world working under the title of ESG analyst. Asset managers and financial institutions also emphasize that ESG information is essential for understanding a company's vision, goals, strategy, and growth potential, and recognize companies that are good at ESG management as exemplary companies.

In Korean society, ESG indicators are emerging as a core value of corporate sustainability rather than an abstract issue of traditional CSR. In particular, young people who are digital natives born between the mid-1990s and early 2000s, who suffer from COVID-19, especially Generation Z, tend to consider economic practicality and social fairness when buying even small things.

> 'Impact Investment' by ESG uses environmental, social and governance factors in investment decisions, so the responsible ESG investing assessment is not a traditional financial analysis but consist of a very wide range of non-financial items related to social issues. For example, how a company responds to climate change and manages water, safety, and health well to prevent accidents, fair treatment of employees, effective supply chain management and creates an organizational culture that promotes trust, fairness, and compliance.

Looking back at the birth of the ESG, it began in 2004 when some fifty CEOs from major global financial institutions participated in a joint project hosted by the UNGC (United Nations Global Compact) supported by the IFC (International Finance Corporation) and the Swiss government.

A key objective of the UNGC project was to find a way to integrate ESG into capital markets. As a result, the *'Who Cares Wins'* report, released a year later, demonstrated that the inclusion of environmental, social and governance factors in capital markets makes sense for companies and leads to desirable outcomes for markets and more sustainable societies.

The UNEP FI (United Nations Environment Program Finance Initiative) published the *'Freshfields Report'* in 2005 and 2009, showing that ESG performance is linked to financial performance. On this basis, the NYSE (New York Stock Exchange) published PRI (Principles for Responsible Investment) in 2006. The following year, in 2007, the UNCTAD (United Nations Conference on Trade and Development) launched the SSEI (Sustainable Securities Exchange Initiative). SSEI is now proliferating as a global initiative, managing over $ 70 trillion in assets by the end of 2020.

> The role of the PRI, supported by UNEP, is to analyze ESG and consolidate investment decisions. Meanwhile, the role of SSEI, supported by UNCTAD, is to provide advice to listed companies on how to request ESG disclosures and ESG reporting.

Institutional investors should conduct analysis and evaluation activities in accordance with PRI standards to enable companies to practice 'good management' to improve ESG performance. Therefore, ESG emphasizes its responsibility as an institutional investor and fiduciary by focusing on the role of analyzing and evaluating ESG performance in accordance with PRI standards.

Responsible ESG management, which companies must support, develops its own expertise and becomes a socially necessary existence, but it is not expected to standardize and level the standardized assessment of ESG management.

In 2015, a report titled *'Fiduciary Duty in the 21st Century'* was published jointly by PRI, UNEP FI, UNEP Inquiry, and UNGC. This report stated that *"If the trustee does not take into account the long-term investment value including ESG issues, it is a breach of fiduciary duty."*

Here, ESG issues have been integrated and standardized through the following decisions: *Publication of a statement integrating ESG issues into investment processes and practices; Policy establishment roadmap to fully integrate ESG issues in the investment processes and practices of the eight participating countries; Expanded and applied investor obligations to six markets, including China, Hong Kong, India, Korea, Malaysia, and Singapore.*

It also issued a joint statement from 22 countries on fiduciary obligations as investors in projects carried out between 2016 and 2019. In particular, the European Union (EU) has fully implemented these recommendations.

The key content of the final report (*fiduciary duty in the 21st century*) is to highlight the fact that *"If you fail to address ESG issues in an integrated manner as an investor, you have failed to fulfill your fiduciary duty, therefore the possibility of legal sanctions will increase".* As such, now is the time to strategically address responsible ESG investment standards.

The problem is that the fiduciary duty is inherent in the responsible ESG investment standards, and it has been established and spread to pursue sustainable management. However, capital markets themselves are by no means sustainable. In other words, although legal regulatory frameworks for investment managers and financial institutions are beginning to have a significant impact on responsible ESG investment standards, little has been done about the impact of these institutional investors' investment decisions on ESG issues. For this reason, a new era role of continuous monitoring and support from ESG initiative bodies and national governments is needed for these institutions.

Institutional investors have rejected these broad ESG concepts because they still emphasize maximizing shareholder value. However, as a result of academic research that started in 2013, evidence that ESG performance directly affects not only financial performance but also corporate sustainability, the situation is changing rapidly. Therefore, the application of ESG standards is emphasized as the duty of institutional investors.

As a result of research showing that stock prices of highly sustainable companies are much higher in ESG evaluation, the perception that high returns can be achieved by investing with ESG risk in mind is rapidly spreading in the capital market. For example, major European pension funds and insurance companies allow new businesses only to asset management institutions with ESG evaluation capabilities, and global investment institutions are developing various methods such as an integrated ESG working guide for stock investment.

Also, unlike Korea, which is emotionally sensitive to corporate governance issues (G), many ESG factors in these countries include those related to climate change (E). Because climate change is not a threat in the distant future, it has become a major threat, costing billions of dollars in economic losses.

To achieve carbon neutrality by 2050, all measures such as electric vehicles, new and renewable energy, and technological innovation are being mobilized. Recommendations made by the Climate-Related Financial Disclosures Task Force (FCFD)[40] on environmental risk preparedness and decarbonization measures are now highlighted as global standards.

Among the ESG factors, the evaluation of environmental performance requires cutting-edge scientific analysis. As Peter F. Drucker put it, *"What gets measured gets managed,"* the heart of ESG management, dealing with non-financial information,

40) The TCFD was established in 2015 under the leadership of the Financial Stability Board (FSB), an advisory body between G20 finance ministers and central bank governors, with the aim of preparing measures to disclose information related to the climate change.

is collecting precise information for each indicator, and applying a series of scientific techniques ranging *'from measurement to analysis, synthesis, and proposal'*.

Failure to comply with ESG standards may result in expulsion from international trade and government regulations. Of course, in the era of artificial intelligence and big data, if only data by ESG criteria are provided in a timely and accurate manner, there will be no difficulties in analysis and evaluation. Likewise, the biggest challenge for ESG management is the accurate and complete disclosure and analysis of corporate information.

Recently, when Korean companies are rushing to report ESG management, there is also a phenomenon that "investors have a greater influence than customers". In other words, companies become more sensitive to the overall evaluation of stakeholders including investors, in relation to fulfilling social responsibility beyond customer value evaluation of products or services.

In general, most of the financial information of a company is presented clearly, but the non-financial and qualitative information required by ESG is naturally selected and provided by frequently manipulating information that is advantageous to the company. In addition, from the perspective of the ESG manager in charge of operation, the more socially important ESG is, the more directly it is directly related to the performance of the department or manager in charge, so manipulations to evade responsibility may follow.

As an evidence of project experience effectuated in 2005, at the request of the Federation of Korean Industries (FKI), the company's ethical management report guideline (FKI-BEX) was newly proposed, and the results were presented in the academic paper *"Establishment of ethical management evaluation indicators for Korean companies. A Study on FKI-BEX Indicators"* has also been published.[41)]

Most of the CSR executives of the FKI member companies agreed with the systematic and practicality of the sophisticated indicators but were negative

41) Park & Cho (2009), "Business Ethics Practice Mechanism and Business Ethics Index Development", *Korean Journal of Business Ethics,* vol.11, No 1. The Korea Academy of Business Ethics.

about external disclosures and inter-company benchmarking. The reaction was that the news article could damage the company's fatal image, cause legal problems, and cause them to resign and take responsibility as responsible executives. As a result, the FKI-BEX standards are not yet widely used. This is also an example of how an ESG system alone cannot change business practices, just as laws alone cannot change society. However, as ESG has become a hot topic of the times, Korean companies are also busy establishing an ESG management committee.

> In January 2020, Laurence D. Fink, chairman of BlackRock, the world's largest investment manager, said: *"Now, when making investment decisions, we will base our investment decisions on sustainability, not on corporate financial performance."* This announcement has a significant impact on the trend toward the transition from shareholder to stakeholder capitalism.

A key task for the proper functioning of the ESG depends on the transparency of information. Then, *"How to standardize these comprehensive assessment indicators and make them available internationally and the attitude of stakeholders to accept the ESG standards?"*

Since the launch of the GRI (Global Reporting Initiative) in 2000, disclosure of information about ESG-related companies has continued to expand, making sustainability reporting based on GRI standards, and the elements of performance.

Overall, the ESG information market is maturing, and information reliability is improving. By using AI and big data, we are already gaining important insights, and we can quickly synthesize and visualize existing financial information and various ESG information. The five global ESG-related organizations (GRI, CDP, IIRC, SASB, CDSB) have already started an international standard integration project for ESG performance reporting in September 2020, and IFRS (International Financial Reporting Standards) is now actively working on ESG standardization.

> In fact, even as evaluation systems and criteria are standardized and disclosure become mandatory, this is only a new standard, and effectiveness depends on stakeholders' acceptance and the transparency of information.

What is important is that even if advanced science such as carbon emission measurement or proof of damage to humidifier disinfectant does everything, it is difficult to measure and analyze all detailed ESG indicators accurately and fairly.

Roles of ESG managemet related Actors

As responsible ESG investment spreads, it leads to legal battles at home and abroad, and ultimately, companies that want to avoid this are expected to consider ESG with minimal disclosure or a passive stance. Nevertheless, recent social interest in global environmental conservation and information technology innovations such as AI is leading to more effective ESG activities such as improved stakeholder understanding and transparency of non-financial information disclosure that reduces ESG data processing time and costs.

Evaluation activities are underway. Since ESG information is seen as a criterion for investors to select good sustainable companies and avoid companies with low performance or high probability of failure, responsible ESG investing is also at the forefront of creating social value for the market and businesses.

4. The trend towards mandatory disclosure of ESG information

At the end of 2020, ESG information disclosure became mandatory in 20 countries around the world and required to publish in the form of a sustainability report. From March 2021, the EU has extended the subject of ESG information disclosure of pension funds to all financial institutions such as banks, insurance companies and asset management companies, and the UK has made it mandatory by 2025. Although the US has liberalized the disclosure of ESG information, more than 90% of US companies are publishing sustainability reports.

In Korea, about 100 companies publish sustainability reports, but only 20 companies declare them on the Korea Exchange. In line with the trend of mandatory ESG information disclosure in developed countries, Korea also announced in March 2021 a plan to make ESG disclosure mandatory led by the Financial Services Commission. Korea entered an era where information can be analyzed with AI to identify 'exemplary companies' in real time.

From 2025 in Korea, companies listed on KOSPI with assets of 2 trillion won (1.5 billion USD) or more must disclose the sustainability report. By 2030, all companies listed on KOSPI will be eligible. From 2021, the *'Corporate Governance Report'* disclosure requirement, which applies to 211 KOSPI-listed companies with assets of 2 trillion won or more, will apply to all listed companies at KOSPI in 2026, after reaching 1 trillion won in 2022 and 500 billion won in 2024.

Since 2018, the Korean Financial Services Commission has assessed the performance of the implementation of the Stewardship Code[42], the *"Principles on the*

42) Stewardship Code: In the UK, this refers to the duty of a butler to take care of the housework. In 2009, the concept of 'Responsibilities of Institutional Investors' was introduced into the financial market, and the stewardship code was used as an obligation to institutional investors in Morgan Stanley's Corporate Governance Report. In other words, it is a system that allows the pension fund to intervene in corporate decision-making with the

Responsibility of Trustees of Institutional Investors", at the level of United Kingdom and Japan, and strengthened the accountability of ESG-related Trustees and Voting Advisors.

The principle of fiduciary duty is the most important system for the proper functioning of the evaluation of ESG management. As such, Korea is at an important turning point in evaluating a company's ESG performance from an investor's perspective. However, the more fundamental task is to understand ESG and provide transparent information, especially scientific analysis of company information and professional interpretation of assessment results.

To this end, France attaches great importance on the annotations and appendices in the Social Report (*Bilan Social*) above the evaluation score for each indicator. In addition, the reliability of the report is ensured by careful monitoring of the accuracy and transparency of information disclosure by labor inspectors in each region of the government for social performance and social audit activities.

In Korea as well, it is important to activate a legally independent official body that oversees the non-financial activities of companies, such as the role of labor inspectors in France, rather than institutional investors or consulting firms, for the performance evaluation, measurement, and disclosure of ESG indicators.

3 Purpose of ESG Management

As investor's influence grows, corporate responsible ESG investment standards are being developed together and many ESG rating agencies are in operation. However, the views and standards for assessing and auditing the social performance of companies, including social responsibility and sustainable management, are appearing differently in each country.

In the United States, items are classified as responsible for the preservation of social organizations or social ecosystems of outside the company, meanwhile, those items are classified as social responsibility of employees inside the com-

guidelines for exercising voting rights. Korea introduced the stewardship code system on July 30, 2018, allowing the National Pension Service to intervene in the management of invested companies.

pany in France. In other words, the French law on the *Bilan Social* promulgated in 1977, requires companies with 300 or more employees to submit reports to labor inspectors and shareholders.

> Therefore, the recent situation in the United States and Korea, which emphasizes ESG management as if it were a new standard for SRI (socially responsible investing), lacks historical considerations and institutionalization of the social performance of the companies, social responsibility, and social performance report etc. compared to those of European countries.

France has been focused on the internal social performance of the company, since 2002, the social performance report included environmental issues as a major indicator, and the Social and Environmental Accounting Report of NCC (National Accounting Commission) which began to publish from 2003 made the preparation of the corporate social performance report compulsory. Now in France, the implementation of social responsibility is more concretely applied than the general ESG indicators. The UK has also required disclosure of relevant corporate information under the Companies Act 2006.

Thus, in Europe, where the importance of social performance has been underlined since the early 1950s, research results have also shown that the societal performance of companies raises the economic performance of companies within a certain limit. In other words, when the external social performance of a company is too high or too low, the economic performance of the company appears relatively poor, but when the external social performance is at an appropriate level, the economic performance appears the most.

> Therefore, for the part of the company, it can be noted that an excessive focus on CSR performance or ESG management would not be desirable for the sustainable growth of a company.

Relationship between economic and social performance (Park, 2015)

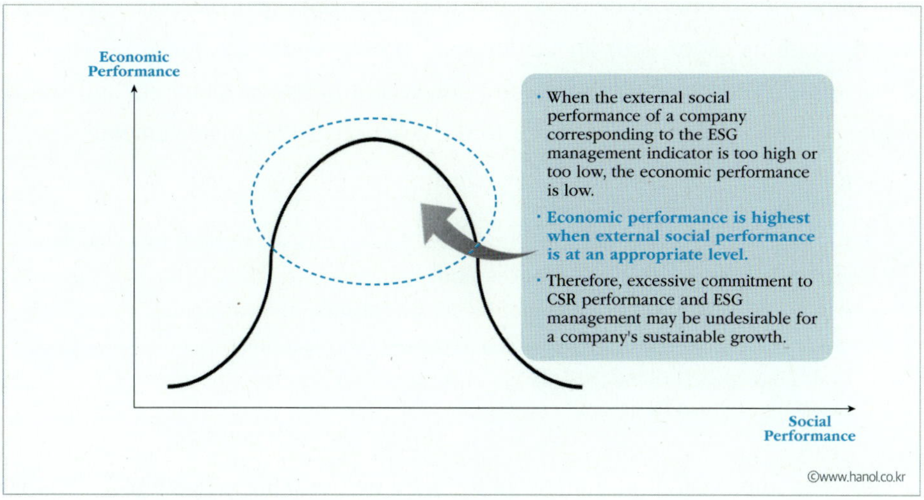

Interestingly, the same type of relationship exists between a company's economic and social performance, which depends on market conditions such as booms and depressions, oil prices, and exchange rates. It is also interesting to note that the economic performance of a company varies according to its value system and its mode of management.

In summary, social, and economic performance is high in companies that practice transparent ethical management through communication and consensus in a climate that emphasizes the value of respect for human beings.

The question of corporate social responsibility issues, highlighted even in French *syndicalism* which appeared as an alternative to capitalism at the end of the 19th century, require a good understanding of the meaning of the word *'social'*. In other words, CSR should be presented as a social contract, or a grand compromise formed by the free consent of all members and stakeholder groups.

So, can these global principles or regulations, which weigh heavily on companies, such as CSR, SRI, SASB, GRI and ESG standards, really be a *'social contract'* made by consensus among members of society?

If the top management and government officials disagree, or if trade unions and employees do not understand why and what ESG management is for, ESG will be nothing more than an institutional power under the guise of 'creating social value'. Thus, understanding and agreement between members and stakeholders is of paramount importance in the practice of ESG management.

Take the example of the *'Golden Circle (why-how-what)'*, a framework for scientific research.[43] "*Why–How–What*" about running a business:

- *'Why'* corresponds to the pursuit of profits and competitive advantage,
- *'What'* corresponds to sales growth and decent job creation, and
- *'How'* corresponds to the formulation of strategy and practice activities.

However, the content and answers to *"why do you run a business"* question are evolving: Even if the heart of the manager is in the search for profit, the thesis officially declared appears to promote social responsibility or the creating shared values. The content and sense of purpose responses of *"what is business management for"* also change. In other words, even the CEO's real dream is set on the market dominance, it is officially disguised as if laid on managing sustainability or creating new customers coming through the social consensus.

In addition, although there are common factors such as digital transformation and entering the platform business, the strategic implementation plan of *"how to create sustainable shared value"* appears in a different way by every single business company.

Even if the Golden Circle of ESG management emphasizes the criteria of SRI (socially responsible investing) and selection of exemplary or good companies, these are all minimum conditions necessary for a sustainable management of a company, and not sufficient conditions.

It is said that the secret to a long-standing Japanese company that has operated Udon (うどん, Japanese noodles) restaurant for over 600 years comes from the craftsmanship itself, not from ESG just like a five-star Michelin restaurant,

43) Sinek S. (2009). *Start With Why: How Great Leaders Inspire Everyone to Take Action,* Penguin.

or Christian Dior. Therefore, *"Isn't the secret of sustainable growth to focus on building differentiated core competencies, already well known in the global market, rather than on ESG management introduced as a fad?"*

One example is 'Blue Ocean Strategy' co-authored by Wichan Kim and Rene Mauborne of INSEAD Business School in France. The blue ocean strategy was a success strategy showing a *'new How'* and spotlighted by LG Group in Korea at one time but fell into the dilemma that *"It is only possible to realize Michael Porter's generic strategy of cost advantage and differentiation at the same time"*. In the end, it became a strategy ignored by the company.[44)]

If ESG degenerates into a trend, the cause will be another burden placed on companies before core competencies, namely the *'good management dilemma'*.

The responsible ESG investing movement has been spreading around the world since 2020, although it is influenced by the results of the US presidential election and the increased interest in investing in equities. The goals and mission of ESG include the desire to practice responsible management based on global 'universalism' to protect the rights and interests of different stakeholders in response to the destruction of the environment, the acceleration of industrial accidents and frequent financial and accounting irregularities.

On the other hand, the key to the success of ESG management ultimately lies in the 'selectionism' of how to implement *'ESG as a firm-specific strategy'*, that is, the company's unique *'How strategy'*. Therefore, in ESG management, strengthening the differentiated corporate core competencies would be an essential requirement.

To become a company loved and respected by society, attracting global investment, and becoming a sustainable business, the followings should be considered:

First, Drucker's PRI (profit, responsibility, and innovation) philosophy must be put into practice. In other words, a company must strive for profit, fulfill its social

44) Park K. (2015), *Professor Kichan PARK on Strategic Management,* IUP.

responsibility, and practice innovation to create customers.

Second, from a methodological point of view, according to the BSC (balanced scorecard) of Kaplan & Norton (1992), a comprehensive assessment including non-financial information such as learning should be performed.

Third, institutionally, it is necessary to operate with a legal authority such as the French *'Bilan Social'*, which assesses the social performance of companies.

Ultimately, sustainability management requires to pursue in a voluntary and selective manner by putting the value of a company's existence on sustainability rather than generating profits, identifying, and evaluating all the 'hidden costs' that companies generate. In short, we may conclude that creating social value became an essential condition for ESG management.[45] Then, *"Can ESG be an effective double bottom line, a new 'smart How', which contributes to the creation of medium-and long-term profits as well as to sustainable growth of a company?"*

The arguments of researchers including Bob Eccles (2014) are very positive. These research findings prove that while ESG and ethical management are not directly related to creating short-term profits, they have a direct impact on long-term corporate sustainability. In the case of practitioners, it is even more positive. Indeed, it appears that the share of socially responsible investing (SRI), which increases in the social value of companies considering the ESG level, represents more than half of the total assets under management in developed countries.

Example of Double-Bottom Line (Profit & Responsibility)

	Assessment of profit creation and CSR activities to select the right companies loved and respected by the society
Drucker (1954)	PRI (*Profit, Responsibility, Innovation*): A company must strive for profit, embrace social responsibility at the same time, and constantly innovate to create customers.
Kaplan (1996)	BSC (*Balanced Scorecard*): In addition to financial performance, it is necessary to prepare a balanced scorecard to assess non-financial information of the company, such as learning, process, and to plan future strategies.

45) Trépo & de Geuser (2003), "Managing the unmanageable: How can SEAM give back to employees and work situations their anthropological original substance?", *Journal of Organizational Change Management*, Vol. 16 Issue: 1, pp.99-106.

Assessment of profit creation and CSR activities to select the right companies loved and respected by the society	
Trépo (2003)	SEAM (*Socio-Economic Approach to Management*): It is necessary to simultaneously seek social and economic performance by understanding the 'hidden cost' of running a business.
France (1977) (2017)	BS (*Bilan Social*): A French social performance report, introduced by the law of 1977, that assesses a company's social performance, and the labor inspectorate submits it to the government to determine the level of government support. Since by the law of 2017, it devoted to the CSE's annual consultation on corporate social policy, working conditions and employment.[46]
ESG	II (*Impact Investing*): Responsible ESG investing rating agencies such as MSCI, Bloomberg, IBD and BlackRock, the world's largest asset management companies, select the 'exemplary (good) companies' through analysis of ESG related information.

The birth of the ESG concept dates to the 1950s, when the focus was on CSR (corporate social responsibility), however on a practical level, institutional investors in advanced countries reflected the GRI and UN Global Compact standards such as the protection of global environment and human rights.

Thus, the ESG is entering into the path of dissemination. Although the implementation of the concept of ESG is insufficient at the academic level, the zeitgeist is in the sense that ethical management and the practice of transparent management of a company that prioritizes the global environment and human society will continuously improve the value of the enterprise.

When global responsible ESG investing rating agencies such as MSCI-Morgan Stanley Capital Investment, Bloomberg, IBD (Investor's Business Daily) and BlackRock, the world's largest asset management firms, focused on information disclosure and declared that they practice responsible investing, the Fiduciary Institution Investors accept ESG as a criterion for selecting an impact company that includes issues related to all stakeholders of the company. As a result, companies are also active in implementing long-term strategic tasks and short-term operational tasks for ESG management.

46) CSE (*comité social et économique*): In-house 'social and economic committee' composed of representatives for a four-year term elected by employees.

4 The Future of ESG Management

1. Development trends related to the environmental issues

The global interest in climate change is unprecedently growing: The GRI, launched in 1997 with the affirmation of corporate environmental responsibility, the Paris Agreement in 2015, the UN SDGs (Sustainable Development Goals) in 2016, and the United States with President Joe Biden returned to the Paris Agreement in 2020, and the recent declaration of carbon neutrality by 2050 by countries around the world would be a prime example.

As such, the protection of the global environment spreads by sharing and creating symbiotic value throughout the supply chain, regeneration, restoration, and building a good company with a humanistic working environment. While cutting-edge technologies in the age of digital transformation such as AI and big data are combined here, the framework and method of analysis are systematized across ESG indicators, including environmental indicators.

> The EU, which advocates carbon neutrality and digital transformation, also plans to create 700,000 new jobs by 2030 with the '3R (Reduce, Reuse, Recycle) circular economy' announced in 2020 to promote resource recycling. This interest in climate and environmental change has been the driving force for ESG to emerge as an alternative to CSR, which has emphasized social contribution conceptually.

ESG is also spreading around the world to address issues of social responsibility, sustainability, and transparent management: Microsoft is already pushing carbon neutrality through technological development with its multi-billion dollar *'Climate Innovation Fund'*, and Bill Gates recently published *"How to Avoid a Climate Catastrophe (2021)"* emphasizing to reduce the effect of greenhouse gas emissions by 51 billion tons per year.

The *'technological-political-market structure'* is proposed by the developed countries to achieve 'Net Zero': Amazon's Jeff Bezos announced a plan to replace 10,000 delivery vehicles with electric vehicles by 2022 and use a total of 100,000 by 2030 to achieve carbon neutrality by 2040, 10 years earlier than the due goal of Paris Climate Agreement.

In August 2021, Korea also presented a policy direction for a sustainable carbon-neutral society with three scenarios *(Proposal 1: 25.4 million tons, Plan 2: 18.7 million tons, Plan 3: Zero) for the 'Net Zero goal in 2050'.*

Therefore, new combinations of industrial structures and technological innovations must be able to achieve these goals. However, it should be borne in mind that the risk of hasty policies that are not bound by speed is too high to cause unexpected social chaos and contradictions in the industrial structure.

So, there is a social contract or social compromise that says, *"If you want to go fast, you can go alone, led by the government, but if you want to go far, the entire society must join hands."* In fact, carbon neutrality and greenhouse gas reduction are not a short-term task at the current government level, but a continuous task at the national level that must be continued.

ESG's environmental challenges require the *'professional effort'* of accounting and finance professionals to develop and internationally disseminate commonly applied indicators. However, it is more important to *'scientific focus'* on R&D activities for a common evaluation method that can analyze information on each indicator more accurately.

2. Development trends related to the social issues

Corporate social responsibility related issues appear both in production activities in the *'upstream sector'* and in consumer activities in the *'downstream sector'*: CSR focuses on social and environmental value creation activities that consider all stakeholders, going beyond existing activities limited to sound management and customer creation as the main body of the current market economy.

Contrary to popular belief, CSR has always been presented in corporate management activities since the early 20th century. First, Frederick W. Taylor's pursuit of *Common prosperity'* through scientific management; Second, it is the practice of *'Profit-Responsibility-Innovation'* based on Drucker's MBO *(Management by Objective)*. Third, Michael Porter's practice of 'Win-win management' based on CSV (Creating Shared Value) is a representative argument.

The biggest problem is that the greater the social influence of a company, the greater its responsibility. Influence comes when we wield power, so we must consider social responsibility based on ethical and moral standards rather than addressing the issue of growing the source of power itself.

Therefore, as a criterion for evaluating influence management, large enterprises with absolute advantages in terms of economic, social, and political influence should preferentially apply ESG standards as a criterion for evaluating influence management compared to SMEs with relatively weak social influence.

3. Development trends related to the governance issues

Governance structure for transparent management of companies, i.e., the issue of governance, has recently become very important in Korean companies where the '*Gapjil* (*abuse of positional power*)' incidents frequently occur. Also, at the global level, it is argued that the role of outside directors, which had only played a limited role in the composition of the audit committee and the board of directors, has strengthened their roles as supervisors and the proportion of female executives has increased with diversity of race and origin.

Examples include BlackRock's announcement in 2018 that it will not invest in companies with fewer than two females outside directors, and Goldman Sachs' announcement in 2020 that it will not undertake IPO (Initial Public Offering) work for companies that do not meet the diversity of the board of directors.

A growing number of women have taken over as CEO, including IBM's *Virginia Rometty,* YouTube's *Susan Wojcicki,* Yahoo's *Marissa Mayer,* and Citigroup's *Jane Fraser.* On the other hand, in Korea, there are only a handful of CEOs from owner families.

With the recent emphasis on ESG management, Korean companies with assets of 2 trillion won or more have made the quota system for female outside directors' mandatory from August 2021. As a result, the number of female non-executive directors more than doubled compared to the previous year, as female professors were the mainstays of outside directors such as Hyundai Motor, Hyundai E&C, Hyundai Mobis, Hana Financial Group, E-Mart, and Naver. However, it is not easy to invite a female expert with sufficient conditions with more than 20 years of professional experience.

In short, ESG management is still in its infancy. The trend requiring *"Management with a Philosophy"* is beginning to coincide with the assortment centered on ESG management, but it is the right time to establish it as a core corporate value and implement corporate social responsibility in stages.

The era of disconnection and uncertainty continues due to the COVID-19 global pandemic. However, K-Management's success philosophy of *"There are opportunities in crisis"* and *"There is no crisis that cannot be overcome"* should lead to disruptive innovation through the rise of ESG management.[47)]

In the end, the challenges for corporate social value creation are tied together from one point of view. A company that practices transparent and ethical management can become a company loved by society and customers thanks to ESG management, which is becoming a new trend.

However, good practice of ESG management does not make a company respected by society. In fact, ESG is another necessary but not sufficient condition for a successful business. Above all, we need to recognize that transparency and accuracy of disclosed corporate information and thoroughness of data analysis and measurement activities are of the utmost importance.

Therefore, 'responsible investment in ESG consulting' and 'creation of social value in a broad sense', which Korean companies must pursue, are only possible when the principle of 'back to basics' is practiced based on corporate ethical management and transparent management.

Technological innovation and advances in AI, big data, and cloud services are opening new chapters in all functions of management, including human resource management and, more recently, ESG management. In particular, the establishment of an effective AI-based HR system for human resource devel-

47) Park Kichan & Woo Kee-hong (2021), "Korean Air's Moment of Truth Realized through the Management Philosophy 『SAFER』", in *K-Management from Incheon,* Knowledge Platform.

opment from recruitment to retirement and employee evaluation (HR evaluation) emphasizes the need for ethical management and integrity management through the introduction of digital transformation technology.[48)]

Although it is still underlined as a trend of the time rather than as an academic dimension, ESG management must also be promoted as a global business strategy that contributes to the creation of environmental, social, economic, and ethical values of the company via the *"Practice of innovation with an emphasis on ESG philosophy and mission as Environmental guardian, Social caregiver, and Ethical steward"*.

48) Chevalier F. & Dejoux C. (2021), "Intelligence artificielle et Management des ressources humaines: pratiques d'entreprises, *Enjeux Numériques*, No 15, Sép. 2021, Annales des Mines.

Ⅳ

『HERI』-Leading ESG Management in Korea

IV

『HERI』-Leading ESG Management in Korea

1. HERI-CSR Management Evaluation
2. Assessment of HERI-ESG Management
3. HERI-EA30 Future Forum
4. CSR2.0 Emerged as ESG

ESG is an acronym for Environmental, Social, and Governance, which replaces the CSR approach as a criterion for evaluating mainly a company's non-financial performance. These include environmental indicators (E) such as carbon neutrality, climate change, environmental pollution, and eco-friendly product development, social indicators (S) such as human resource management, industrial safety, subcontracting, product and service safety, and fair competition. And governance indicators (G) include elements such as shareholder rights, composition of the board of directors, audit system, and dividend system.

> The problem is that, in a situation where the difficulties of corporate management are further aggravating due to the global pandemic, it is another regulation of companies to place importance on ESG management and many evaluation indicators, which may be a necessary burden to invest in additional time and money.

ESG management, which is being promoted as a global standard for corporate sustainability management, is expanding the responsible ESG investment market, centered on institutional investors, such as pension funds, despite controversy over on-site effectiveness. As the analysis method using artificial intelligence and big data is advanced, the value evaluation activities of asset management companies and specialized research and advisory institutions are rapidly increasing.

> As such, companies, pension funds, and government agencies around the world are announcing ESG implementation programs that the world calls 'ESG boom'. Then, in the case of Korea, *"Did there not be any research and effort on ESG and socially responsible management of companies?"*

If we talk about CSR or ESG as in our history, we can also find many exemplary virtues: Operation of the *Kaesong Merchants Cooperative* since Koryo Dynasty (918-1,392 AD), *Park Seungjik Store* (Doosan) and *Dongwha Pharma* (Dongwha Pharmacy) in 1896, *Hansung Bank* (Shinhan Bank) in 1897, *Daehan Cheonil Bank* (Woori Bank) in 1899, *Kyungsung Textile* (Gyeongbang) in 1919, *Yuhan Corporation* in 1926, *Gu Inhoe Pomok Sanghoe* (LG) in 1931, Samsung Sanghoe (Samsung) in 1938, *Burim Sanghoe* (Daelim) in 1939, are some representative companies. In fact, the history of growth from the time of their founding to the present day reflects their support for the independence movement from the 35 years' Japanese occupation and the spirit of patriotism.

CSR and ESG through the History of Korean Companies

1. **Koryo & Lee Dynasty: Cooperative by Kaesong Merchants**
2. **1896: Park Seungjik Store (Doosan) and Dongwha Pharma**
3. **1897: Hansung Bank (Shinhan Bank)**
4. **1899: Daehan Cheonil Bank (Woori Bank)**
5. **1919: Kyungsung Textile (Gyeongbang)**
6. **1926: Yuhan Corporation**
7. **1931: Gu Inhoe Pomok Sanghoe (LG)**
8. **1938: Samsung Sanghoe (Samsung)**
9. **1939: Burim Sanghoe (Daelim)**

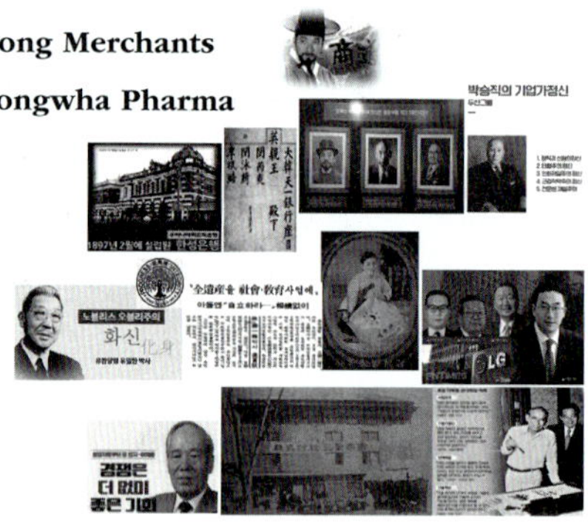

©www.hanol.co.kr

If the philosophies of these predecessors and their *'entrepreneurial spirit'* continue, it can be expected that the ESG management practices of Korean companies and their results will be highlighted as a world-class example representing the *'Spirit of K-Management'*.

Yuhan Corporation with the founder Dr. New Il-han (1895-1971) respected as a pro-independence activist, entrepreneur, educator, and social entrepreneur, has been practiced since its foundation in 1926 the philosophy of stakeholder capitalism which emerged and spread widely since 2008 global financial crisis.

Management philosophy of Dr. New Il-han is based on the principle of ownership for all employees and the exclusion of those close to the front line of management, strongly embodies the spirit of corporate social responsibility. Of course, at that time there was no movement or mention of the environment, such as the climate change etc.

- The very life of a company comes through and laid on honesty & trust (G)
- Corporate profits should be returned to their society that has fed them (S)
- The search for profit is an essential prerequisite for corporate growth (G)
- Business cannot be a means for entrepreneurs to increase their wealth (G)
- The owner of a company is the society, only the individual manages it (G)

- The production of high-quality and low-price products is a fundamental duty for the success of the company and a responsibility to the society (S)
- All people of the company have a common destiny through businesses (S)

This may be the answer to Peter F. Drucker's lifelong search for *"What is a business?"* And *"What is the mission of the company?"* Therefore, Yuhan Corporation's *'Seven Management Principles for Coexistence and Prosperity of Society and the Underprivileged Since 1926'* is being evaluated as the standard for ESG practice that Korea should present to the world.

On the other hand, CSR-related norms in Korea are more prominent in the role of NGO groups such as the CCEJ (Citizens Coalition for Economic Justice) formed in 1989, rather than the roles of government or the National Assembly.

In 1992, KEJI (Korea Economic Justice Institute), an organization affiliated with the CCEJ, introduced the following 10 standards (KEJI index) to focus on ethical management and corporate social responsibility, which contain and comparable most of the key indicators of global ESG standards.

① Companies that prevent industrial pollution and improve environmental pollution (E)
② Companies that faithfully abide by Fair Trade Order and Business Laws (S)
③ Companies that faithfully disclose corporate information and strive for customer satisfaction (S)
④ Companies contributing to economic development through the effective increase of employment and globalization (S)
⑤ Companies that achieve employ-union harmony by developing employee skills, promoting well-being, and preventing accidents at work (S)
⑥ Companies that faithfully fulfill community social roles such as social welfare, culture, and local community support (S)
⑦ Companies that strengthen technological innovation with creativity and entrepreneurship (G)
⑧ Companies that reduce the concentration of ownership by business owners and specialize in management (G)
⑨ Companies that are faithful to their core businesses by avoiding financial

techniques and unhealthy expenses (G)

⑩ Companies that promote productivity improvement and maintains a sound financial structure (G)

On this basis, the 'KEJI index' is a set of 58 indicators in 7 evaluation elements, in particular the solidity of the company's activities, equity, social service, environmental protection, consumer protection, employee satisfaction and contribution to economic development.

KEJI reminded us of the importance of socially responsible management by annually evaluating and announcing the *sociality and ethics* of Korean companies and by awarding the *'Economic Justice Award'* based on the KEJI index. In particular, the emphasis placed on the need to combine ethics and transparency is highly commendable.

1 HERI-CSR Management Evaluation

Recently, ESG advisory agencies and asset managers assess and rank companies' responsible ESG investment activities using AI and big data. However, these activities are evidenced in the support and efforts of the Hankyoreh Newspaper and HERI (Hankyoreh Economy & Society Research Institute), which began already in 2008.

As the authors participated in the expert committee since 2008, through the content of the Hankyoreh articles, we will examine in detail the evaluation process and the main contents of Korean, Chinese, and Japanese companies, focusing on ESG indicators.[49)]

① **Evaluation model:** HERI used the standards for social responsibility management assessment developed in the West, such as the UNGC, GRI, SDGs (MDGs), ISO26000 and ESG. However, on this basis, the "East Asia 30" evaluation model of HERI was developed in 2008 for the three East Asian countries (Korea, China, and Japan), operating in different business environments.

49) This content is based on the Hankyoreh Newspaper articles, and the authors synthesized.

Using ESG data from EIRIS in the UK up to 2012 and from Bloomberg since 2013, a *'quantitative assessment'* was carried out by HERI according to the following process, and a *'qualitative assessment' f*ocused on negative screening by means of data disseminated in the media was carried out in parallel.

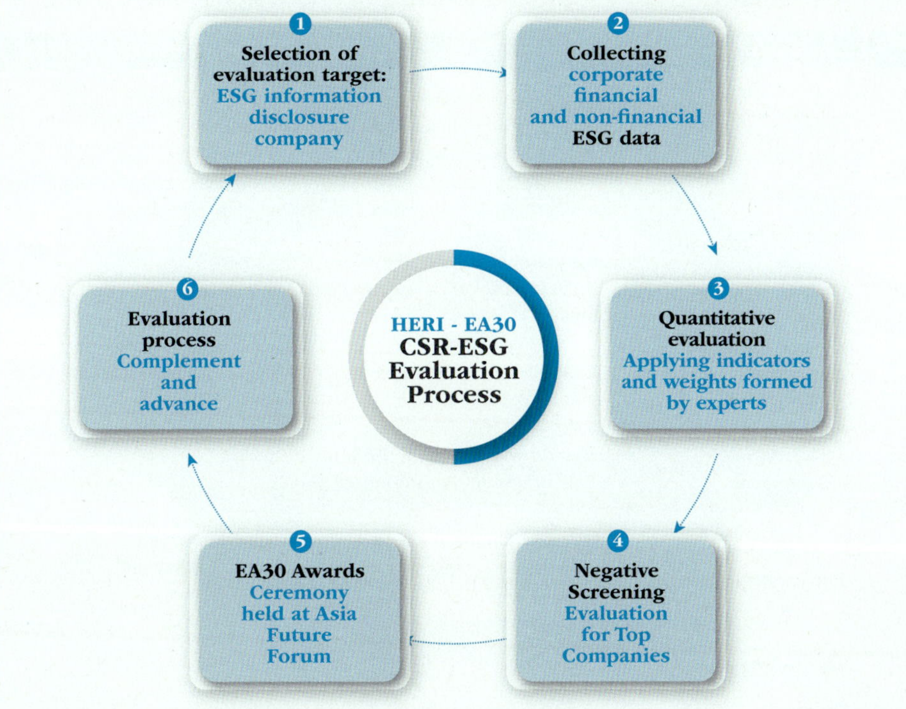

©www.hanol.co.kr

② **Quantitative evaluation:** HERI's quantitative evaluation framework was established in 2010 by the Korea, China, and Japan CSR expert committee as an international standard for corporate sustainable management such as *'10 principles of UNGC'*, *'G3 guidelines of GRI'*, *'17 goals of SDGs (MDGs)'*, and *'7 principles of ISO26000'*. In addition, reflecting the internal and external environmental characteristics of East Asian companies, a total of 20 detailed indicators including 6 environmental (E), 8 social (S), and 6 governance (G) sectors have been reorganized into a total of 70 sub-indices which are very similar to the current *K-ESG 2021*.

The detailed ESG related indicators aimed to verify the relations between corporate governance and stakeholders, whether companies are well equipped with policies, implementation, performance, monitoring, and evaluation systems for each ESG area, and whether the issues are managed in an efficient and transparent manner.

EA30 Quantitative Assessment Indicators and Weights (HERI, 2010)

	Indicator	Weight	Description
ENVIRONMENTAL	Climate change	25	• How do companies cope with the climate change? • What are the policies, systems, and results?
	Environmental core	20	• What are the company's environmental policies and commitments, and is there an environmental management system and a reporting system? • Is it closely linked to the heart of business? • What is the level of improvement in terms of environmental impact?
	Eco-friendly products	15	• What percentage of sales or new business or products come from green solutions?
	Water management	15	• How do you deal with the water scarcity crisis? (Policy, System, Performance, etc.)
	Chemical safety management	15	• Are there chemical safety policies and systems? • How does the company approach chemical safety and sustainability issues?
	Biodiversity	10	• Do you have a biodiversity policy? • How do you deal with this?
SOCIAL	Dialogue with stakeholders	15	• Is there a clear system for maintaining good relationships with customers and suppliers? • At what level is the relationship with stakeholders? • What about the management system and reporting?
	Health and safety	15	• Is there a clear system in place for health and safety policies?
	Job creation and guarantee	13	• How clear is the evidence regarding systems and practices for job creation and stability?
	Supply chain management	13	• What are the policies, systems and scope of labor standards reporting in the supply chain?
	Labor issues	12	• Are industrial relations management policies and systems in place?
	Equal opportunity	12	• Are equal opportunities and diversity policies in place?

	Indicator	Weight	Description
SOCIAL	Human rights	12	• What are the human rights policies and systems and the scope of reporting on them?
	Social contribution	8	• How clear is the company's commitment to community and philanthropy?
GOVERNANCE	Board of Directors execution structure	23	• Do you have a system in place for transparent governance to function? • Is it a system in which the board and management can control and cooperate equally? • Are there elements that allow transparent communication with internal and external stakeholders?
	Anti-corruption	20	• What are the company's anti-corruption policies, systems, and reports? • What about the monitoring and complementarity system?
	Ethics	16	• The company has a code of ethics (policies, systems)? • How comprehensive is it?
	CSR risk management	16	• How well do boards and management manage companywide ESG risks and opportunities?
	CSR leadership	13	• Are the elements of socially responsible management reflected in the company? • Are you looking for a new company or a new product from a CSR perspective? • How many socially responsible management issues are there and how many stakeholders are included on the board of directors?
	Women's participation on BOD	12	• How many women executives and members of the board of directors are there? • Do you have a system to block the glass ceiling?

③ **Evaluation Strategy:** Since 2010, the "Korea, China and Japan Social Responsibility Management Expert Committee" has annually determined the priority of each assessment indicator and applied it to strategically assess ESG indicators in assigning weights within or between each ESG sector.

As for the weight of each indicator, the total score and the ranking for the quantitative evaluation were calculated based on 100 points for each domain of E·S·G, for a total of 300 points. In the event of a score below 30 points in only one of the three sectors, a failure criterion has been introduced. At the same time, negative screening, a qualitative assessment method, was introduced as follows to complement the quantitative assessment.

④ **Qualitative evaluation:** The purpose of *'negative screening'* is to judge whether a company's social responsibility management policies and practices are being implemented in actual business operations and to verify the company's efforts for sustainability.

Negative issues were investigated for companies which had primarily been quantitatively assessed and evaluated by HERI and the expert committee reflecting the impact of the issue on society, the severity of the issue, and the will of the company to improve the current issues.

Public data such as the website of assessment target companies, business and sustainability management reports, data from government agencies, reports from NGOs and research institutes, and media articles were targeted for evaluation. The company is finally eliminated from the evaluation according to the following negative screening criteria:

- Tobacco, pornography, and weapons manufacturing industries
- Chronic personnel accidents due to unethical management activities
- Prosecuted or convicted by law enforcement authorities
- Fines or sanctions from government agencies

In addition, companies involved in issues that were continuously reported by media and NGOs were asked to confirm company awareness of related issues and follow-up actions and prevention activities through written questionnaires.

Examples of negative screening that were published in the media for exemplary ESG candidate companies at that time in 2010 to 2021 are expressed in various ways as follows:

Example of HERI's Negative Screening (2010-2011)

Amore Pacific	Rectification order by the Fair Trade Commission on the discovery of the ban on discount sales
Korea Gas Corporation	An outside director resigned after participating in a tender for a project commissioned by KOGAS

Hyundai Motor	Intervene directly and systematically in disciplinary action and the dismissal of the company's subcontractor workers. 13 employees, including former and current union officials, were convicted of habitual gambling
LG Electronics	Prosecutor's office charged with extortion of trade secrets from former employer in same company move
KIA	About 500 Kia Motors internal contractors have requested direct employment and class action lawsuits against Kia
POSCO	Prosecutor's Office arrests POSCO employee for receiving 100 million KRW from POSCO ICT partner
Samsung Electronics	Minister of Employment and Labor ordered Samsung Electronics to draw up health management plan costing around 100 billion KRW, causing leukemia death controversy among its employees
KT & SK Telecom	Prosecutor's office requested arrest warrant against POSCO ICT manager and KT team leader for receiving large sum of money from subcontractor for promotion of Seoul Metro project
	The Korea Communications Commission imposed fines of KRW 2 billion and KRW 1 billion, respectively, as SK Telecom and KT were found to restrict USIM's mobility and hamper user profits
Doosan Infracore	Doosan Infracore, which develops the K-2 Black Panther Tank engine, inflated the unit supply price, and misrepresented 7 billion won from the national budget in the past five years
Kepco	Electricity construction officials commissioned by Korea Electric Power Corporation donated 1.5 billion won in cash and entertainment
SK Innovation	On December 20, 2010, a worker was killed, and 6 others were seriously injured in an explosion at SK Energy's Ulsan plant
Shinhan Bank	Prosecutor's office indicted former president with embezzlement
STX	A worker was killed in an electric shock and another worker died after falling from 15 meters
Hankook Tire	Former Hankook Tire manager indicted for trade secret disclosure
LG Chem	On October 30, 2010, an explosion occurred at the product factory
Hyundai Steel	Dangjin Hyundai Steel rebar factory office fire killed an employee

2 Assessment of HERI-ESG Management

1. Evaluation of ESG management 2009

In 2009, HERI assessed the corporate social responsibility level of 111 Korean companies included in the UK's Financial Times Stock Exchange (FTSE) index of developed countries for the first time on a global scale. ESG social responsibility management, which consists of three areas E (environmental), S (social) and G (governance), is a core and basic management element that global companies must have within the international community.[50)]

In the first phase, HERI requested data collection and baseline business assessment from EIRIS and KOCSR, which were selected as partners. IRIS is an independent global corporate social responsibility (CSR) and socially responsible investing (SRI) research organization, headquartered in the UK, providing ESG data to key managers of global funds and asset investors. EIRIS has a reputation for not providing advice to companies assessed for the fairness of the investigation.

> The assessment of the first stage was carried out based on 2008 data published by the target companies of the assessment. In addition to the sustainability report and annual report, data and documents disclosed on the company's website and various disclosures were investigated.

Therefore, even if only an annual report focused on financial performance or a sustainability report was released, companies that did not disclose relevant data had no choice but to receive lower evaluation scores. According to the EIRIS model, the assessment domain consists of three main sectors: environmental (E), social (S) and governance (G). Each area includes detailed corporate social responsibility issues that are important to global investors.

The total score for each of the three sectors was obtained by adding the scores for each detailed problem thus calculated, and the final score (final score / achievable score) divided by the perfect score was expressed as a ratio.

50) Although the debate on the area of CSR is still ongoing, HERI has assessed the level of CSR management based on the EIRIS ESG index, with an emphasis on the concept of SRI (socially responsible investing).

The final evaluation of the second stage was carried out by forming a committee of six experts (Chairman: Professor Kichan Park) based on the results of the first stage evaluation. The selection committee examined the feasibility of the detailed elements in each environmental (E), social (S) and governance (G) sector and selected the final exemplary companies.

Among the 111 companies, the nominees for the *'EA 30 Award (30 exemplary companies)'* were selected first, and the grand prize was awarded to the company with the highest overall score in three ESG sectors. For the companies selected for the award, the committee examined whether there had been any negative cases that could lead to serious disqualification for ESG-related issues in the past three years. If there were several companies with the same highest score in each category, they were all recognized as joint winners.

1) CSR-ESG level of Korean companies

As a result of the assessment, there was a difference in the level of social responsibility management among the 111 global companies. The difference between the highest and lowest scores in the assessment results, which was scored out of 100, exceeded 70 points. Eight companies received only 20 points or less.

A significant number of Korean companies do not know or understand international practices for assessing socially responsible management. They missed that socially responsible global investors will receive zero points in the rating of relevant items if they do not publish the Global Standard Sustainability Report or actively disclose information through public disclosure.

In the next step, HERI divided a total of 111 Korean companies into 5 deciles, and among them, 21 companies with the best score of 20% (1st decile) were first selected as exemplary global companies in CSR practices.[51)]

51) Among manufacturing industries, Kia Motors, Samsung Electro-Mechanics, Samsung Electronics, Samsung SDI, Amore Pacific, POSCO, Hynix Semiconductor, Korea Gas Corporation, Korea Electric Power Corporation, Hyundai Motor Company, Hyundai Steel, LG Chem, LG Display, LG Electronics, SK Energy, S-Oil and 16 companies were included, and in the service sector, 5 companies including Daegu Bank, Daewoo Securities, Dongbu Insurance, Samsung Card and KT were included.

Using these 21 exemplary global CSR companies as candidates, one company (POSCO) that received the highest score in all areas was awarded the grand prize. The companies with the highest scores in each of the manufacturing (Korea Gas Corporation) and services (KT: Korea Telecom) sectors were selected as the industry grand prize, and the top companies were selected in each of the three ESG (environmental, social and governance) areas.[52)]

2) Evaluation of ESG management by sector and industry

There were also clear differences in each ESG area and industry. Looking at the average score for each area of 111 companies, governance (G) had the highest score of 49.6 points, and the average score for social (S) and environmental (E) areas was only 41.9 and 35.8 points respectively, showing the lowest score in the environmental area. However, 21 companies belonging to the global CSR model group are exceptional, with an average score of 66.9 points in the environmental area, higher than that of governance (64.1 points) and social (63.8 points).

The environmental area score showed a marked difference between manufacturing and service industries. In the case of the banking sector, all but one of the assessment targets were in the lowest quintile in the environmental area. In the general financial sector, including insurance and securities, all but two of the companies in 10 were in the lowest quintile for the environment.

The main feature of the service industry was that the assessment of the environmental area was low. Of the 45 companies in the service sector, only 2 companies obtained a score of 60 or more in the environmental area, and 29 companies (more than half) were judged to be below 20, which corresponds to the level of virtual absence environmental management.

In contrast, in the manufacturing sector, there were 18 companies with a score of 60 or more, and there were only 19 companies with a score of 20 or less, much lower than in the service sector.

> This shows that Korean domestic service companies, including financial companies, still neglect environmental management, or mistakenly believe that environmental issues are the responsibilities of the manufacturing industry.

52) HERI, "The appearance is world-class, but the practice of social responsibility appears in various ways.", *HERI Review No. 10*, 2011.06.24.

3) Limits and perspectives of the evaluation of ESG management

The HERI 2009 assessment is significant in the in-depth examination of the level of socially responsible management of Korean companies based on global standards. It can be said that this is a differentiated valuation in that it is valued based on data used by investors to make investment decisions, and not on commonly used reputation data.

Corporate sustainability is the most important survival strategy in the 21st century global economic system and can be sustained when trust and responsibility are recognized by domestic and foreign customers and investors. As a result of the assessment, it was estimated that the level of corporate social responsibility management of Korean companies in each of the ESG areas is quite far from that of global companies. It was found that the level of awareness and response to environmental issues should be significantly improved in the case of financial companies.

However, the Korean companies selected for the award demonstrated a level of sustainability that was not lower than that of global companies. In addition, it is an important achievement to form a group of *'exemplary companies'* which can serve as an index of socially responsible investing in the future. However, it is necessary to compensate for the fact that the comparison with the world competitors was not made since only the superiority and the inferiority of the national companies were distinguished.

Founded by religious institutions in the UK, EIRIS is a global research organization providing data on 3,000 companies worldwide to global financial institutions, pension funds, fund managers, religious institutions, foundations, and consumer groups. Korean companies' data is transmitted to EIRIS after being evaluated by KOCSR, EIRIS's Korean partner. Based on assessment data from EIRIS and KOCSR, HERI conducted a quantifiable assessment of the ESG performance of 111 Korean companies included in the list of the FTSE.

The *Asian Expert Committee*[53)] selected two companies each for the Grand Prix (manufacturing industry, service industry) and the Grand Prix for each ESG

53) Chairperson: Park Kichan, President of the Korean Society for Business Ethics, Inha University. Judges: Kim Seong-cheon, from Korea Consumer Agency, Yang Chun-seung, Executive Director, Korea Socially Responsible Investing Forum, Lee Jang-won, from Korea Labor Institute, Jeong Jae-gyu, Korean Corporate Governance Center, Jeong Kyung-su, Professor of Law, Sookmyung Women's University.

area. By carefully selecting exemplary companies with exceptional efforts and a willingness to practice social responsibility and environmental management, the aim is to enable all Korean companies to learn from them. The Hankyoreh newspaper's Global CSR Grand Prix, which took its first steps in 2009, was expected to become a reliable coordination for global investors as they accumulate years of experience.

2. Evaluation of ESG management 2010

The *"Asian Expert Committee on Social Responsibility Management"* composed of economics and management experts from Korea, China and Japan finally confirmed and announced the 'East Asia 30' in 2010, which included 30 companies with outstanding CSR activities in three countries. For the fairness and benefit of the assessment work, experts from Korea, China and Japan had extensive discussions with the HERI research team to develop ESG assessment criteria and analysis models.

> The expert committee focused on completing the valuation model based on international standards, but also on some different features of the Asian region. Through this process, differences and commonalities between Korean, Chinese, and Japanese companies were found, and evaluation indicators were selected and weighted according to the content that could be commonly applied to the three countries. Based on the completed evaluation model, 708 representative companies in Korea, China and Japan were evaluated, and among them, 'East Asia 30' exemplary companies were selected for recommendation.

CSR (Corporate Social Responsibility) theory was developed and introduced in the West and has had a great impact on innovation and business reform in East Asian countries. This attempt is very meaningful in that it prepared and implemented evaluation standards more suitable for the environment of the three East Asian countries.

Based on this assessment work, it is expected to greatly contribute to the strength of Northeast Asian enterprises and the fulfillment of ESG by strengthening and mainstreaming social responsibility, which is accepted as a common value in Korea, China, and Japan.

3. Evaluation of ESG management 2011

In 2011, anti-corruption, social responsibility management leadership, participation of female on the board of directors in the field of governance (G), and human rights management (S) in the social sector were added as new evaluation indicators. Meanwhile, in the environment area (E), evaluation indicators for each issue such as climate change, water management, and chemical safety management were newly introduced and the scope of research by Korean, Chinese, and Japanese companies was expanded.

'East Asia 30' selects the 30 most advanced companies in social responsibility management in Korea, China, and Japan. 10 people participated in the expert committee.[54)] The committee divided into three ESG areas and held an award ceremony with the presentation of the assessment results of representative East Asian companies at the '2011 Asia Future Forum' hosted by Hankyoreh. Joo Cheol-ki, chairman of the Expert Committee, said: *"Including human rights and the proportion of women on the board is very forward-looking."*

3 HERI-EA30 Future Forum

1. Asia Future Forum 2012

In 2012, 'East Asia 30' covered topics related to ESG, including various social issues and phenomena. It stressed that the session on *socially responsible investing (SRI) in East Asia"* provided a venue to discuss the real obligations of an asset manager as a fiduciary, the topic of responsible investment. Thanks to HERI, in 2012, discussions about ESG and impact investment started in earnest in Korea.

Here it was pointed out that the starting point of the economic crisis that spread around the world due to the subprime mortgage crisis in the United States in 2008 was the unethical management case of financial institutions. In other words, by observing the immoral management behavior of financial companies, investors realized that sound corporate governance and disclosure of

54) Including Joo Chul-ki, Secretary General of the UNGC Korea Association, Yang Bin, Director of the Leadership Center at Tsinghua University in China, Takashi Evashi, Director of the UNGC Research Center at Hosei University in Japan, Park Kichan, Professor of Inha University, and Lee Young-myeon, Professor of Dongguk University.

corporate information was necessary to protect their interests.

In addition, social and environmental issues such as population growth, aging and climate change in Asia have prompted global companies and investors to pay attention to *"sustainability"*. Now is the time for investors to prepare for a future that is different from the past, away from the investment method that focused only on financial performance.

> Investment institutions that make long-term investments need to consider various factors that affect value and performance. However, in East Asia there is still prejudice and skepticism that *"socially responsible investing (SRI) has a low return" or "investing against fiduciary obligations"*.

Maria Tinelli, president of the UN Principles for Responsible Investment (UN PRI) global network, said the criticism of SRI stemmed from a misconception that *"there is a conflict between fiduciary duties"*. It is to predict long-term performance considering ESG (environmental, social and governance) factors. Tinelli explained what a true fiduciary duty is in a time when capitalism is in jeopardy and how ESG issues can be applied to investment activities:

- *"A 2011 study by Harvard Business School professor Robert Eccles and George Serafeim confirmed that high sustainability companies outperform their competitors in terms of price and stock returns.*
- *In other words, since SRI (socially responsible investing) deals with both ESG opportunities and risks beyond the simple financial dimension, it deals with opportunities and risks at a much broader level than ordinary investors."*
- *"Socially responsible investing does not need to fundamentally change the way investors invest. Because SRI improves the breadth and depth of investment analysis by additionally integrating ESG factors into traditional investment analysis, thereby increasing returns and reducing risk."*

Therefore, asset management institutions should establish clear investment beliefs and policies based on abundant corporate information and monitor asset management companies such as investment trust companies. They should also focus on research, measurement, and analysis to find the link between long-term performance and SRI with a clear responsible investment policy.

2. Asia Future Forum 2013

Since 2013, we have been evaluating social responsibility management by applying the indicators and weights finalized by the expert committee, starting with ESG-linked non-financial data provided by Bloomberg.

In 2013, new governments took office in the three countries (Korea, China, and Japan), and while negotiations on the Korea-China and Korea-Japan free trade agreements (FTA) were on track, the CSR activities in Northeast Asia also increased the attractiveness of domestic and foreign investment. It has become a determinant of customer satisfaction.

In Korea, 247 companies, which more than doubled from last year, were evaluated by environmental, social and governance indicators. As a result, companies from the electronics, steel, cosmetics, chemicals, and automobile industries accounted for most of the top 30 applicants, while telecommunications, shipbuilding, services, and construction were relatively few. Above all, from January 2012 to July 2013, there were many companies that did not pass the negative screening for corporate corruption, unfair trade, security accidents, and follow-up measures that appeared in the media and society.

The superiority of candidate companies by each ESG area was also differentiated. Awareness of the environmental issue was high in hi-tech industries, and the social area was similar among industries, while most governance structures have barely passed the failure point. Problems such as the composition of the board of directors and the transparency of the operations of Korean companies were said to be always serious.

Professor Park Kichan said, *"Through the annual evaluation, we are realizing that the realization of the win-win value of corporate management and social responsibility is the cornerstone of economic prosperity in Northeast Asia. I hope that experts from East Asian countries and the Asian Social Responsibility Management Expert Committee will always be together to create Asian values in corporate management."*

The governments of Northeast Asia are shaping the political, social, and economic values of the new rulers: the *"Economic democratization and Creative economy"* of Korea, the building of the economic, political, social, cultural, and ecological civilization of Korea. China *'Five-point unity theory'*, and Japan is looking forward to the glory of *'Strong Japan with Abenomics'*. A new approach to business is always at the heart of the new government's policies. Indeed, business activities not only generate economic benefits, but also have various spillover effects on the environment and society.

Changes in government and policies can directly or indirectly affect socially responsible management, which is seen as an autonomous area of action for companies. As an example, if we look at Korean society over the past five years, we can see that the policy framework of *'Green growth'* has been applied to corporate management activities in various ways.

By applying the *'Low Carbon Green Growth Act'*, a greenhouse gas and energy target management system was established, and many companies are participating. Businesses were reorganized according to the government's policy stance, and low-carbon industries and their products were subsidized by the government. Companies are carrying out activities such as reducing greenhouse gas on their own centering on social responsibility, and the government's political efforts and speed have accelerated even more.

1) Asia Future Forum 2014: CSR Exceptional Management Assessment

In 2014, the *negative screening* (eligibility assessment) was reinforced. About ten Korean, Chinese, and Japanese companies were eliminated from the valuation, when accidents such like human losses occurred due to the negligence of the company and when the collusion or embezzlement of the management, and the tax evasion or breach of trust has occurred.

The *"Expert Committee on Social Responsibility Management in Asia (Chairman: professor Park Kichan)"*, made up of social responsibility management experts from Korea, China, and Japan, interviewed 1,544 companies, including companies listed in Korea, Japan, and China for the environment, social and governance assessment. After 3 months of verification and screenings by country, 29 exemplary companies including 9 in Korea, 10 in Japan and 10 in China have been confirmed.

The selected companies have extended the disclosure of non-financial corporate information not only to their head office, but also to business sites, affiliates, and supply chain business partners abroad, while launching products for the disadvantaged or activities aimed at inducing business partners to improve their business practices.

As exemplary companies, LG Electronics introduced a digital device that improves accessibility for the disabled and the elderly, Samsung Electro-Mechanics with an environment-friendly electronic price indicator that replaces existing paper labels , and LG Hausys produced a flooring that reduces the noise between floors and wall-papers that minimize emissions of environmental hormones, and POSCO by developing a system that induces prompt payment from primary suppliers to secondary suppliers, they all received excellent reviews.

The average score for each area of 29 exemplary companies in Korea, China and Japan was in the order of environment (62.24 points), society (53.30 points) and governance (44.95 points). In the environmental area, Japanese companies obtained the highest score of 71.69.

The expert committee explained that this is because already an eco-friendly management system has been in place in Japan, and the business results are disclosed in a transparent and specific manner. Korean companies came out on top with an average score of 60.42 in the social area, and most importantly, they received relatively high scores in the 'social contribution' category. In contrast, governance structures in Korea, China and Japan have remained relatively weak.

The Expert Panel said: *"Among the companies in the three countries, few companies faced business opportunities or the risks of socially responsible management on the board of directors. There have been very few cases in which social responsibility management was linked to the evaluation of board or corporate performance."*

Industries such as tobacco, gambling, pornography, and the manufacture of mass-produced weapons were excluded from 2014. In addition, negative screening that appeared in the media over the past year has been more carefully verified. As a result, companies regulated or fined by government or public institutions due to chronic collusion and problematic businesses in the telecommunications, oil refining and construction sectors have been eliminated.

In addition, companies involved in embezzlement, breach of trust and management corruption due to social responsibility and those that caused chronic industrial accidents were also excluded.

In the event of a business accident or unfair transaction, the questionnaire was reviewed to determine if there were follow-up measures for improvement. Since it is important to prevent corruption or accidents, it is necessary to verify the company's forward-looking efforts by simultaneously applying the evaluation of response activities after an accident.

ESG assessment domain and applied index (HERI, 2014)

Area	Environmental (6)	Social (8)	Governance (6)
Indicator (20)	Environment core	Health and safety	BOD structure
	Climate change	Stakeholder dialogue	Anti-corruption
	Water management	Job creation/security	Ethics
	Eco-friendly products and services	Supply chain management	SRI and Risk management
	Chemical safety	Labor issues	CSR leadership
	Biodiversity	Equal opportunity	Women in BOD
		Human rights	
		Social contribution	

In the case of Korea, the number of applicants for assessment was relatively low in the financial sector, and it did not even meet the negative screening (eligibility) criteria. Therefore, when it comes to corporate social responsibility, the financial sector needs to be proactive. Due to the full evaluation and reinforced negative screening results, expected 10 Korean winners have not been fully provided in 2014.

EA30 targets companies belonging to major stock indexes in Korea, China, and Japan. KOSPI 200 in Korea, TOPIX in Japan, Shanghai, Shenzhen in China, and the SRI index of the Hong Kong Stock Exchange. In 2014, 247 Korean companies, 744 Japanese companies and 553 Chinese companies were assessed to select the 30 exemplary companies in total from the three countries.

The assessment was conducted based on the disclosure of non-financial information provided by Bloomberg. The non-financial information was collected based on the annual corporate sustainability management reports, websites, corporate annual business reports, and through government agencies or related associations.

The evaluation framework consists of 20 detailed indicators in the area of ESG. After evaluating the CSR performance of companies according to the evaluation framework, a negative screening was conducted by expert committees in each country. This task was to reflect negative issues that cannot be detected only with the content disclosed by the company in the review. After completing the negative screening of each country, *the Asian Social Responsibility Management Expert Committee* cross-checked the full list of companies exchanging through online and went through the final confirmation process.

2) Global Social Responsibility Management in Transition

Managing corporate social responsibility is important in the implementation of a *'sustainable society'* and a *'human-based economy'*, as it becomes a key tool and a metric. The *"Global CSR Management in Transition"* session was held at the Asia Future Forum 2014, moderated by Professor Park Kichan, President of the Korea Society for Sustainability Management. Participants confirmed that the idea of CSR management, which was once seen as an *'advertising'* marketing tool for large corporations or a kind of philanthropy, has undergone a huge change both internally and externally.

> Professor Park said that *"The reason I dared to use the term 'transition period' on the topic of CSR management and SRI is that the disclosure of ESG related information is not only voluntary but now becomes legally mandatory."*

In fact, there is a growing trend that stock markets, institutional investors, and financial supervisors around the world are required to disclose information on the corporate non-financial performance through *'socially responsible management' or 'sustainability management'* reporting. It means evaluating sustainability by assessing the ESG related issues, such as carbon emissions, biodiversity conservation, respect for human rights and corporate governance in business activities.

CSR consultant Enrique Torres said: *"Ten years ago, only a handful of leading companies in the world published a CSR report. However, a 2013 study showed that 93% of the world's 250 largest companies and more than 70% of the 100 largest companies in 41 countries publish the related reports."*

Torres, who served as CEO of the Global Reporting Initiative (GRI), a non-profit organization that provides standards and guidelines for sustainable management and socially responsible management, pointed out that *"CSR around the world is changing rapidly"*. In fact, in April 2014, the European Union (EU) made it mandatory for companies with 500 or more employees to disclose socially responsible management information, and the Hong Kong Stock Exchange introduced the "Hang Seng Sustainability Index" in 2013.

Michiyo Morisawa, director of the Japanese UN PRI (United Nations Principles for Responsible Investment) organization, explained the growing importance of socially responsible management information from an investor's perspective: *"Institutional investors who manage tens of billions to hundreds of billions of dollars should aim for medium to long term profits, so they are increasingly aware that when deciding which company to invest, it is necessary to assess the sustainability of the company in terms of ESG as well as financial performance."*

Morisawa said that *"The fact that SRI (socially responsible investing) also improves long-term performance is proven by research results and has been adopted as a major investment principle by pension funds in the United States and in Europe. The Financial Supervisory Authority and the Japan Stock Market introduced regulations to disclose sustainability management information earlier this year, followed by the Japanese Government Pension Investment Fund (GPIF) which introduced the concept of SRI."*

Liu Xuezhi, professor of Economics at Beijing University of Chemical Technology, presented the changes in Chinese society and business movements, where concerns about a sustainable society have deepened due to worsening pollution of the air. He said, *"In China, it has been concluded that 70% of the total environmental pollution is caused by industrial activities." He asserted in detail that "Among the 2,400 listed companies in China, 680 are expected to publish social responsibility management reports in 2014. In other words, as public demand to disclose what Chinese companies are doing in environmental matters increases, efforts to assess and standardize corporate social responsibility management information are advancing rapidly."*

3) Japan's 'Environmental (E)', Korea's 'Social (S)', and China's 'Women Participation in BOD (G)' scores are highlighted

The *"Asian Expert Committee on CSR Management"* composed of experts from Korea, China and Japan selected the top 30 companies with excellent CSR, regardless of the country. Now that CSR management based on ESG indicators has spread widely, it means that it is time to go further and find implications through country-by-country comparisons focused on the sharing of cases by company. In addition, the *'negative screening'* criterion, which excludes companies with negative factors, has been strongly applied. For this reason, only 9 Korean companies were selected. Park Kichan, Chairman of the Korean Expert Committee that evaluated Korean companies at the award ceremony of the Asia Future Forum 2014, intends to develop the cases of award-winning companies which will be used as course materials and research subjects in the universities by putting them in contact with academic societies. In particular, he stressed that these exemplary cases to be disseminated through periodic academic seminars such as the Korean Academic Society of Business Administration.

4) Asia Future Forum 2015: Corporate Governance Crisis and Solutions

Professor Park pointed out that *"There are many successful companies in Korea, but there are few respected companies and CEOs. In a book already published in 1954, Drucker stated that the mission of a company is profit first, CSR second, and third, innovation for the creation of customers. Social responsibility now became such important in the management of companies."* East Asian companies, the fastest growing in decades, have also been criticized for being insensitive to CSR. Recent discussions aimed at eliminating such stigma converge on CSR for sustainability. At the Asia Future Forum 2015, experts from Korea, China and Japan discussed the *"Crisis and Solutions for Corporate Governance"* and suggested practical measures to overcome corporate governance issues backlogged business and strengthen CSR:

Song Min-kyung, researcher at the KCGS (Korea Corporate Governance Service), pointed out that due to the outdated governance structure, 'accidents of chaebols' such as the Lotte Group's *'Brother Rebellion'* keep on happening. Researcher Song asserted that *"The board of directors is powerless, the general meeting of shareholders is formal, and the role of shareholders is insignificant, which amplifies the problem."* In Korea, among the companies that make up the KOSPI 200, the number of cases where the CEO is also chairman of the board is around 83%, suggesting that the board is most likely a mere handful of hand. Therefore, the solution could be to give substantial powers to the board of directors and to the general meeting of shareholders while strengthening the *'SRI (socially responsible investing)'* measures of institutional investors.

Seo Jae-kyo, head of the HERI's CSR team, also pointed out that *"In the case of the national pension, there is a problem of independence from the government. We need a system that allows institutional investors to have a voice without outside influence."*

> Japanese and Chinese experts have also expressed similar issues and concerns. In other words, strengthening CSR management, including ESG improvement, is a common task for companies in East Asia.

Eiichiro Adachi, director of the ESG Research Center at the Japan Research Institute, said: *"Japanese companies always tend to be family-run. In 2013, about 600 of the 1,400 large companies had no outside directors". "The number of outside directors is not a panacea for some outside directors to come in, and there is no guarantee that the CEO will listen to them on sensitive issues."*

Peiyuan Guo, CEO of Xintao Consulting in China, said: *"The Chinese government is encouraging more companies to disclose information related to SRI, such as the environment, amid severe air pollution". "Apple did not comply with environmental regulations and then changed its attitude when a Chinese NGO recommended a boycott of consumers."*

They also suggested that it is important to spread the awareness that CSR and ESG are conditions for sustainable growth of companies, not costs.

Jang Ja-young, ESG analyst at Bloomberg, said: *"A month before the emissions handling issue erupted, Bloomberg warned that the Porsche family's influence in Volkswagen was so great that the independence of the BOD was threatened".* She also presented an international survey which found that 73% of investment professionals, including securities analysts, consider SRI management criteria in their analysis and investment decisions.

4 CSR2.0 Emerged as ESG

The pioneering role of HERI's research team Lee Hyun-sook, Cho Hyun-kyung, Seo Jae-kyo, Yang Eun-young, and Park Eun-kyung to make CSR management a framework suitable for Asian values and culture for 8 years from 2008 centering on ESG, can be highly appreciated. Here is a summary of HERI's accomplishments ahead of times:

- First, weights were assigned to each ESG area and detailed indicator through the Korea-China-Japan CSR Expert Committee.
- Second, the ESG exemplary companies from Korea, China and Japan were selected by quantitatively and qualitatively analyzing the large amount of company information from Bloomberg.
- Third, an international seminar was organized and held in Korea to stress the importance of CSR management.

These HERI activities should be reviewed by Korean companies considering the era of ESG management. However, since 2016, the activities of the Asia Future Forum of the Hankyoreh Newspaper have dealt with huge speeches such as *"the happiness of citizens"*, *"the world economy"* and *"the era of coexistence with the COVID-19 pandemic"*, with an emphasis on investors as stakeholders in the discussion, it is regrettable that the discussion on SRI and ESG management to strengthen the sustainability of companies has not been deepened.

Therefore, ESG for *"Zero Carbon (E) · Zero Corruption (S) · Zero Abuse of*

Power (G)" is welcome. However, there is also a counter-question: *"Why is the company's interest in ESG so hot again replacing the long history of the CSR?"*

> Recently, in the *"ESG Readiness and Perception Survey"* for the 500 largest domestic companies conducted by the FKI (Federation of Korean Industries) in April 2021, it was stated that *"66.3% of CEOs treat ESG as a top priority"*. The most striking expression of the CEO group is that *"ESG is no longer an option for companies, but now a compulsory subject"*.

The difficulties encountered by CEOs with ESG also appear to be an urgent priority to be resolved: *"What exactly is ESG?", "How does ESG relate to our business?", "Why do different assessment agencies have different assessment methods?"*

There are also complaints that ESG comes at additional costs and that ESG related regulations are overly introducing. On the other hand, the answer worth paying attention to is that over 43% of the total consider ESG as the goal of improving the image of the company. As such, the core philosophy of Korean business leaders on ESG appears still poor and rare.

ESG seen by CEOs of Top 500 Korean Companies (FKI, 2021.04.05)

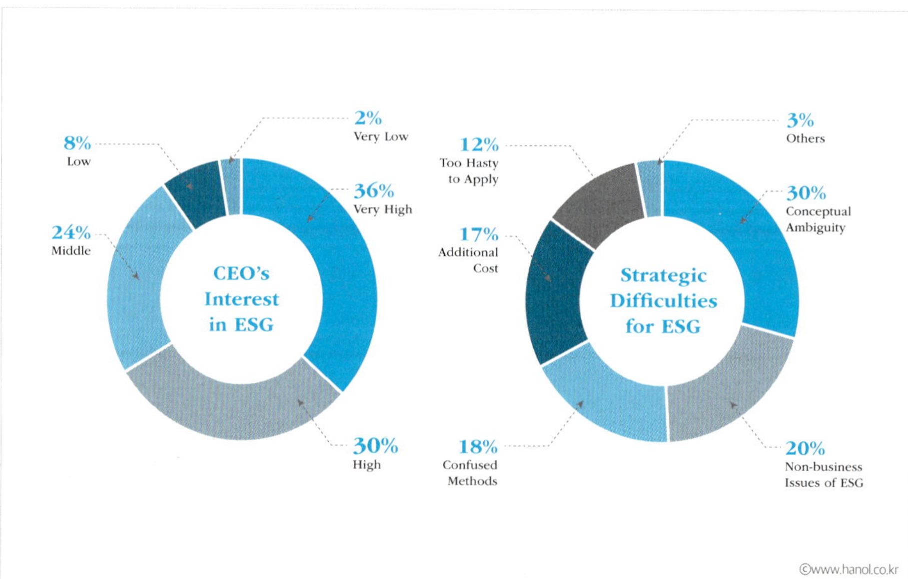

According to Wayne Visser's 5 stages of CSR evolution,[55] ESG needs to shift from current defensive (stage 1), philanthropic (stage 2), and promotional (stage 3) activities to corporate strategic (stage 4), and integrated (step 5) level 'CSR 2.0' which can be conceived as the strategic ESG management.

Of course, there are ESG concepts and purposes that overlap and diversify to the extent that CEOs interest them: CSR (corporate social responsibility), sustainable development management, CSV (creating shared value), corporate citizenship management, sustainable development, and SRI (socially responsible investing), social audit, and TBL (triple bottom line)[56] etc.

ESG focuses on non-financial risks or related investment decisions and non-financial factors that can affect the long-term financial value of a company. For this reason, the difficulties in industries that frequently generate by nature pollutants and industrial accidents such as petrochemicals, petroleum products, steel, semiconductors, machinery and shipbuilding, and automobiles are expected to be much higher than other industries.

In summary, among ESGs, the environmental sector is institutionalized with global consensus and contracts such as *'Net Zero'*, and each country is taking the process of legal obligations accordingly. Therefore, in the environmental field, the government-led role should be emphasized, in line with the global trend.

After President Biden took office, the United States returned to the Paris Agreement on climate change. Korea has also actively declared to achieve carbon neutrality by 2050. Since the core tasks of ESG and the source of the difficulties are particularly in the environmental elements, strict measurement of detailed environmental indicators and disclosure of information must be substantiated.

---

55) Visser W. (2011), *The Age of Responsibility-CSR 2.0 and the New DNA of Business*, University of Cambridge Programme for Sustainability Leadership.

56) A term that emphasizes the role of business in social equity and environmental sustainability as well as economic efficiency of the business.

For environment-related indicators (E), global standards, target levels and achievement points are clearly presented, and measurements can be carried out scientifically. Therefore, as a representative element of the ESG index, it should be subject to international regulations and to a *competitive advantage of nations*. On the other hand, social indicators (S) and indicators linked to governance (G) can be considered as areas of *'comparative advantage of enterprises'* which must consider the context by country, sector, company, size, and generation.

Therefore, in the environmental indicators, government-led legal and institutional regulations are set in accordance with global standards, and the importance of negative screening based on these should be emphasized. Meanwhile the social responsibility indicators and corporate governance indicators for transparent management are conceived as voluntary ones in accordance with corporate strategies.

When the Hankyoreh Newspaper and HERI dealt with the issue of responsible ESG management in 2008, it has probably been considered just an event by a progressive Korean media company. But in fact, HERI carried out ESG responsible management assessment with Korea, China, and Japan CSR Expert Committee far ahead of other institutions. And the Committee deliberately provided *'Prioritization and Weighting'* for each ESG indicator and identified *'Common factors and Differentiated factors'* for each indicator. As the like in Korea, HERI has played a pioneering role in spreading ahead of the time the importance of ESG management since 2008.

V

Patagonia - A Leader in Global ESG Management

V

Patagonia - A Leader in Global ESG Management

1. Outdoor Apparel Industry and Patagonia
2. Foundation for Growth of Patagonia
3. Think-Tank Leadership that Drives Change
4. Corporate Environment and Strengthening Strategies
5. Core Competencies and Major Resources
6. Mechanism for Managing the Virtuous Cycle
7. Future Prospect of Patagonia

Patagonia

After two years of preparation, the Hankyoreh Newspaper, HERI and the Asian CSR *Management Expert Committee* developed ESG indicators and assessment methods in 2010. And it was used to measure the level of CSR management in Korea, China, and Japan. Through this procedure, LG and Doosan, the Central Bank of China and China Mobile, and the Japanese Ajinomoto and Fujitsu have been highlighted. However, compared to Patagonia, an outerwear manufacturer recognized as a global representative of ESG management, there is a long way to go.

Patagonia is a valued company by customers and society with continuous sales growth by producing environment-friendly clothing as well as various donation activities for environmental protection, and achieving zero pollution of environment, and toxic substances in the manufacturing process.

Patagonia, which has practiced socially responsible management with an eco-responsible philosophy rather than *'show-off'* management, is strategically sustainable beyond the dimension of *'consensual responsible ESG investing'*, which deals with non-financials that affect a company's financial performance from an investor's perspective. As the like, Patagonia strives to practice *'responsible management of ESG in the broad sense'*.

"Patagonia is not a 'Sustainable company'.
Patagonia is a 'Responsible company' for all the impacts we have."

This is the management philosophy of Ryan Gellert,
CEO of Patagonia, who took office in 2020.

Gellert is also running a global campaign called *"Buy Less, Ask More"* which stems from his coherent management philosophy that reducing overconsumption can protect the global environment. As such, Patagonia shows the essence of ESG management in the business model: [ESG management → Performance creation].

Prior to the appearance of the term ESG, ESG management was already embedded in organizational culture as Patagonia's unique *'Green Business'* philosophy and practiced daily. Patagonia's socially responsible management practice mechanism, based on the corporate strategy of *'empathetic leadership'*, *'TBL* (*triple bottom line*) *competence'* and *'environment friendly product'*, can be particularly highlighted as follows:

Patagonia's Virtuous Cycle Management Mechanism

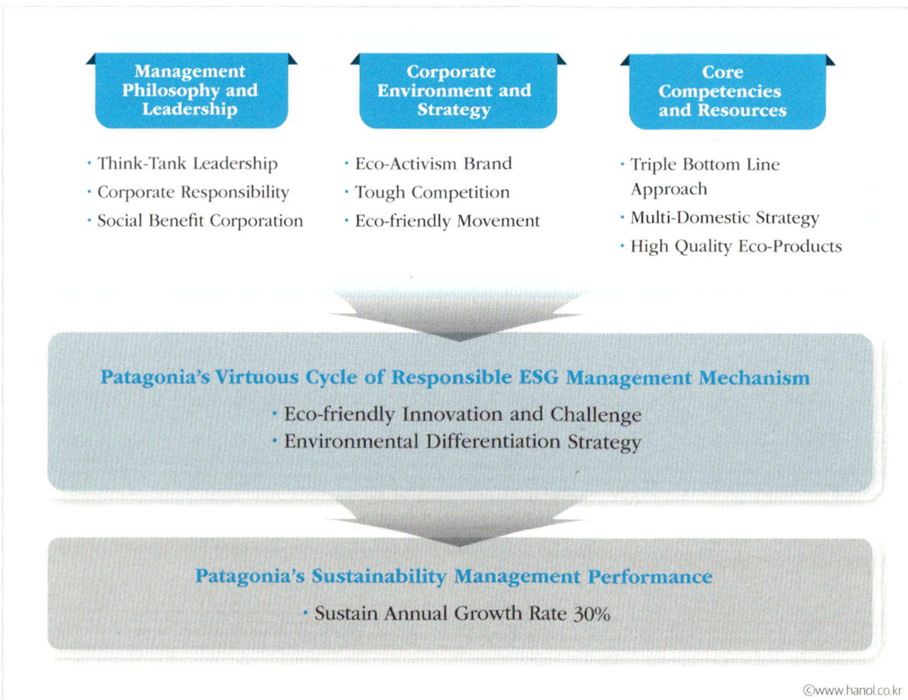

1 Outdoor Apparel Industry and Patagonia

In a context of globalization, most clothing companies manufacture their clothes in developing countries, where labor costs are cheaper, laws are more flexible, raw materials are cheaper among other factors. This phenomenon can be understood by looking at the world map highlighting the global clothing trade flows by continent in 2016. Indeed, for the United States and Europe, we can see that most of the trade flows originate from Asia. Thus, to be competitive in the clothing market, global companies tend to have a cost reduction approach in which offshoring plays an important role in their strategy.

Global Apparel Trade Flows in 2016 (INTRACEN, 2016)

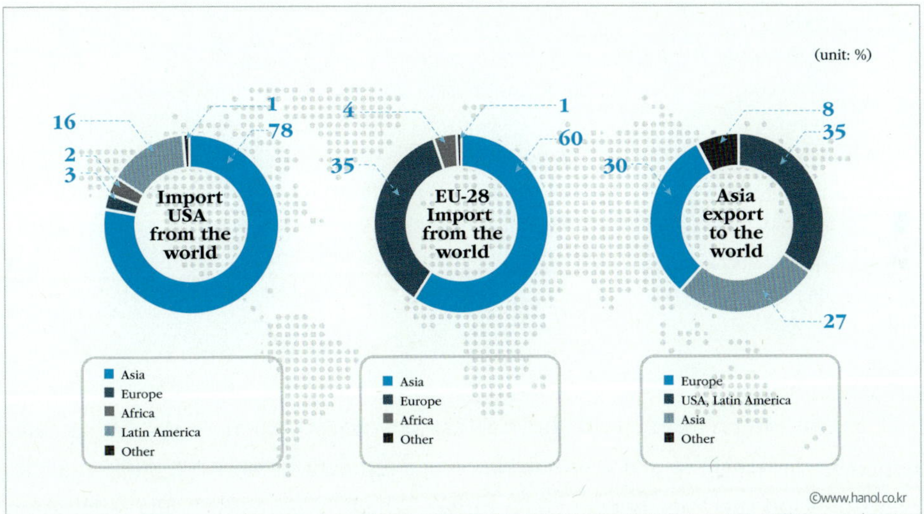

However, with the new trend of concern for sustainability and consumer awareness, buyers are examining the ethical dimensions as well as the satisfaction of companies' downstream activities.[57)]

In response, the goal of the strategy is also to shift from product quality to downstream activities to create value for the customer. The downstream argument of finding the source of innovation with customers rather than within the company is well known through Peter F. Drucker's emphasis on *"innovation for customers"*. Professor Niraj Dawar at Ivey Business School presented again the

57) The business process is divided up and down the supply chain. Upstream corresponds to activities related to purchasing-production-distribution: *"What a company does and how to sell it"*. Downstream refers to activities that take place at the point of sale (POS); *"what can a company do to its customers"*. While the *'source of competitiveness'* comes from upstream purchasing and production activities in developing countries, the *'creation of value and income'* is mainly exploited as a mechanism occupied by companies in developed countries through downstream activities.

following specific innovation strategy for customers:[58)]

- *Should the sources of competitive advantage exist within the firm? – NO*
  : Values evaluated by customers (brand, trust, quality, etc.) exist outside the company.
- *Does innovation always mean better products and technologies?* – NO
  : The purchasing method, cost and risk reduction are also important innovation activities.
- *Should the voice of the customer be obeyed unconditionally? – NO*
  : In some cases, customers may not be able to accurately understand their own needs.
- *Does the competitive advantage tend to weaken over time? – NO*
  : Identifying and reinforcing strengths will give you a sustainable competitive advantage.
- *Is innovation a product of technology-based laboratory?* – NO
  : Technological innovation is not the only, but more innovation can come from the field.
- *Can you change or choose your competitors yourself? – YES*
  : Changing the category of a product or service can also change competition and markets.

If ESG is simply seen from the *narrow* perspective such as the SRI (socially responsible investing), it will come under other regulations and pressures that depend only on the ESG performance rating, which is far from being such innovative management activities. However, when you consider ESG from a strategic perspective, it emerges as a new solution for sustainability that could be applied to all the upstream and downstream processes, like Patagonia.

The specificity of Patagonia, which has driven '*5R* (*Reduce, Repair, Reuse, Recycle, Reinvent*)' ecological strategy in upstream activities, is more evident in downstream activities: Patagonia practices socially responsible management and shares all the benefits with stakeholders such as customers and investors related to in-depth and environment-friendly upstream activities and POS (point-of-sale)-based downstream activities. Patagonia's management philosophy and strategy, which has pioneered maximizing value for customers and stakeholders rather than maximizing shareholder value, is based on the following mindset:

58) "When Marketing is Strategy" (Niraj Dawar, Dec. 2013, *Harvard Business Review*).

Patagonia's Customer Creation Mindset

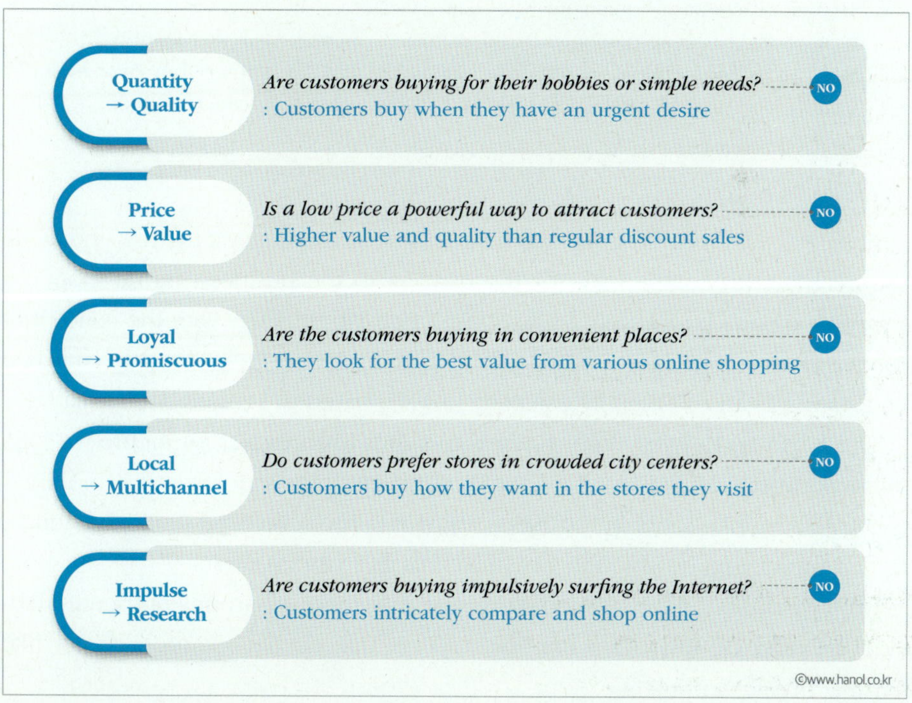

Here, the differentiation of views and values pursued by each area of ESG is evident. First, since environmental issues (E) are expressed mainly in upstream activities, a company must ensure that production and distribution management problems do not arise. At the same time, social (S) and governance (G) issues linked to transparent and ethical management are expressed mainly in downstream activities directly linked to customers.

2 Foundation for Growth of Patagonia

Yvon Chouinard, the founder of Patagonia, born in 1938, has loved mountaineering since his very childhood. Beginning in 1957, he set up a small workshop in the backyard of his home and roamed the California coast selling handmade climbing gear. In 1965, he teamed up with famous engineer and climber Tom Frost to expand his business into exceptionally designed products. In 1970, *'Chouinard Equipment'*, which gave his name, became the largest supplier of climbing equipment in the United States.

> However, Chouinard Equipment has been criticized as an *'environmental villain'* because the climbing equipment sold damaged the rock and was toughly influenced by public opinion. In response, Chouinard and his partner Tom Frost took drastic environmental protection measures to phase out the activity of making pitons for climbing.

In fact, at the time, piton was the main business, and he took the risk and made the decision. To compensate for the damage to the business, he developed a climbing apparel business, but it was just a side job. In 1972, with the concept of *'Clean Climbing'*, the first catalog of the clothing brand Patagonia was launched and started as an eco-friendly company in 1973, based in Ventura, California.

The goal was to encourage climbers to climb with respect for nature. Its logo is the outline of Mount Fitz Roy, border between Chile and Argentina, in the region of Patagonia. Later, in the 1980s, Patagonia revolutionized the textile industry by introducing eco-friendly raw materials and vibrant colors.

Until then, they have continually researched more environment-friendly fabrics and offer clothing lines for *'silent sports'* that do not require a motor like surfing, hiking, and biking.

The History of Patagonia's Green Business

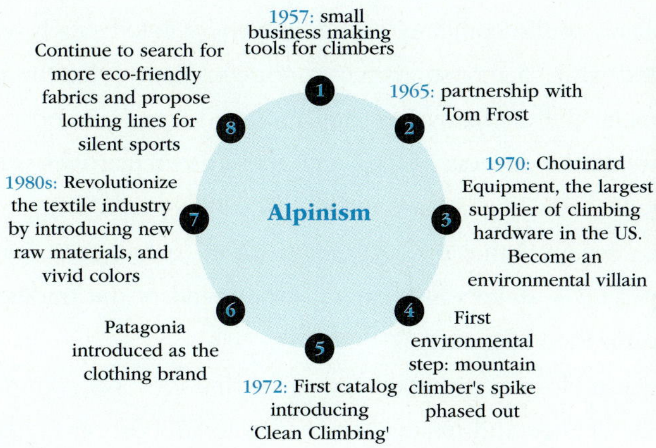

Yvon Chouinard
Patagonia's founder and American alpinist.

©www.hanol.co.kr

3 Think-Tank Leadership that Drives Change

In keeping with the company's mission *of "To make the best products, not to cause unnecessary harm, and to grow our business to provide and implement solutions to the environmental crisis,"* Patagonia focuses, aligned with leadership, all its activities on the ecological philosophy of the CEOs.

Patagonia's DNA is anchored in the core value of collaboration with the following three principles:

- Management of stakeholders based on sincerity and mutual respect
- Performance of individual and corporate roles based on environmentalism
- Development of innovative methods that are not bound by existing customs

Chouinard's leadership is focused on building consensus with its members. To this end, Patagonia encourages all employees with good ideas to express and share them with confidence, even though there are upper and lower hierarchies. Thanks to Chouinard's *'Brain Group Empathic Leadership',* which he calls *'Think-Tank Leadership'*, all Patagonia employees create a climate of collaboration with a sense of shared responsibility to contribute to the company with their ideas.

Patagonia's movement to protect the environment based on collaboration is embodied in both the policies of the company and its members. Interestingly, even if employees are arrested while demonstrating in a non-violent way for the protection of the environment, the company has well prepared a support policy in which the company pays all the deposits. Along with these green activities within the organization, Patagonia actively promotes external social responsibility.

In fact, Patagonia has received the *'B Corp Certification'*, a balanced corporate certification that practices 'stakeholder capitalism' instead of the traditional shareholder value maximization approach."[59]

In addition, exemplary ecological activities such as caring for local communities vulnerable to climate change and paying *'Earth Tax'* to support on site environmental protection activists and NGOs each year have a great impact on other companies. As such, Patagonia receives frequent requests from global companies to learn how to meet their social and environmental responsibilities.

Patagonia's Organizational Leadership

Internal Focus	External Focus
• **Patagonia Mission Statement** : *"Build the best product, do no unnecessary damage, use companies to inspire and implement solutions to the environmental crisis"* • **Patagonia Core Values** : *Quality, Integrity, Environmentalism, Not bound by custom* • **Think-Tank Leadership** : *"When you have a lot of independent people working for you, you can't tell them what to do, or you'll get a passive-aggressive response. Instead, you have to build consensus."* • **Activism, anchored in the brand and in all staff** : *"We even have a policy that employees can be refunded their deposit if they are arrested during a non-violent protest."*	• **Certified B Corporation Movement** : The practice of 'stakeholder capitalism' • **Patagonia 'Earth Tax'** : A self-imposed tax to ① Defend vulnerable communities in face of climate change ② Support local activists and NGOs • **Influence other corporations with best practices** : Patagonia often receives requests to help large companies guide them on how they could become more socially and environmentally responsible.

59) Certified B Corporations (Certified Balanced Corporations: B Corps): To certify a new type of business that pursues a balance between goal and profit. Certified balanced companies legally consider the impact of their decisions on employees, customers, suppliers, communities, and the environment. A Certified Balanced Company is a community of leaders who lead a global movement of people who use business as a good driving force.

4 Corporate Environment and Strengthening Strategies

1. Competitive Environment

To understand the eco-friendly business environment that Patagonia creates, let's start by comparing it with its major competitors. Patagonia's biggest competitor is *'The North Face'*. Both companies are leaders in outdoor clothing, general clothing, and hiking products. Sure, The North Face is way ahead of Patagonia in terms of sales, however Patagonia is showing its unique strength as a strong environmental movement group that can grab the attention of customers before it becomes a business.

Commercial Features of Patagonia and The North Face

Patagonia	The North Face
· **Created in 1972** : Outdoor clothing company with a history of environmental conservation and activism · **Sustainability** - 1% of annual net revenues to support nonprofit charitable organizations that promote environmental conservation and sustainability - 2018 → launched *ReCircle collection* using REFIBRATM lyocell fibers composed of 80% wood pulp and 20% recycled cotton scraps - Fabrics made from recycled (31%) or renewable (21%) sources · **Total Revenue 2018**: $ 800M · **Global Presence** : 80 countries (mainly e-commerce), 107 points of sales and high prices	· **Created in 1966** : High performance outdoor clothing, footwear, gear, accessories · **Sustainability** - Expanded its Climate Beneficial Wool collection, launched in 2017 → made in the USA from sustainable farms - Launch of the *Renewed collection* in 2018 by selling used, damaged and repaired or second-hand products · **Total Revenue 2018** : $13.8B (company owned by the group VF Corporation) · **Global Presence** : 60 countries, 500 points of sales and high prices

To understand the environment in which Patagonia operates, it is important to analyze its competitors. Patagonia was officially created in 1972, so a little later than the North Face which was created in 1966. The North Face and the Patagonia are both very similar in face value, but they differ in some areas: Patagonia is more environmentally focused than The North Face, with strict environmental guidelines on materials and a focus on recycling.

Patagonia is also less growth-oriented and more interested in its impact on the planet. Nevertheless, The North Face tries to implement sustainable activities by launching, for example, the *'Renewed Collection'* in 2018 by selling second-hand, damaged, and repaired or second-hand products.

Regarding their mission statement, Patagonia's goal is to build the best product, not to cause unnecessary damage, to use companies to inspire and implement solutions to the environmental crisis. They were born as a company providing equipment to the climbing community but have since grown into more premium and stylish outdoor gear.

Their passion for the outdoors means that they try to reduce their environmental impact (less dyeing, organic cotton, etc.) and that they donate at least 1% of their time, services, and sales to various environmental causes every year. They focus very heavily on ensuring that their materials are sourced from quality suppliers using ethical principles.

In the case of The North Face, they have grown into a huge outdoor equipment company offering everything from extreme ski gear to running shoes. They strongly support exploring the outdoors which they love and protect the environment in every way possible. They also state that they believe in improving environmental performance and social responsibility in the supply chain.

When it comes to pricing, in general, Patagonia products tend to cost more than The North Face equivalents. This is usually because Patagonia goes the extra mile with the quality of its materials and production. Regarding their global presence, The North Face is present in 60 countries and has approximately 500 outlets, and Patagonia is present in 80 countries and has 107 outlets.

Finally, regarding their total turnover in 2018, Patagonia earned $ 800 million, and The North Face, as part of the VF corporation group, earned $ 13.8 billion. An interesting fact is that The North Face, which has become the largest outdoor equipment company in the world, has also confirmed a new marketing mechanism that reinforces the image of its products, leading to immediate profit creation. What The North Face learns about Patagonia, which accounts for only 5% of its revenue, is reflected in this eco-friendly ESG management.

Patagonia was born as a company that provided equipment to the rock-climbing community, but now, as a high quality and stylish outdoor equipment company, they are passionate about eco-friendly business environment which is ahead of The North Face by reducing the use of dyes and dramatically increasing the use of organic cotton. For example, Patagonia donates more than 1% of its sales to the fund, as well as more than 1% of its working hours and service activities as talents to improve environmental issues.

Patagonia, which applies strict ethical principles to all *upstream activities* from material sourcing to manufacturing, also applies a strict duty in *downstream activities*. In other words, Patagonia established [Eco-friendly Strategy → Create new Market and Generate Profit → Voluntary Donation for Activism → Create new Customer] a virtuous cycle of business mechanism.

However, as Patagonia invests more in sourcing eco-friendly raw materials and in the quality of its products, Patagonia products are generally more expensive than The North Face products. Since there is no guarantee that a *'good (exemplary) company'* will succeed in the competition, Patagonia overcomes this trade-off issue with a strategy to maintain its share in the global market by strengthening the e-commerce sector rather than developing new stores compared to The North Face.

2. Environmental analysis

Whether it is a business or an individual, when your strength is combined with a good opportunity, the road to success will be widely open. As the like, Patagonia's sound future lies in growing opportunities outside of the business, such as the ecological trend included in ESG movement and the era in which social responsibility and communication with stakeholders became highly important and more and more well appreciated by customers.

The mechanism of creating a more positive brand image by providing attractive and sustainable products in terms of quality as well as the brand of an environment friendly company is spreading mainly through SNS based communication.

In addition, they are proud of being an exemplary ESG company in the world with *think-tank leadership*, high job satisfaction, low turnover rate, and an organizational atmosphere where free communication is possible through securing

SWOT Analysis Comparison of Patagonia and The North Face

	Patagonia	The North Face
S	• Sustainable/qualitative products • Good brand image • Sustainable brand • Low employee turnover • Strong distribution network • Qualified workforce (skilled, innovative, and diversified) • Strong presence on SNS	• Good quality products • Strong brand awareness • Focus on product technology • Commitment to sustainability • Large range of product portfolio • Good geographic presence in different regions • Strong online presence
W	• Limited advertising • High product costs • Few customers loyalty initiatives • Less fashionable clothing compared to competitors • Relatively high prices	• Difficult communication with customers • Expensive products • Low employee morale and lack of opinions on management • Lack of marketing campaigns
O	• Enter new outdoor markets, increase brand exposure, and expand product lines • Increase in online spending • Growth of eco-friendly products and services • The government offers grants on these eco-friendly products	• Set up training for the senior management so that they welcome and encourage feedback from their employees • Improve internal culture • Increased involvement of the community to improve the company reputation
T	• Fierce competition: Existing market obsolescence	• Fierce competition: Regulations and damage to brand image

innovative and diverse professional manpower.

These core competencies of Patagonia also serve as a cornerstone for the expansion of the global distribution network. Interestingly, Patagonia's weaknesses stem from their strengths. In Patagonia, because it does not force customers to buy excessively, it advertises in a limited way and uses recycled and organic cotton, so the production costs and the prices of the products are relatively high. And customer surveys show that Patagonia products lack a fashion sense compared to their rival The North Face.

Meanwhile, The North Face's strength lies in its solid brand reputation for selling high-quality products with high functionality and comfort, and its global distribution network with constant technological innovation and cutting-edge fashion products. However, The North Face, despite being the largest outerwear company in the world, has weaknesses in its organizational climate, such as low employee morale and lack of communication both internally and externally.

While there are many common aspects in terms of strengths and weaknesses, the reason Patagonia is better than The North Face like Goliath can be seen in the strong passion and pride of its employees for sustainability, and the low turnover rate. Both brands have the fundamental problem of high prices. Therefore, it will be interesting for Patagonia to develop a strategy to increase its market share with a 'good price', because the future competitive advantage is not guaranteed only by an environment friendly ESG management.

> The opportunities and threats in the external environment are forcing both companies to expand their business online, increase environment friendly products and services, fiercely compete with low-cost products, and innovate in products and services for generation MZ after generation Y. Now for Patagonia, competing with low-cost products such as Columbia Sportswear is emerging as a difficult but challenging strategic task.

3. Strategies to build Strengths

Patagonia's strategy to strengthen its strengths, which has been successful as an environment friendly company, is being implemented in various forms in line with the current trend in which ESG management, including social responsibility of the company, is put forward:

- *The first is a strategy to attract consumers as environmentalists.* In fact, Patagonia continues to build leads by leveraging its strong social media presence to entice young people to visit its web pages through word of mouth.
- *The second strategy is to develop innovative low-cost and environment friendly products and sell them at low prices.* This has been made possible through government support for eco-friendly companies, and it has the effect of purchasing Patagonia products preferentially from customers who show a strong commitment to protecting the global environment.
- *The third strategy is to develop the outdoor business market itself.* Patagonia actively promotes the importance of outdoor activities for health and happiness

as well as enhancing the branding of environment friendly products, and the efforts of its employees to listen to and reflect the opinions of customers, are followed up by working with customers through various environmental protection events.

Patagonia's Strengthening 4P Strategy

Place

Develop market penetration strategy to attract consumers as environmental activists

Product & Price

: Development of innovative low-cost, eco-friendly products and low sales prices

Promotion

Promote the importance of outdoor business activities to improve brand image

©www.hanol.co.kr

4. Risk analysis and risk management

As their mission statement emphasizes, *"We do business to revive our home, the planet,"* all of Patagonia's product brands are focused on the environment rather than profit. To defend these values, Patagonia employees are trained as environmental activists, and they actively practice even risky behaviors.

- Patagonia donates 1% of its total sales in cash each year, and since 1985, it has primarily been used to support non-profit environmental organizations.
- In November 2011, a photo of a fleece jacket with the phrase *"Don't Buy this Jacket"* was posted in the New York Times, campaigning for consumers not to overspend.
- In 2016, the $10 million in Black Friday sales was donated to non-profit environmental organizations, in addition to giving 1 % of annual sales.
- In November 2018, Patagonia donated $10 million to environmental organizations opposing the Trump Administration's corporate tax cuts.
- On September 20 and 27, 2019, all 107 stores around the world were completely closed to allow customers to take part in the climate strike.

5 Core Competencies and Major Resources

1. Core competence

TBL (triple bottom line) proposed by the GRI (Global Reporting Initiative) launched in 1997 is an accounting framework made up of the three components: Social, Environmental (ecological), Financial performance. TBL is used as a guideline for companies to prepare sustainability reports.

Meanwhile, in Patagonia, the 'Patagonia-TBL' framework that assesses corporate performance from a broad perspective to create more ambitious business value than GRI-TBL, the *'3P: Planet, People, Profits'*, proposed first and performed by John Elkington in 1997.

❶ **Planet** Patagonia produces the best clothes without harming the environment. This is possible thanks to the materials they use: In 1993, they started using fleece made from recycled plastic soda bottles; in 1994, they switched to using only organic cotton. In addition, the wish of the brand is to produce products only when customers need them. Thus, customers have always been asked to think twice before purchasing a product. Patagonia encourages customers to donate or sell used products to charity and does everything to protect the environment. In addition to switching to organic cotton and using recycled products in its manufacturing process, Patagonia has regularly donated to environmental causes since the beginning of the business. Initially, they donated 10% of their profits to environmental causes. In 1985, Patagonia increased it to 1% of their sales. In 2002, they created an organization; *"1% for the planet"*.

❷ **People** Patagonia, since its foundation, has employed quite independent people who care about the environment and love the outdoor activities, and teaches the business through OJT (on-the-job training) and education. It is not just graduating from a top university and entering a business after passing an exam. This is the reason why the turnover rate of internal customers (employees), who jointly carry out eco-responsible activities, appears low.

Patagonia's TBL: *Planet - People - Profits*

Planet	People	Profits
· Produce the best clothes without harming the environment. It starts with the used materials. · In 1993, started to use fleece made from recycled plastic soda bottles. · In 1994, switched to using only organic cotton · Wish: make products only when customers need them → also encourages customers to donate used products to charity or sell them. · Since 1985: donate 1% of sales to environmental causes → "1% for the Planet"	· Customer loyalty · Hire independent, environmentally conscious outdoors people and teach them about business. · Treat them well: Work-Life Balance (WLB) is a hallmark of the company. · Day care centers · Employees set their own work hours. · Covers 100% of the health insurance costs of employees. · Mothers/Fathers can take paid parental leave for up to 2 months. · Employee turnover rate is low (25% compared to the industry average of 43%).	· Patagonia faced bankruptcy twice : 1970's: sourced poor quality rugby shirts from a factory in Hong Kong. : 1991 Recession, when credit dried up → could not get loans & had to lay off 120 employees. · Quadrupled profits and revenues → today without debt. · The Founders are billionaires, but you wouldn't know it by their way of life : Fly coach to redirect money to environmental causes. : Take very little money out of the business.

Patagonia emphasizes the Work-Life Balance (WLB) and allows employees to define their own daycare operation and work schedules, so that employees are highly satisfied with their work. Patagonia hire people who enjoy the outdoors, and corporate policy ensures that they can stop working early on and enjoy surfing or hiking any time. Field trips to learn rock climbing and fly fishing are also provided as educational courses. Therefore, it can be said that it is natural that the competition rate for Patagonia's job is 900 to 1, which roughly provides up to two months of paid parental leave and 100% of health insurance premiums. In contrast, for external customers, customer loyalty counts the most important. In fact, Patagonia manages everything that is responsible for its own products. If the customer is not satisfied with the product at any time, it can be returned, and if the product is worn out, the company will fully repair it.

❸ **Profits** Today Patagonia is an exemplary company with great commercial success outside of its ESG management, but like most companies Patagonia has been on the verge of bankruptcy on two occasions: The first was when Patagonia was supplied with shoddy rugby jerseys at its Hong Kong factories in the 1970s, and the second when the 1991 recession ran out of credit lines and eventually forced 120 employees dismissed. Since then, Patagonia's profits and sales have quadrupled over the past 10 years as they reinforced their *'Green Philosophy'* with high quality financial products and credits and became a debt free business.

2. VRIN competency factor

Let's analyze the core competencies of Patagonia, which has established itself as a model company in ESG management, with the VRIN framework[60], to see if it is a source of sustainable competitive advantage. Indeed, Patagonia's ESG management resources and capabilities must be valuable (V), rare (R), inimitable (I) and non-substitutable (N) to form the basis of a sustainable competitive advantage.

❶ **Valuable** Business activities that emphasize unique corporate value are seen as environment friendly. In 1985, Patagonia launched the *'Product Lifecycle Initiative'* to reduce the environmental footprint of its products, with a commitment to devote 1% of its annual sales to the conservation and restoration of the natural environment. This plan contains the '5Rs' including, *Reducing Patagonia product consumption, Repairing, Reusing, Recycling, and Reimagining.* Since 1994, decided to use only organic cotton. Patagonia's *"Textile Exchange Program"* teaches intermediary retailers, producers, and

60) VRIN Framework (Barney J., 1991): A framework for analyzing valuable, rare, inimitable, and non-substitutable competencies as sources of sustainable competitive advantage.

key stakeholders to understand how using eco-friendly raw materials can deliver significant social and environmental benefits to brand value.

❷ **Rare** Patagonia's economic activity lies in environmental giving beyond imagination. As a pioneer in the use of organic cotton and a leader in sustainability and recycling, Patagonia donates 1% of its sales to environmental organizations around the world, and voluntarily levies a global tax to save the planet, in the interests of public. At the same time, Patagonia is a global leader in technological innovation and innovative ideas to provide high-quality and low-cost products.

❸ **Inimitable** Patagonia's hard-to-emulate business activities are reflected in the long-term investment of enormous costs to fulfill its mission of protecting the planet environment. In fact, Patagonia faced a financial crisis that required an additional 20 per cent (roughly $20 million) of the company's stake to use only organic cotton, which is three times the price of the regular cotton used by its competitors and has grown into a global leader. In addition, Patagonia invests huge amounts of money in the *'5R Practice'* recycling initiative and in its own R&D related to raw materials.

❹ **Non-substitutable** *"Why are The North Face or Columbia Sportswear so hard to make them like Patagonia?"* The fact that it is difficult for an outerwear company that can replace Patagonia comes from the recycling rate that Patagonia pursues and achieves. Patagonia's goal is to increase the recycling rate of all its products from 65% to over 90%. Patagonia sells over 8% more of its organic cotton products than the total of its giant rivals The North Face and Columbia Sportswear.

The practical competency that gives Patagonia a competitive edge is in a word, sustainability. Patagonia is practicing sustainability management as an *'environmentally responsible company'*, maintaining an average annual growth rate of 30% with its multinational strategy of providing products that meet the needs of customers differentiated by country and an eco-friendly strategy of business marketing activities.

6 Mechanism for Managing the Virtuous Cycle

1. Business model for creating balanced performance

An analysis of Patagonia's business model, rated as a global exemplary company in ESG management, with the Balanced Scorecard (BSC) from Kaplan and Norton, shows the following outstanding activities:

- Meets the needs of customers through the *'Environmental Stewardship'* activity inherent in the organizational culture and solve the problem.
- The creation of environment friendly customer value is highlighted.
- Through the customer value created, it is expressed as a mechanism of [ESG management → Performance/Profit], creating financial results such as improved profitability, increased sales and expanding market share.[61)]

Patagonia's successful virtuous cycle mechanism is not simply made up of eco-friendly business and ESG management, but it is the excellence of the internal organizational management system that has created lifelong employment, continuous technology development and ideas, understanding of customers and immediate customer response activities. Thus, it must be understood that they are working together like assembled Lego Pieces:

- *Learning and Growth for Sustainable Value Creation*: Patagonia's corporate culture of lifelong employment is imbued with a philosophy of respect for people that treats employees as lifelong customers, and the role of *'Environmental Stewardship'* is rooted in the management of ethics and integrity.
- *Internal Business Process for Excellence*: Patagonia is committed to reducing unnecessary costs and waste throughout its business-related supply chain activities. In addition, Patagonia maintains close relationships to understand its customers and solve their problems and continues to explore new ways to produce *'Green Products'* through innovation. Environmental stewardship activities

61) Balanced Scorecard (BSC): It is a strategic management system that reorganizes the vision and strategy of the company into key performance indicators (KPIs) inside and outside the organization so that the whole organization can focus on activities to achieve the goal. It was developed in 1992 by Professor Robert Kaplan and Dr. David Norton of Harvard University to measure and manage the business performance of companies from a perspective balanced between internal and external, tangible and intangible, short and long term. As the BSC is used as a means of developing a sustainable strategic process, it is receiving new attention as a tool that shares the objective of ESG management and sustainable growth.

Patagonia's Learning Organization Strategy on BSC

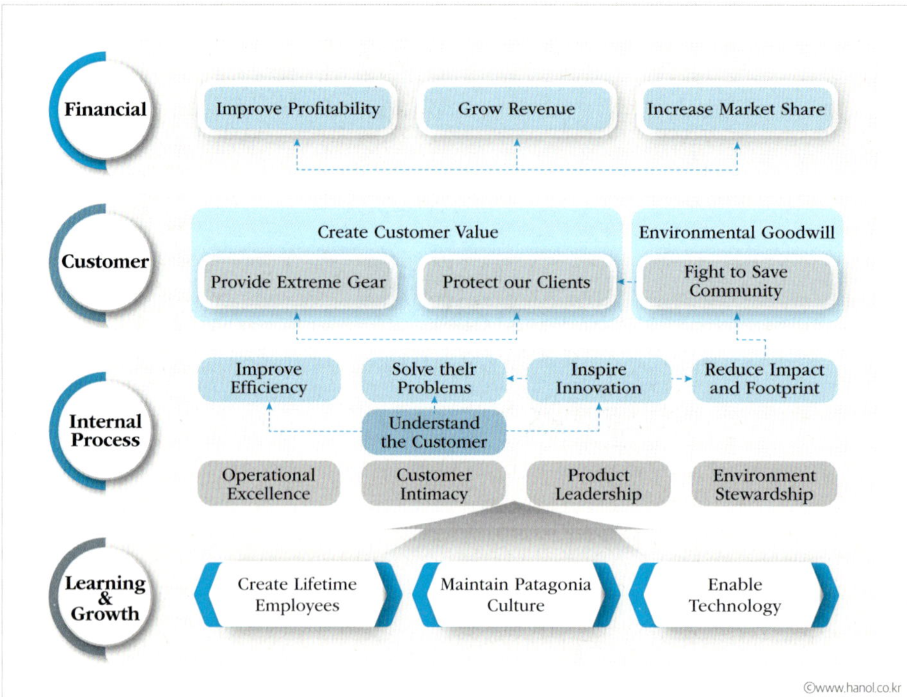

aimed at reducing environmental damage in the manufacturing process are presented as an example of ESG management.

- *Customer in the mirror looking at Patagonia:* With the capabilities built through all these internal management processes, Patagonia demonstrates *'Agility Management'* that responds to customer complaints at supersonic speed while pursuing the creation of environment friendly value of the customer.
- *Financial performance for all stakeholders as well as shareholders:* Patagonia's *'Eco-friendly Business Philosophy'* has led to financial performance of over 30% annual increase in profitability and an increase of over four times the market share in the last 10 years.

2. Environmental differentiation strategy

Michael Porter's *generic strategies* and Boston Consulting Group's *BCG model* present the actual conditions and types of business and encourage each company to find a strategy which fits the situation. In contrast, Peter F. Drucker who emphasizes in his *'The Practice of Management'*, and entrepreneurs who value the practice like Steve Jobs, pointed out that the *'differentiation strategy'* is the only and the best strategy for success that companies should pursue, whatever the size of the company or market conditions.

Patagonia's unique strategy, differentiated by environment friendly business management, broadens the path to contemporary success. Patagonia is a non-listed company, so there is no need to follow the management practices of listed companies that are obliged to report sales and profits monitoring the shareholders.

Patagonia's Sustainable Circular Economy Mechanism

As such, Patagonia's core concept of environment friendly business is to *"Manufacture-Repair-Recycle"* so that its products last a lifetime. Therefore, once a Patagonia product is sold, the relationship with the customer does not end with revenue and sales.

In other words, Patagonia creates value for the *'bona fide'* customers, and customers and companies participate together in the manufacturing-repair-recycling *'Circular Economy'*, where *"Thinking production and Waste-free consumption"* takes place. To this end, Patagonia has implemented the *'Common Threads Recycling Program'*, encouraging customers to reduce consumption and to repair, reuse and recycle their products.

For recycling, Patagonia strives to recover products from landfills or incineration, and sells returned products and used items at lower prices through a separate website. Products reached the end of their useful life are recovered and used entirely as materials for manufacture of new products. Therefore, Patagonia is praised for saying that *"Patagonia's products contain infinite love!"*

3. Patagonia's business performance

In fact, academics are skeptical of the difficulty of converting business activities into an *'environment friendly circular economy'*. However, Patagonia, a successful green business, uses up to 65% recycled or renewable raw materials, with a target of 90%. As the like, Patagonia demonstrates a theoretically difficult mechanism into practice as a living model of ESG management. In particular, the argument that *"ESG management should be carried out by companies, not initiated by government"* can be clearly confirmed through the case of Patagonia.

Patagonia has donated $150 million to environmental projects since 1985 and approximately 550 employees directly supported environmental organizations. As an example of a circular economy, more than 100,000 garments were recycled around the world in 2018 alone. In 2019, the fund was invested in the production of approximately 13 million kilowatts of solar power. Collecting for recycling costs more than buying organic cotton, but the results paid off for Patagonia's financial performance.

> Patagonia is committed to creating sustainable solutions based on its eco-friendly philosophy: Internal recycling, selection of organic raw materials, use of clean electricity, reduce carbon emissions from manufacturing processes, analyze environmental footprint and practice self-auditing and transparent disclosure of information. As a company loved by the customers, Patagonia is leading the way to *'Save the Earth'* more than any other companies.

7 Future Prospect of Patagonia

The secret to the success of Patagonia, once branded as an *'environmental villain'* early in its business, lies in the CEO's philosophy of not producing products that harm the environment with an immediate and daring decisions. In addition, treating Patagonia as a model of ESG management has also become an important evaluation criterion for the influence of the current trend of global environmental protection, including carbon neutrality:

- First, Patagonia is a pioneer in environment friendly companies and has set ambitious goals for itself since its foundation. All strategic decisions are scrutinized and evaluated around this goal for sustainability. Patagonia's mission statement, *"We are in a business to save our home planet,"* was also expressed as an ambitious but even dangerous goal and strategy.
- Second, Patagonia pays huge amount of money to support environmental activists. For example, during Black Friday in 2011, *"Don't Buy this Jacket"* was announced. Although this was a risky strategy for short-term earnings, it became an opportunity to gain attention and love from media and customers.
- Third, Patagonia doesn't take anything for granted. Responsibility to customers and stakeholders, not just to shareholders, is defined as the *'economy of conscience',* resulted in high profits as well as opportunities for sustainable growth. To uphold the philosophy and beliefs of an eco-responsible business, Patagonia boldly takes risks that build customer trust.

It is difficult for individuals or businesses to be successful with weaknesses. In other words, we must compete with our strengths. Patagonia's strength is shown as a successful case of a differentiated strategy that puts all the effort into areas that others overlooked or didn't want to do, such as *"eco-friendly, donation participation, and consumption reduction".*

The consistency and reliability of the eco-friendly business that Patagonia has built facilitates communication with all stakeholders, including customers, and the overconsumption prevention campaign and the circular economy recycling mechanism '5R' now require the participation of other competitors. These are the future goals of Patagonia.

Just as Tesla maintained a financial surplus by selling carbon credits rather than income from the sale of electric vehicles, Patagonia also presents an eco-friendly business model that pursues substantial growth with the competitive advantages in carbon credits and circular economy.

Patagonia's future vision, which focuses on an eco-friendly and ESG-based business model, will become brighter as environmental issues are highlighted. Of course, there are many companies that are successful in SRI (socially responsible investing) and there are also many companies that are successful in transparent and ethical management as their core competencies.

> However, what must be evaluated here is social sympathy and the values expressed in the spirit of the times (zeitgeist): *"Do we really give more the meanings to successful companies or more to those we love?"*

If the number of companies that have always been with our company as successful and respected managers through ESG management increases, the ESG value will increase over time. Efforts have already been made to prepare an assessment and analysis framework for responsible ESG investing, including not only Korean companies, but also China and Japan, that we have seen through the Hankyoreh newspaper and HERI's East Asia 30 Future Forum.

In the future, we want to give our society a value for the future of eco-friendly ESG management while hoping that there will be more the loved companies and respected CEOs assessed by ESG standards including carbon neutrality etc.

VI

Ethics and Transparency to Lead ESG Management

VI

Ethics and Transparency to Lead ESG Management

1. Making Profits with Corporate Social Responsibility
2. Ethical Management for Corporate Sustainability
3. Respected Executives of Successful Companies
4. Historical Examples of Compliance Programs
5. Ethical Management Learned from History
6. Transparent Information and Scientific Measurement

"Aux Grands Hommes La Patrie Reconnaissante"
There are no mausoleums for the President or dignitaries in the Paris Panthéon, a national cemetery dedicated to the Great personages.[62]

If we are like them, who should we serve first? The people who made France like France were people who showed the values of the time and of society with their intelligence and their dedication. We, who live in the 21st century, are losing such ideas and philosophies, and pay more attention to every word from the CEOs of the world's biggest companies called MAGA (*Microsoft, Apple, Google, Amazon*), NFT or FAANG (*Facebook, Amazon, Apple, Netflix, Google*) than do political leaders or social thinkers.

The impact of businesses on the economy and society is getting bigger and bigger, especially if they are large corporations, they must not only contribute to the national economy but keep pace with the times for future generations.

For this reason, the *'management with philosophy'* of the entrepreneur, the ethical conscience, and the values of the manager as a social leader, should be

62) A post-revolutionary figure in 1789, writer and revolutionary *Honoré Gabriel Riquetti Comte de Mirabeau* (*except François Marie Arouet dit Voltaire and Jean-Jacques Rousseau*), great writer *Victor-Marie Hugo, Émile Zola, André Malraux, Alexandre Dumas,* and war hero *Léon Gambetta,* union activist *Auguste Marie Joseph Jean Léon Jaurès*, Nobel Laureates in Physics *Jean Baptist Perrin and Pierre Curie, Marie Curie*, Nobel Peace Prize Laureate *René Cassin*, Resistance Leader *Jean Moulin*, Economist and Father of the European Union *Jean Monnet*, including Poet from Martinique *Aimé Césaire*, 80 people are enshrined (as of 2021). Meanwhile, in the center of each village, a small memorial with the names of veterans of World War II engraved on a copper plate or slab shows another meaning as a philosophy in the lives of French people.

the most important *'karma(業)'*. We are waiting for the CEOs respected by society, and furthermore, the nation and honored through their management philosophy'.

Except for Dr. New Il-han, the founder of Yuhan Corporation, who has been rated historically as Korea's most respected CEO, it is hard to find a businessman who has not made a splash in the company, to be honest. However, as Drucker praised, *"The history of the 20th century cannot be understood without looking at Korea's economic growth,"* it must be recognized that their challenges and efforts were the driving force behind the development of Korean economy.

> *"Shouldn't they be able to be enshrined in the National Cemetery after being passed away?" "Why is it difficult for business leaders to be revered as the nation's heroes, both at home and abroad?"*

The political collusion and corruption associated with the business are not just the product of underdeveloped countries, but also appear in developed countries. When Enron Corporation, one of the great companies admired, went bankrupt in late 2001 due to accounting fraud, tens of thousands of people lost their jobs and Arthur Anderson, the accounting firm responsible for the audit of Enron, was also dissolved. This is a typical example of the loss of confidence in *'The Corporation USA'*, which represented capitalism.

> In the sudden changes of government or unexpected changes of top management in company, the lack of ethics and accountability follows like a shadow with almost no exceptions. Even religious groups are the same cases.

According to Peter Drucker, a company's mission is to generate profits, be socially responsible, and innovate for customers. This is the argument that if only one of the three missions being emphasized or even one is abandoned, the company is already running a business that cannot be fulfilled successfully.

Therefore, to generate profits, *'check and balance'* is essential for social responsibility, including fair trade and social contribution, and management rights focused on innovation for customers. Likewise, the power relations between businesses and governments, and between businesses and customers, should not be concentrated in one side. To this end, employee empowerment, win-win cooperation between organizations and responsible management activities for customers and stakeholders should be established as organizational culture and management philosophy of the leaders.

Arguably the importance of corporate social responsibility began in Drucker's *'The Practice of Management (1954)'*. The problem is that Korean companies are too much interested in profit making, but the social performance and innovation activities for customers are relatively weak. Thus, the true innovation activities of a company for its customers and the leadership of the top management are important. And inevitably, companies and leaders must strive to be respected by society through ethical and responsible management practices.

> *"A country where there are many successful companies but few respected companies", "A country where there are many global companies but few sustainable companies..."* This is the real business context in Korea.

1 Making Profits with Corporate Social Responsibility

In order for a company to grow continuously, in the market competition, the price determined by supply and demand must be higher than the cost of production activities to make a profit, and the utility evaluated by the customer must be greater than the price paid by the customer. Since profit is only created when customers and potential customers are created, increasing the utility valued by customers is considered an essential activity for the sustainable growth of a company from a traditional point of view.

The view of corporate management focused on retaining customers like this is evolving into one that emphasizes emotional management that treats customers as if they were invited guests as we can see at Disneyland. Recently, the issue of creating social value, which comprehensively evaluates the value of companies and management activities, from the perspective of the stakeholders, especially investors, has emerged.

Management function of the corporate sustainability

	Cost	Price	Utility	Value
Pro-Sustainability	Cost Down	Profit Up	More Satisfaction	Value Creation
Principal Actor	Corporation & Manager	Market & Competitor	Customer & Guest	Stakeholder & Society
Evaluation Criteria	Input based	Process based	Output based	P-R-I[63] based
Focus of Control	Cost	Competition	Needs	Ethics
Corporate Goals	Financial Profit → Customer Satisfaction Social Value → Sustainability			

Basically, the survival and growth of a company is only guaranteed when the price received from the market is higher than the cost of product or service, and the utility valued by customers is greater than the price set in the market.

The recently emerging ESG management, which includes both corporate social responsibility and sustainable management activities, emphasizes the argument that the social value of a company assessed by all stakeholders, including investors, should be greater than the utility of products and services valued by customers.

> In economics, the production function is represented by the two main factors that are capital (K) and labor (L): [P=f(K·L)]. However, the production function of business administration targeting enterprises not only deals with these two authentic factors (K·L) but [P=f(K·L·M·I·C·T·LO·KM·HN·EE·SM·TG·SV·RI)] has evolved by focusing on various artificial factors of customer value creation.

Thus, business activities include marketing (M), information (I), culture (C), time (T), learning organization (LO), human networks (HN), knowledge management (KM), environment and ethics (EE), sustainability management (SM), transparent governance (TG), social value (SV), and responsible investment (RI), as well as capital (K) and labor (L).

All independent variables of management functions that have appeared in

63) P-R-I: Profit, Responsibility, Innovation.

different eras are all important, but recently emerging sustainability management, transparent governance, compliance management, corporate social responsibility, and social value creation are all responsibilities to shareholders and customers. Now, it is being emphasized as an essential condition for becoming a *'Good to Great'* company by fulfilling its obligations and responsibilities to all stakeholders.

The evolution of the management function (Park K., 2021)[64)]

Factor	Period	Representative Books and Cases
Kapital	18C.	A. Smith: *The Wealth of Nations*
Labor	19C.	K. Marx: *Das Kapital*
Marketing	1950s	P. Kotler: *Marketing Management*
Information	1970s	D. Bell: *Post-industrial Society*
Culture	1980s	E. Shine: *Organizational Culture & Leadership*
Time	1980s	P. Drucker: *The Essential Drucker*
Learning	1990s	P. Senge: *The Fifth Discipline*
Knowledge	1990s	I. Nonaka: *Knowledge Management*
Networking	1990s	D. Morgan: *Human Networking*
Ethics	2000s	A. Carroll: *Corporate Social Responsibility (CSR)*
Sustainability	2000s	F. Spreckley / J. Elkington: *Triple Bottom Line (TBL)*
Governance	2000s	P. Sarbanes / M. Oxley: *Sarbanes-Oxley Act (SOX)*
Social Value	2010s	M. Porter / M. Kramer: *Creating Shared Value (CSV)*
ESG & SDGs	2020s	CERES / UNEP: *Global Reporting Initiative (GRI)*

Then, "How are managers to overcome all the regulations and crises on business management? And what kind of regulation and support should the government provide to ensure that the business is running properly?"

64) Park K. (2021), *ESG and Sustainable Society,* Oct. 2021, https://youtu.be/mpvi_6F1c84

It is necessary to discuss fundamental philosophical and practical issues by asking the following questions about CSR performance, sustainability management, and ESG management, which have been continuously emphasized since the publication of Peter Drucker's *"The Practice of Management'* in 1954.

- Do the integrity and ethics of the CEO have a positive effect on the business performance of the company?
- Do successful companies in Korea have a CEO who is highly respected by the society?
- Where to present an exemplary company that has created a desirable ethical climate?
- How does the evaluation standard of the value of the time, so called the 'public sentiment law' appear?
- What is the mission of CEO for the continuous practice of ethical management and ESG management?

2 Ethical Management for Corporate Sustainability

"Ethics can be money in business, but money can hardly be ethics." This connotation is also verified by academic research.[65] Samsung Electronics, which have become world-famous companies, and Hyundai Motor Company, never reach the world level in terms of business ethics. Transparency International (TI)'s *'2020 National Integrity Ranking'* of Korea is still ranked 23rd out of 37 OECD countries, which is in the low-middle range, especially in the level of corruption and bribery practices.

If then, *"What are the roles and performance of ethical and integrity in actual corporate management activities?"*

According to the results of previous research on this subject, even if the activities of ethical and integrity management are insufficient, the output profit appears rather high in many cases. In other words, ethical and integrity management act as moderators of corporate profit creation, but their roles as causal

65) Carroll A. (2015), "Corporate social responsibility", *Organizational Dynamics*, 44(2).

variables or mediators rarely appear as is shown on the following figure.[66]

Meanwhile, it has been proven that ethical and integrity management play an important causal or mediating role for the sustainable growth of a company. Therefore, if a company expects sustainable growth as well as temporary or short-term profit creation, a culture of integrity and ethical management must be a prerequisite.

Ethical and Integrity Management as a Parameter of Sustainability

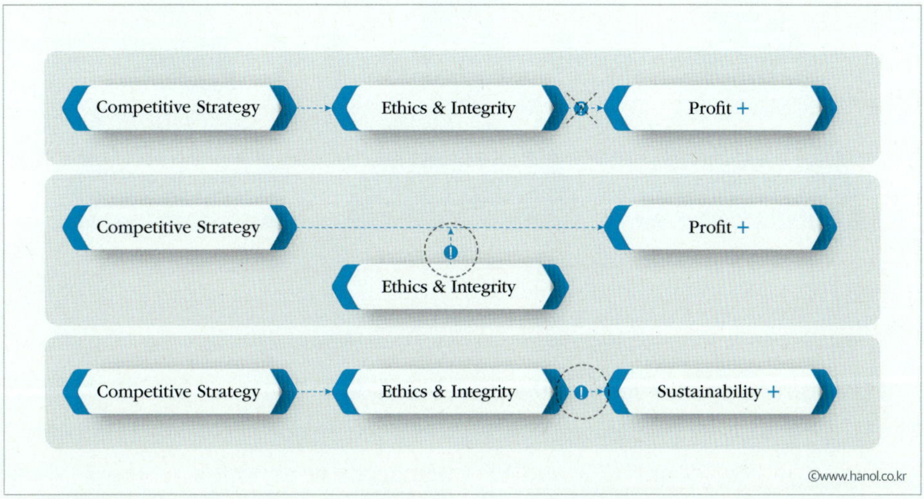

There is *Heinrich's law* (*1931*), '1: 29: 300'. The statistical logic behind a serious accident (for example, a fatality) is that 29 minor accidents (for example, minor injuries) have the same cause, followed by about 300 signs of related accidents (for example, accidents without injury).
Frank E. Bird interpreted this again and revealed the *Bird's Pyramid* (*1966*), '1 (dead): 10 (minor): 30 (property damage): 600 (Oops accident)'. These are all claims based on statistical analysis that *"Great disaster always happens when trivial things are overlooked"*.

The reason Heinrich's Law is important in ethical and integrity management, or CSR and ESG management, is that it can be applied as a negative screening

66) Park et al. (2012), "Desirable ethical climates on Organizational effectiveness, *AJBM,* 6(14).

criterion in evaluation and measurement. According to Heinrich's Law, it can be assumed that when one case of corruption in a company is revealed, there are already over 300 signs of such case.

Heinrich's Pyramid and Similar Studies[67)]

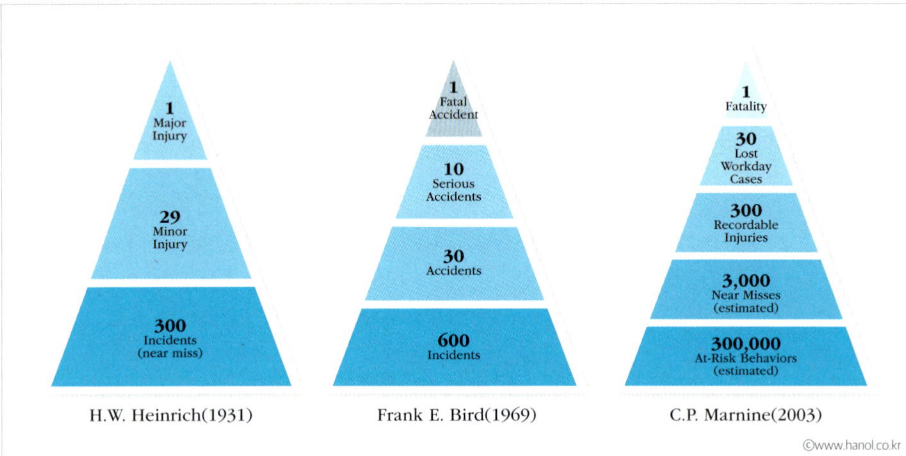

It is like the tip of an iceberg that is submerged in water, so it is hard to see, but looking at it is the driving force to prevent major accidents in advance. Therefore, in considering CSR and ESG management as well as sources of unethical management beyond legal and institutional devices such as disclosure obligations, ESG indicators are important control variables for corporate sustainability management.

3 Respected Executives of Successful Companies

"There are many successful companies in Korea, but few respected CEOs." This applies not only to business, but also to politics and government. It is said that *"In Korea, there are many bureaucrats and members of the National As-*

67) Heinrich W. H.: *Industrial Accident Prevention*, 4th Edition. New York: McGraw-Hill Book Company, Inc., 1959. Bird, Frank E., and George L. Germain: *Loss Control Management: Practical Loss Control Leadership*, Revised Edition, Det Norske Veritas (U.S.A.), 1996. ConocoPhillips Marine: *Safety Pyramid based on a study*, April 2003. Freibott B.: *Sustainable safety management: incident management as a cornerstone for a successful safety culture*, Safety and Security Engineering V, WIT Press, 2013.

sembly who succeed through individual efforts, but there are few who are truly respected by the people."

> There is a saying from the great Buddhist monk Beop-jung who called *"to possess nothing"*, and Cardinal Kim Soo-hwan who said *"The length from the head to the heart is only 50 centimeters, but it took 70 years to walk down this street"*. This echoes the importance of integrity and ethics in business and social life.

However, in the era of global competition, we cannot demand 'super ego' like a religious leader from business leaders, public officials, and politicians. Indeed, as the saying goes, *"Where there is income, there is tax"*, churches and temples are also subject to tax payment, so it is time for them also to lead sustainable growth, such as carbon neutrality, as well as increase in business performance.

1. Management with the philosophy of a loved company

Without doubt, there are business leaders in Korea respected by foreign scholars and business leaders. In his book *"Mintzberg on Management (1989),"* Henry Mintzberg pointed out *'Management by Intuition'* that should be learned from the founder of Hyundai Group, chairman Chung Ju-young.

Chinese leaders praised that *"Only three people like the founder and chairman of POSCO Park Tae-jun can make China the center of the world"*, and Chairman Lee Byung-chul and Lee Kun-hee (Samsung), Cho Choong-hoon (Hanjin), and Choi Jong-hyun (SK), who are the subject of case studies in major business schools. There is also Dr. New Il-han, the founder of Yuhan Corporation, who has still been Korea's the most respected CEO for almost 100 years.

What the respected CEOs have in common is the fact that they are all people who have made the company with *"management with a philosophy"*. The *'philosophy to repay the gratitude of the nation and society'* is in the management philosophy of the founders, who solidified the foundation for Korea's economic growth, such as patriotic medicine, steel, and business.

The culture of integrity and anti-corruption is reinforced with laws and systems, and ethics and integrity management are emphasized as slogans, but management with a philosophy is required in the deep base of business activities. Indeed, the more laws and systems impose ethical and anti-corruption management philosophy, the more it is clear that companies will rush to invest and prepare countermeasures to avoid evasion.

Respected CEOs of the Successful Companies

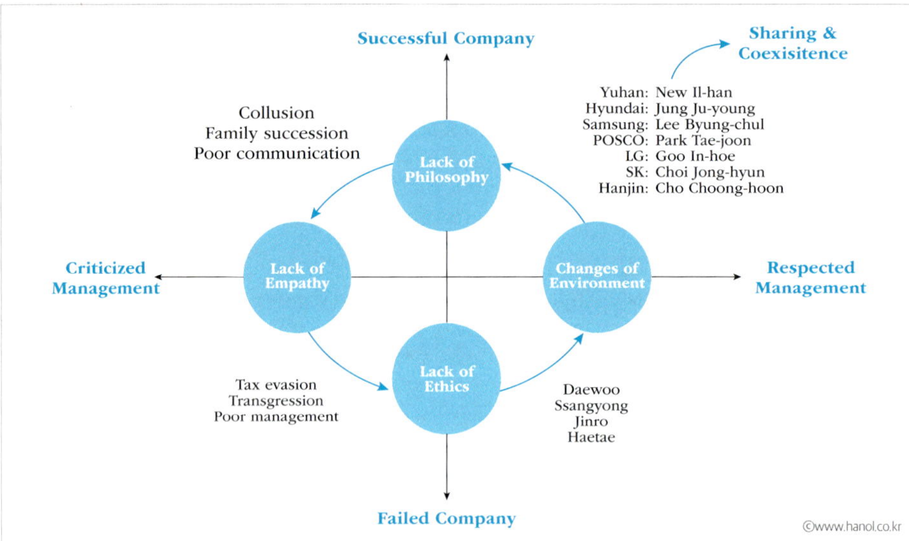

Therefore, management with a philosophy such as eco-friendliness is not systematically applied, but rather a direction for a sustainable growth which comes from the practical wisdom voluntarily built by the business leaders.

2. Practice of ethical management as an ESG foundation

Take the case of creating a list of strategic tasks considering the *'urgency'* which determines the priority of a decision and the *'importance'* which determines the weight, called the Eisenhauer Matrix: *"What do you think should be the most urgent and important task for Korean companies?"*

> While only pursuing economic growth as a corporate strategy of competitive advantage, in fact, even the CSR and ethical management have been seen as important by CEOs, they were not implemented as urgent corporate tasks.

Perhaps therefore the satire says, *"Korean entrepreneurs are people of interest who narrowly walk between prison walls and business opportunities in the market."* So, if we look at our current situation, CSR and ethical management are still at the *'Rain Check or Do Later' l*evel, which is forced to respond or procrastinate depending on the times and the social atmosphere.

The Importance and Urgency of Ethical Management (Park K., 2015)

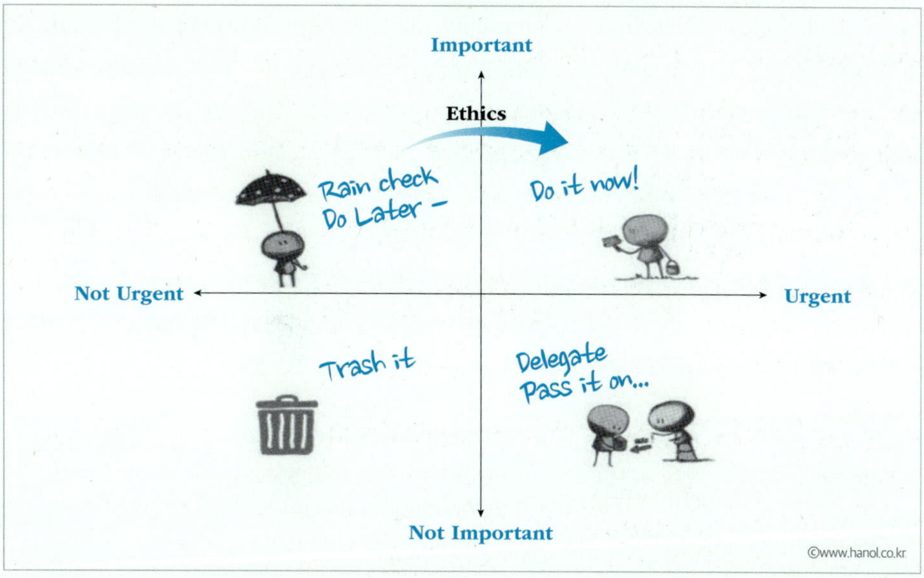

> Therefore, corporate ethical management and social responsibility should be used as a sustainable competitive strategy as well as the best practices through active positive screening rather than focusing on passive negative screening.

If responsible ESG management indicators are overstated or imposed as a measure for capital market investors rather than innovative management for *physical market customers,* companies conceive it as new regulations or a troubling threat. And the social vicious cycle of finding another way to avoid the law will only repeat itself.

> Obviously, mandatory disclosure of ESG information and standardization of indicators are important. However, even for this, CEOs must understand current trends

and values in ESG management and write practical reports to prepare immediately as a *"Do it now"* strategy.

The initial objective of ESG management is to participate voluntarily in corporate social responsibility and sustainability management, however the ESG index is often interpreted as another institutional regulations for the socially responsible investing (SRI) by asset managers. Aristotle said, *"Among the three factors that move people-Rules, Incentives, and Practical wisdom-the most important is 'practical wisdom' that everyone can relate to. Practical wisdom comes from the combination of moral skill and spontaneity."* French sociologist Michel Crozier asserted that *"Institutions alone cannot change society."*[68] *Taking these wisdoms into account, the limits of the role of ESG indicators, which are becoming institutionalized as a new standard, are clearly highlighted.*

As such, the performance of ESG management does not depend only on its principles and indicators, but on the practical wisdom of companies which voluntarily put them into practice with the philosophy arose by the CEO.

There are also fears that if indicators related to ESG management are institutionalized as rules and incentives such as the *'Must-Do'* item of the company, the moral spontaneity and the judgment of the company will weaken, and only the managerial activities that support *"Do the Things Right"* will be carried out. In other words, it is difficult to avoid the risk of not realizing the philosophy and wisdom of ESG management that comes from the courage, honesty, and consideration that lead leaders to *"Do the Right Things"* because of the institutionally reinforced UN PRI (Principles of Responsible Investment).

3. The value of the company reflected in the mirror of the society

The era of *"customer is the mirror of company"* now emphasizes ESG indicators as if *"investors were the mirror of company."* As ESG is highlighted as the indicators related to responsible ESG investing, companies are already again ab-

68) Michel Crozier (1982), *"On ne change pas la société par décret"*, Collection Pluriel.

sorbed by the ESG assessment results and scores.

In fact, the essence of ESG management with environmental preservation (Guardian), social responsibility (Caregiver) and transparent governance (Steward) lies in the emphasis on CSR for a sustainable society.

This thesis is a concept that has already been introduced in the field of business administration via CSV (creating shared value) in a 2011 paper by Michael E. Porter and Mark R. Kramer. CSV is different from CSR (corporate social responsibility) practices such as citizenship and philanthropy and volunteer work, which have been stressed to the top management but recognized as costs to companies.

Creating Shared Value (Porter & Kramer, 2011)

Social Value	→ Creating Shared Value ←	Business Value
Business and investment activities that can achieve social and environmental goals	Business and investment activities that improve a company's long-term competitiveness and meet social and environmental goals	Business and investment activities that can enhance a company's long-term competitiveness

In other words, *"Companies should be the object of a win-win game that simultaneously creates business value, eliminates absurd social practices and takes the lead in preserving the environment."* Just like you look at yourself in the mirror and take care of yourself in the morning on the way to work, CSV aims to identify the social needs of the community by looking at the *"value of a company reflected in the mirror of society"* and to create both economic profits and social values in the process of resolving them.

Examples of CSV practices can often be found in eco-friendly businesses:

- Patagonia for its eco-friendly outdoor sports brand
- Dow Chemical developed trans-fat-free cooking oil
- Nestlé invested in sustainable businesses in Africa and India.
- Walmart reduced unnecessary packaging, improved inventory management

Not only at a business practice, but the academic community sees CSV as an area of CSR that emphasizes creating corporate social value, rather than considering as a new movement. As such, the thesis put forward at the academic and conceptual level has been put into practice as a business model and is now systematized as an internationally accepted index and integrated into environment friendly ESG framework after long debates by academics on CSR and CSV.

> However, as ESG assessment indicators are too complex to specify objectively and difficult to write a sustainability report, there is always a risk of relying on the results of the conversion of subjective information provided by companies in quantitative evaluations by asset managers or rating agencies.

Therefore, as the former chairman of GE Jack Welch has pointed out, it can become an exemplary leading company in ESG just by keeping only one standard: *"If you think it is okay to appear in the mass media, do it as it is!"* Conversely, ESG index management and sustainability management reporting activities that are not based on ethics and integrity will act as regulations that will make companies more suffering while inducing another game of hide and seek.

4. The effect of negative screening in the SNS era

Our zeitgeist is also changing rapidly. The generation of baby boomers, born after the war, knows well the authoritarian and collectivist culture as the main driving force of strong economic growth.

In contrast, the MZ Millennial SNS generation is quite open and individualistic, and the top-down type of one-sided instruction is not reflected as a communication activity at all, and social equity and fairness are their precious values. As such, in the age of longevity in a super-aged society, several generations live together, but each generation has different growth histories, consumption patterns, and judgement values.[69]

69) Generation M (Millennial Generation): In the United States, it refers to a new generation born between the early 1980s and early 2000s. They are also called Generation Y because they were born after Generation X born in 1970-1980. They think and express themselves mainly, and they are familiar with SNS (Social Networking Service). Meanwhile, Generation Z, born after 1997, is the offspring of Generation X, called *'Digital Native'*, and enjoys video content on smartphones, YouTube, and Netflix rather than TVs or computers.

In addition, the Internet and SNS have opened a new chapter where you can immediately check the status of ESG management and ethical management of a company and express yourself through comments. When academic societies and large institutions select applicants for the exemplary CEO Award or Ethical Management Award, they often start with negative screening (qualification checking and eligibility review) through internet searches to prevent the nominated companies from causing a social scandal.

> The stinginess of praise is a common phenomenon throughout Korean society across generations. Western education teaches us to grasp the strengths of others first, but our attitude is that we easily attack and criticize the weaknesses of others rather than encouraging their strengths.

ESG management clearly consists in selecting excellent companies in the creation of social value by a *'positive screening'* rather than *'negative screening'* and recommending them as candidates for qualified responsible investment. It is debatable whether Korean companies can establish ESG management system successfully following the original purpose of ESG. Meanwhile, it has become very difficult to cover up corporate corruption in the current era of SNS.

Although media agencies have specialized in reporting activities, netizens and bloggers criticize beyond the level of professional reporters, and the checks by various NGOs are also seen as beyond the investigative powers of the Board of Audit and Inspection, the Prosecutor's Office, and the National Police Agency.

> Alvin Toffler, in his book *'Revolutionary Wealth (2006)'*, stated that if a company runs at 100 mph, NGOs are chasing it at 90 mph, and housewives are also running at 60 mph. In contrast, government is 25 miles an hour, universities 10 miles, politics 3 miles, and the legal profession just 1 mile an hour. On the other hand, SNS sometimes speeds up, but the forces of the SNS and NGO are already playing a leverage role in stemming the tyranny of power held by business leaders, government officials, and politicians, emerging as subjects of new social contracts and reciprocal empathy.

So, *"Would it be a fair society for lazy third-class bureaucrats, academics, and politicians dare to criticize the first-class companies that work such hard?"*

It should also be recognized that new ESG standards and government regulations and guidelines are forcing even startups that are struggling to attract investment to do practice ESG standards as they are, in fact, could be a stumbling block.

> Therefore, before ESG management spreads, even to take hold, innovation in government policy that sufficiently relaxes all regulations on business activities to a level satisfactory to business leaders, must be at the top priority.

The ESG on UN PRI (principles for responsible investment), which has risen above existing regulations on companies, will never escape the social negative screening, and as a result, companies will once again wear the mask of ESG index management and write a sustainability report for advertising purposes. Therefore, ESG management that is not based on ethics and scientific analysis can become a subject of investigation as difficult as the case of drug control.

> Thus, the bold deregulation of government and the ethical integrity management of companies would be the key factors that allow ESG impact management to function successfully for corporate sustainability.

In Japan, where administrative reform and deregulation is slow, the last 20 years of companies are immersed in *"easy business"* and young people having their dreams stolen now could become the Korea's next 20 years. On the other hand, although China is slow in its culture of integrity and ethical management, thanks to deregulation, Chinese companies have been *"running without obstacles"* for 20 years, and young people were able to realize their dreams especially by startups. China's past 20 years may now be the next 20 years for other developing countries. To that extent, Korea's future is as bleak as Japan's past 20 years, and too regulated to run as fast as China.

> *"Then, can ESG become a new growth engine for Korean companies? If not for growth, will it provide a guarantee for sustainability? And how to establish ethical management and transparent management, which are basis of ESG?"*

4 Historical Examples of Compliance Programs

Germany and Denmark are often cited as countries where business deregulation and a voluntary ethical climate have been harmoniously established. If the spirit of compliance combined with regulation and ethics is not respected, how big an event will appear can be seen through the case of Siemens in Germany. If sustainability is the goal of ESG management, Siemens which has grown steadily for more than 170 years, its corruption scandal and subsequent initiatives for *'zero corruption'* clearly show that *"the ethics is competitiveness"*.

> At the end of 2006, Siemens was on the verge of bankruptcy due to corruption scandals such as embezzlement, tax evasion, black fundraising, and bribes. Siemens was fined 390 million euros in 2007 for manipulating prices in the European electricity market by partnering with 11 multinational companies, including ABB, Fuji, and Mitsubishi from 1988 to 2004.[70)]

In addition, unethical behavior has been rampant at Siemens over the past 20 years, such as bribing a former Nigerian minister in exchange for a construction order in 2007. At that time, public funds from the company extorted by management exceeded 100 million euros, and tens of millions of euros were found in the accounts of Siemens executives in Switzerland, Greece, and Austria.

Out of a total of 332 projects, 4,283 cases of corruption were exposed, and the number of bribes was estimated at $ 1.4 billion. When the incident first broke, CEO after CEO resigned, hundreds of employees were fired and sanctioned, and the number of fines and unfair profits recovered reached $ 1.6 billion. As a result of such unethical management, Siemens suffered a total loss

70) [Siemens Scandal (Sep. 21, 2015). Rebecca Ray, DeVon Toler, Monica Canales, Matthew Nyfeler]. In late 2008 Siemens AG was accused by the United States and German governments of bribery in different countries to win multibillion dollars contracts. In the early 90's bribery was a big part of business around the world and Siemens was no stranger to this practice. When Germany finally passed a law in 1999 abolishing this act, Siemens saw itself hiding their wrongdoings from the government and hiring over 2,700 'consultants' who would deliver the money to government officials, or people in a position high enough to get the contract accepted. These bribes were as early as 1999, where Siemens supposedly paid over 1.4 billion USD in bribes in countries such as Bangladesh, Nigeria, Israel, Argentina and among other countries. In 2006, Siemens started to feel closed out. Several of their executives had gotten arrested for their illegal practices and finally in 2008 they paid a total of 2.6 billion USD in fines and improvements to their compliance process.

of 10 billion euros and the confidence and status of Siemens, once the pride of Germany, fell overnight.

> A company that has grown despite numerous wars and global economic crises is on the verge of shutting down 159 years after its founding in 1847 due to a corruption scandal. In 2007, Siemens implemented an immediate and strong self-cleaning strategy by establishing an ethical management system and a company-wide *'compliance program'* with the corporate missionary slogan *"Challenge to Zero Corruption"*.

First, the leaders who did not closely monitor corruption resigned and the Chief Compliance Officer system was introduced to strengthen the compliance program, especially the auction system which was the main cause of corruption.

At the time, Chief Compliance Officer Josef Winter said, *"Eradicating corruption and preventing breaches of fair competition are the top priorities of Siemens' sustainability agenda. Siemens' principle of ethical and integrity management is that the only business Siemens does is a clean business."*

- First, all Siemens employees around the world are expected to adhere faithfully to Siemens' anti-corruption-focused business conduct guidelines and international anti-corruption conventions and recommendations.
- Second, the most important role of management is to accurately and thoroughly convey the desire to create a clean business to the employees.
- Third, in any Siemens meeting, we need to talk about ethics and the spirit of compliance and aim for a state in which cases of ethics and compliance violations are void.

To support these guidelines, Siemens applied the *'principle of zero tolerance'* for corruption in management and introduced the world's first *'Compliance Compensation System'* in 2008. For employees, since 2007, more than 300,000 Siemens employees in the world received compliance training and focused on ethical management practices such as operating a whistleblower hotline.

Of course, top management was no exception to ethics and compliance training, and in particular, employees working in sales, marketing, purchasing and law have been managed more strictly. As a result, Siemens was reborn as a company that has not only restored its corporate image but is also internationally recognized as an exemplary company.

As for the performance reflected in the stock price, the Siemens stock price, which plunged from 96 euros per share in 2007 to 66 euros in 2008, is rising steadily to 90 euros per share at the end of 2013, 117 euros at the end of 2017, and 141 euros at the beginning of 2021.

Thanks to Siemens' compliance management efforts, physical market sales increased, and stock prices continued to improve. Additionally, as if to rekindle Siemens's pride, it was awarded 100 out of 100 points in the 2012 DJSI (Dow Jones Sustainability Index) compliance management category.

Siemens's corruption scandal and efforts to reinvent itself

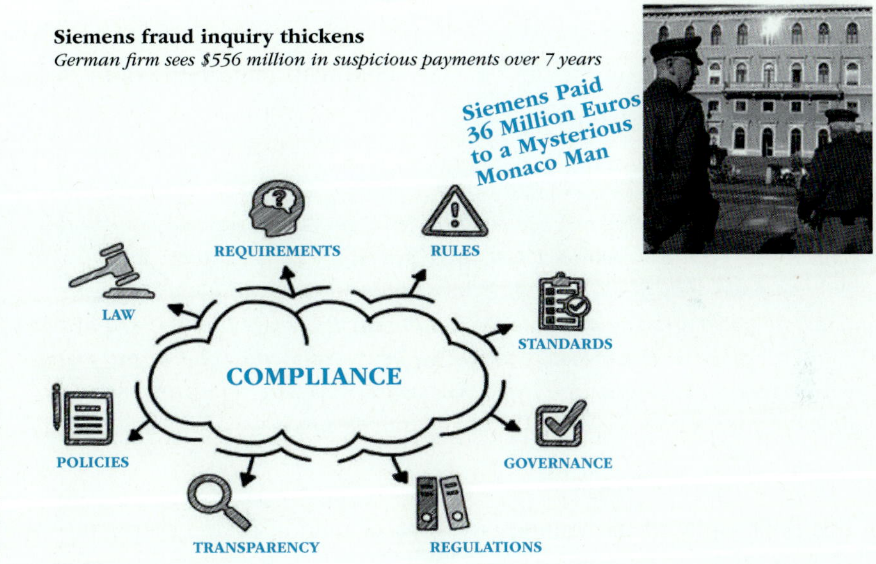

©www.hanol.co.kr

In 2017, Siemens was selected as the *World's Most Respected Company* according to Forbes' comprehensive assessment of the reliability, honesty, product and service, and CSR performance of 15,000 people in 60 countries around the world. Siemens, reborn through integrity and ethical management, leads by example by becoming the world's best sustainable company for 173 years from 2022.

5 Ethical Management Learned from History

As with ESG indicators, the Western standards for analytical and rational management is based on the practicality of the system. On the other hand, the valuation standards of the East, including Korea, emphasize the implicit and moral philosophy and spirit etched beyond times.

To this extent, to deal with ESG issues, it is necessary to understand the different Eastern and Western philosophies toward ESG management, rather than focusing on the ESG indicator itself. And on the other hand, for every company to practice *'Management with Philosophy',* rigorous measurement and analysis activities are compulsory for systematized indicators on a global scale such as ESG standards.

In this regard in Korea, Kyobo Life Insurance Group, founded in 1958 under the banners *'National Education Promotion' and 'National Capital Formation',* presents a quite interesting history of integrity management. First, in the following sentence, we can clearly see the management with philosophy of the founder and chairman Shin Yong-ho:

> *"If only aims to make money, we must put in a beautiful, upscale mall in this location. But even if there is a deficit, there are things we need to do. What is the founding philosophy of our company? Isn't this the promotion of national education? How about creating a wonderful opportunity for young people and citizens in the best place in Korea that is connected here and there? Think of the young people who read and grew up here to become great writers, university professors, entrepreneurs, Nobel laureates and Presidents in the future."*

In this philosophy of the founder, the idea of patriotism and corporate social responsibility is strongly anchored. In addition, it is worth to engrave the philosophy of current chairman Shin Chang-jae, who is practicing ethics and integrity management as that: *"The first-class ethics is to do the right thing and make a profit"*. In Kyobo, the four ethical standards enunciated by Jeong Yak-yong (Dasan)[71], a public official in the early 19th century who has been appreciated as a monumental teacher of Korea.

71) Dasan (茶山) is the pen name of Jeong Yak-yong, a scholar of the late Lee Dynasty (1762-1836). Dasan compiled the real-life science when he was exiled to Gangjin for 19 years.

> *"In order to end my exile, you wrote a letter to Mr. Hong, asking him to take good care of me, and said that he would beg for sympathy from Mrs. Kang and Mrs. Lee. However, this is a matter of adopting a third-degree ethic. And in the end of course, I am falling into a fourth-degree ethic, so why should I do it?"*

The 'Moment of Truth'[72] *outlined in Kyobo's ethical management begins by asking the following questions according to the standards expressed by Jeong Yak-yong. Kyobo's ethical management practice standards show us 'Thinking Business Ethics' with a simple and strong philosophical perspective:*

- Will I ever think that I was right about this?
- Would it be fair for this to be known to customers, colleagues, and family?
- Will it result for others in any unreasonable gains or losses?

The Four Ethical Grades of Dasan (Jeong Yak-yong)

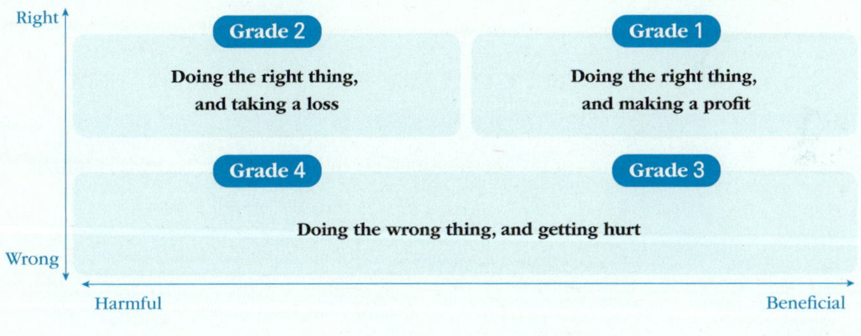

©www.hanol.co.kr

72) Swedish economist Richard Norman describes the moment that leaves a decisive impression on customers as a 'Moment of Truth'. In 1987, Jan Carlzon, president of Scandinavian Airlines (SAS), used it to promote business, emphasizing the need to prove to customers that their service was a good choice within 15 seconds of customer-employee interaction. In the case of Korea, the founder of Samsung Chairman Lee Byung-chul who entered the semiconductor industry, POSCO Chairman Park Tae-joon who pioneered the steel industry, Hyundai Chairman Chung Ju-young who pioneered the shipbuilding industry in wasteland, and Hanjin Group founder Cho Jung-hoon who pioneered the world-class air transportation business etc. they are representative figures who showed the 'Moment of Truth' for customers and the 'Moment of Decision' for business.

As such, the four ethical ratings of the great master Dasan (Jeong Yak-yong) suggest us how to compensate for the complexity and difficulty of measuring ESG indicators, and above all, the *'Poverty of Philosophy'*, which is often seen not only from the CEOs but also from the investor's point of view.

In other words, the practice of integrity and ethics is one's own subject, and the practical wisdom. In a word, it is never composed only of complex indicators and standardized systems as we are encountered with the ESG related standards and principles. And firmly we can say that it is clearly contained in the four ethical grades of great master Dasan.

6 Transparent Information and Scientific Measurement

We have been taught since childhood that newspaper articles should include *when, where, who did what, how,* and *why* in accordance with the *"Principles of 5W 1H"*. If the key evaluation indicators for a company's ESG (environmental-social-government) framework can also be explained in the 5W 1H method, the successful operation of ESG could be expected more clearly.

Scientific measurement and disclosed accurate data are required to evaluate

5W 1H of ethical practice for successful ESG management

<table>
<tr><th>Focus of Leadership</th><th>WHEN</th><th>WHO</th><th>WHAT</th><th>WHERE</th><th>WHY</th><th>HOW</th></tr>
<tr><td>Decision: Timing</td><td>Quick Response</td><td colspan="5">"If you miss the golden time, you are already half way through."</td></tr>
<tr><td>Management: Responsibility</td><td></td><td>Leader's Initiative</td><td colspan="4">"Even if authority is delegated, responsibility remains with the supervisor."</td></tr>
<tr><td>Objective: Challenge-MBO</td><td></td><td></td><td>Zero Corruption</td><td colspan="3">"Let's practice ethical management at the 6 Sigma level."</td></tr>
<tr><td>Stakeholder: Emotion</td><td colspan="3">"If it is okay to be published newspaper, practice it as it is."</td><td>Social Sentiment</td><td></td><td></td></tr>
<tr><td>Shared Value: Cooperation</td><td colspan="4">"If you want to go fast, go alone; if you want to go far, go together."</td><td>Win-Win Gaming</td><td></td></tr>
<tr><td>Must-Do: S-O Strategy</td><td colspan="5">"Implement the 'To-do List' strategy based on the Eisenhower Matrix."</td><td>Priority & Weights</td></tr>
</table>

the implementation of internal and external SRI (socially responsible investing) and transparent management such like the carbon emission issues of a company. In other words, as a company, to achieve its strategic goals (To-Be) at the current level (As-Is), it is necessary to establish and plan a strategy to fill this gap and put it into action within a given period. And the evaluation of the results should be strictly measured to ensure the feedbacks.

Therefore, for the success of ESG management, accurate measurement and analysis based on the scientific techniques and transparent disclosure and provision of information are of paramount importance.

1. Corporate information without concealment or manipulation

Recently, there has been a case of conflicts between the assertion that *"The economic valuation of 'Wolsong Nuclear Power Plant Unit 1' was manipulated for the early shut down of the nuclear power plant"* and another assertion that *"It was a national project that puts the safety of the people first"*. These examples demonstrate the importance of scientific measurement and transparency of information in government policy or long-term project evaluation.

In a study on the export of nuclear power plants to the United Arab Emirates (Park & Chevalier, 2010)[73] and a study on the culture of nuclear safety (Park et al., 2015)[74], AREVA, a French company of nuclear power, showed that human error appeared 80% as the cause of the accident, while Korea Hydro and Nuclear Power (KHNP), it was only 20%. *"How many people really believe in this data?"*

After the establishment of *'The Board of Audit and Inspection of Korea'* in 1963, there have been many complaints in the public service community saying that *"We cannot work because of the terrible Board of Audit and Inspection!"*

But now even the Board of Audit and Inspection is entering an era where the power of the SNS cannot be avoided. Media and video surveillance also play a whistle-blower role, and difficult to escape the obsession of civic groups as NGOs. This is because the public sentiment shows much faster and stronger

73) Park K. & Chevalier F. (2010), "The Winning Strategy of the Late-comer: How Korea was awarded the UAE Nuclear Power Contract", *International Review of Business Research papers,* 6(2), pp.221-238.

74) Park K. et al. (2015), "Competence-Evaluation Modeling for Positive Safety Culture: In and Around of Nuclear Power Industry", *Creativity and Innovation,* Peter Drucker Society of Korea, 8(2), pp.197-235.

The power of law on social sentiment in the era of the SNS

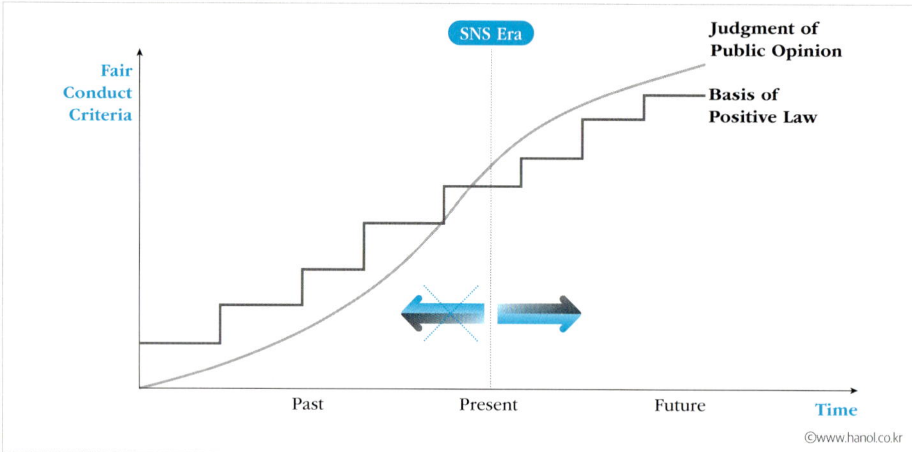

than the obsolete standard of positive law or the governmental policies.

The National Sentiment Law (國民情緖法) requires persuasive scientific analysis with transparent business data from companies. Thus, for sustainable ESG management, not only changes in the attitudes of stubborn government officials, but also business leaders to adapt to the times expected by society and industries.

2. The importance of leader's ethical management

Every country has a different culture that has long been developed with history, and such the like, every company also has a different and unique organizational culture. Of course, it has its own strengths and weaknesses.

In the case of Korea, the first thing we might say when we are frustrated with a problem that we cannot resolve on our *own is, "Do any of you know anyone who can help us?"*

As much as that, there is a strong ethnocentrism in which people try to solve problems through personal connections. Korea is a society where academic alumni and innate local ties are strong enough to call it a *'know-whom'* culture. On the other hand, there are comparative studies which show that the United States has a pragmatic *'know-how'*, Japan has a *'know-what'* of learning and France has a climate of *'know-why'*.[75)]

75) Park K. (1997), *Team Performance Evaluation*, Korea Management Association.

To successfully introduce and develop ESG management, it is above all necessary to create a transparent and ethical climate. Therefore, it is difficult to hope for success in ESG management in a society where people are trying to overcome a crisis through personal relationships or to seize opportunities for business growth as can be seen easily in many developing countries.

Cultural characteristics of each Coutry (Park K., 1997)

Actors and Systems		System's Rule	
		Principled & Positive	**Heuristic & Skeptical**
Actor's **Role**	Logical & Mechanistic	JAPAN **know-WHAT** Mechanism	FRANCE **know-WHY** Mechanism
	Practical & Organic	U.S.A **know-HOW** Mechanism	KOREA / CHINA **know-WHOM** Mechanism

"In Denmark, there is absolutely no reason for business leaders to meet with government officials or politician. If necessary, a lawyer can meet with them."

This is a self-assessment of Denmark, one of the cleanest countries in the world. The answer is that integrity is embedded in their culture and that ethical management is rooted in the business activities of leaders, whether national or corporate. Therefore, at a time when the world demands ESG management based on global standards, the first step required by ESG standards is not the legal system but the foundation of business and society with integrity and ethics.

Since the 1960s, Korea's vicious cycle of high economic growth, its *'fast-paced' and 'career-oriented'* culture, which has been nurtured by networking and kinship as a lube, should now be cut off with the scissors of ethical management. However, Korean managers have so much reason to meet public officials. If necessary, human networking is mobilized, and a person recruited as a public official or external director is placed in front of the hall for lobbying.

As former chairman of Alibaba Jack Ma once said, *"All success will come when we train hard and practice it hard again."* Integrity and ethics, which are

Common success factors for Creating an ethical climate

Common Factors for Violation of the Code of Ethics	Common Success Factors in Ethical Management
Intentionally violate laws and company policies	The tone at the top
Hide or distort errors	Systematic code of ethics and rigorous implementation
Breaking the rules is okay if it helps the business	If there is no problem even if it appears on the newspaper, practice it
It's good to break the rules because there is nothing to gain personally	Constant focus in a changing environment
Personal interests take precedence over the interests of the company	Offer continuous and regular training programs
Thinking that small amounts of violations won't be a problem	An environment where inquiries and reports can be easily accessed

the foundations of ESG management, will also be successful when we train hard and practice it hard again.

Although each country or organization have different cultural characteristics, the commonalities of corruption and unethical behavior are emerging in the same manner. And the requirements of creating an ethical climate appear in common. Therefore, efforts to establish an ethical climate by taking the lead in the ethical practice of managers, applying the legal system without exception, and continuing education on compliance are needed. In particular, the example of the CEO will be an essential requirement for the adage *"If the water above is clear, the water below is also clear"*.

> Carbon neutrality and ESG management, which have become global trends and new corporate tasks, are important not only as evaluation criteria for institutional investors, but also as tasks for the whole human race to pursue together for the sustainability of companies, society, and our hometown planet. Therefore, the practice of ethical management, which should be created as the basic climate of ESG management, is recognized far more important than ESG outcome measurement activities.

In Korea, a social contribution team, a CSR team, and now an ESG team or an ESG management committee are newly organized, mainly in large companies.

However, if only the current *Ethics Management Committee or the Compliance Committee is* strategically operated as follows, desirable performance of ESG management, including CSR activities, can also be expected.

- First, don't miss the *'golden time'* of ethical management given by ESG management.
- Second, induce *'lead by example'* through CEO's strength and corporate social responsibility.
- Third, achieve the goal of *'zero corruption'* on time through 6 Sigma ethical management.
- Fourth, listen the *'diverse opinions'* of NGOs and stakeholders through SNS and various media.
- Fifth, always check and verify monopoly status by creating a win-win CSV *'collaborative ecosystem'.*
- Sixth, define the weight of each ESG management indicator and the *'priority of the execution strategy'.*

Therefore, responsible ESG management, which is introduced as a mandatory requirement for large companies, is not a trend but to be used as a common standard for sustainable growth in the global village. Here we would like to conclude by suggesting two conditions for ESG management to be established in Korean society:

First, it should be established as *'ethical ESG management'* based on transparent governance.

Second, it should be implemented through a social contract or a social compromise between workers, management, government, and employees, as is called stakeholders.

The Practice of
ESG Management

VII

The Practice of ESG Management

VII

The Practice of ESG Management

Since the early 1950s, the focus of *'the Social'* has been on corporate social responsibility (CSR) and various methods have been developed to put it into practice. However, while active discourses of information and specific guidelines are being established on the global climate crisis, the environmental crisis, the labor crisis and the human rights crisis, issues related to standards based ESG management or global standards became hot global concerns.

Especially, advanced countries promote the legalization of ESG management practices by introducing in a form of management certification system. In fact, corporate sustainability reporting and ESG management practices have been underway since the early 2000s and have grown remarkably over the past 20 years. In addition, based on corporate sustainability reports, the performance evaluation of ESG management and socially responsible investing (SRI) activities are now spreading globally.

1 Practice by Norms

As various global standards related to ESG are being promulgated, national level of standards to comply with them are also on their way of establishment. However, rather than establishing ESG as an integrated standard, the introductory method is divided into three sectors such as environmental (E), social (S) and governance (G), and further, detailed indicators and evaluation issues are more differentiated by countries.

In fact, there is no environmental expert, neither in business nor in government, who can understand and implement them all together. As a result, companies complain that it is not easy to understand the whole norms or systems related to ESG in a holistic and integrative way at the level of international laws as well as the level of each national laws. As such, there is a need to understand and practice ESG management from a more professional and practical perspective focused mainly on the *'10 Principles of UN Global Compact (1999)'* elaborated by the participation of 13,000 companies from 17 countries, which provide global standards and guidelines as the basis of ESG management.

1. Environmental norms

In the environmental sector, international agreements have been promulgated dividing air emissions, energy, raw materials, sewage and waste, biodiversity, transport and environmental accounting, and related national standards have been newly introduced to regulate or support the environmental management practices of companies.

10 Principles of UN Global Compact (UNGC, 1999)

Division	Contents
Human Right	1. Businesses should support and respect the protection of internationally proclaimed human rights; and 2. Make sure that they are not complicit in human rights abuses.
Labor	3. Businesses should uphold the freedom of association and the effective recognition of the right to collective bargaining, 4. The elimination of all forms of forced and compulsory labor, 5. The effective abolition of child labor; and 6. The elimination of discrimination in respect of employment and occupation.
Environ-ment	7. Businesses should support a precautionary approach to environmental challenges, 8. Undertake initiatives to promote greater environmental responsibility. 9. And encourage the development and diffusion of environmentally friendly technologies.
Anti-corruption	10. Businesses should work against corruption in all its forms, including extortion and bribery.

The most important international standard in the climate disaster crisis is the *Paris Agreement*, a treaty adopted at the UN Climate Change Conference in 2015. The Paris Agreement was adopted on December 12, 2015, and is entered into force on November 4, 2016, as international law with full application.[76)]

Despite the one-sided withdrawal of the United States from the Paris Agreement in June 2017, 200 countries, representing 87% of global carbon emissions, continue to implement the agreement. Thereafter, following the election of President Joe Biden in 2021, the United States returned to the Paris Agreement, and

76) The main issue lies in the international commitment to keep the global average temperature rise below 2℃ compared to pre-industrialization, and to work together to limit the rise in temperature to 1.5℃ or less. In other words, each country must set its own greenhouse gas reduction goal, promise to the international community, and implement the proposed goal, and the international community will jointly verify the implementation.

in November 2021, President Biden personally apologized for the past withdrawal of the United States from the Paris Agreement.

In the meantime, issues related to environmental standards are specified in the following conventions, agreements, or protocols.

1) Air pollution

- United Nations Framework Convention on Climate Change, UNFCCC or FCCC, 1992
- Kyoto Protocol to the United Nations Framework Convention on Climate Change, 1997
- IPCC (Intergovernmental Panel on Climate Change) Climate Change 2001, Working Group I: Scientific Foundations
- Paris Agreement, 2015
- Montreal Protocol on Substances that Deplete the Ozone Layer, 1987
- Vienna Convention for the Protection of the Ozone Layer, 1985 (Acidification, Eutrophication, and Surface Ozone: Revised 2012)
- Geneva Protocol to the Convention on Long-Range Transboundary Air Pollution, 1979
- Geneva Protocol to the Convention on Long-Range Transboundary Air Pollution, 1984 (Collaborative program for evaluation and monitoring)
- Helsinki Protocol to the Convention on Long-Range Transboundary Air Pollution, 1985 (30% reduction in sulfur oxides)
- Sofia Protocol to the Convention on Long-Range Transboundary Air Pollution, 1988 (Nitrogen oxide suppression)
- Geneva Protocol to the Convention on Long-Range Transboundary Air Pollution, 1991 (Reduction of volatile organic compounds)
- Oslo Protocol to the Convention on Long-Range Transboundary Air Pollution, 1994 (Additional sulfur oxide reduction)
- Aarhus Protocol to the Convention on Long-Range Transboundary Air Pollution, 1998 (Reduction of heavy metals, revised 2012)
- Aarhus Protocol to the Convention on Long-Range Transboundary Air Pollution, 1998 (Reduction of POP-persistent organic pollutants, revised 2009)

- Gothenburg Protocol to the 1979 Convention on Long-Range Transboundary Air Pollution to abate acidification, eutrophication, and ground level ozone, 1999
- MARPOL: International Convention for the Prevention of Pollution of Ships, 1973
- Stockholm Convention on Persistent Organic Pollutants, 2001

2) Energy

- Kyoto Protocol to the United Nations Framework Convention on Climate Change, 1997
- GHG (Greenhouse Gas) Protocol Initiative
- World Resources Institute & World Business Council for Sustainable Development: Corporate Accounting and Reporting Standards (Revised 2004)
- IEA's Energy Balances for OECD and non-OECD countries & ISO's Energy efficiency standards and related inspection procedures
- IEC (International Electrotechnical Commission): Energy efficiency standards and related inspection procedures

3) Raw materials

- OECD: Recommendation of the Council on Material Flows and Resource Productivity, 2004

4) Waste water and wastes

- OECD: Working Group on Waste Prevention & Recycling
- Ban Amendment to the Basel Convention on the Control of Transboundary Movements of Hazardous Wastes and their Disposal, 1989
- Rotterdam Convention on the Prior Informed Consent (PIC) Procedure, 1998
- London Convention on the Prevention of Marine Pollution by Dumping of Wastes and Other Matter, 1972

5) Biodiversity

- IUCN's Red List: Ramsar Convention on Wetlands, 1971
- UNESCO: World Heritage Sites
- UN: United Nations Biosphere Reserves
- Conservation International: Biodiversity Hotspots and Wilderness Areas

- WWF: Global 200 Ecoregion
- Bird Life International: Important Bird Areas
- IUCN: Centres of Plant Diversity
- GRI Cross-Reference: GRI Biodiversity Resource Document

6) Transport

- UN: United Nations Recommendations on the Transport of Dangerous Goods

7) Environmental accounting

- UNDSD: United Nations Division for Sustainable Development, 2003
- Environmental Management Accounting Procedures and Principles
- EMARIC: Environmental Management Accounting Research and Information Center, 2003
- IFAC: International Guidelines on Environmental Management Accounting, 2005

2. Human right norms

Article 2 of the United Nations Declaration of Human Rights, enacted by the UN General Assembly in 1948, states; *"Everyone is entitled to any kind of distinction based on race, color, sex, language, religion, political or other opinion, national or social origin, property, birth or other status, etc. without, entitled to enjoy all the rights and freedoms set forth in this Declaration. Furthermore, no discrimination shall be made based on the political, judicial, or international status of a country or territory to which an individual belongs, whether independent or trustee med, non-autonomous or subject to other sovereign limitations."*

Accordingly, it was introduced as a model for human rights norms that basically protect employees in ESG management.

- Universal Declaration Rights, 1948
- International Covenant on Economic, Social and Cultural Rights (A): ICESCR, 1966
- International Covenant on Civil and Political Rights (B): ICCPR, 1966
- International Convention on the Elimination of All Forms of Racial Discrimina-

tion: ICERD, 1965

- Convention on the Elimination of All Forms of Discrimination against Women: CEDAW, 1979
- UNGC, 1999
- International Convention for the Protection of All Persons from Enforced Disappearances, 2007
- Convention on the Rights of Persons with Disabilities: CPD, 2007

3. Labor norms

The 189 International Labor Conventions and 205 Recommendations of the ILO and labor-related norms among the UN's human rights norms were enforced as practice items in 'Society (S) sector of ESG'.

- Since its establishment in 1919, the ILO has enacted 189 International Labor Conventions and 205 Recommendations.
- Declaration of Purpose of the ILO (Philadelphia Declaration, 1944 - Annex to the ILO Charter)
- The ILO Code of Conduct on the Protection of Personal Data for Workers (1996) and the ILO Declaration of the Fundamental Rights of Workers (1998)
- United Nations Supplementary Convention on the Abolition of Slavery, the Slave Trade, and Institutions and Practices Similar to Slavery, 226 U.N.T.S.3, 1957
- Declaration on the Elimination of All Forms of Intolerance and of Discrimination based on Religion or Belief, 1981
- Convention against Torture and Other Cruel, Inhuman or Degrading Treatment or Punishment, 1984
- United Nations Convention on the Rights of the Child, UNCRC, 1989
- International Convention on the Protection of the Rights of All Migrant Workers and Members of Their Families: ICPRMW, 1990
- UNGC, 1999
- Declaration on the Rights of Persons Belonging to National or Ethnic, Religious and Linguistic Minorities, 1992

4. Anti-corruption norms

In accordance with the international anti-corruption related norms presented by the UN, OECD, and agreements in the Americas, etc., the 'Governance (G) sector of ESG' became mandatory as an ethical management practice.

- Inter-American Convention Against Corruption, 1996
- OECD Convention against Bribery of Foreign Public Officials in International Commerce, 1997
- UNGC, 1999
- OECD Guidelines for Multinational Enterprises, 2000
- UN Convention Against Corruption on the Prevention of Bribery of Foreign Public Officials in International Commerce Transactions, 2003
- Business Principles for Countering Bribery, 2003
- OECD Corporate Governance Principles, 2004

2 Practice by Self-Diagnosis

The global trend is to provide a methodology for the self-practice of ESG management within the company, so that ESG management is observed as a self-diagnosis method for ethical management and human rights management.

As a self-diagnosis guideline for corporate social responsibility, the Danish Institute for Human Rights (DIHR) developed *'Human Rights Compliance Assessment (HRCA)'* to promote human rights impact assessment.

The DIHR has released HRCA self-diagnosis tools to the world after frequent consultation with stakeholders including for example, the Denmark Enterprises Federation, and test operation for large corporations. DIHR is a detailed human rights norm that embodies individual human rights depicted in the UN Declaration of Human Rights.

In addition to the human rights standards, the HRCA includes guidelines for the overall implementation system, corporate self-diagnostic standards for human rights policies and implementation status, training courses on policies and implementation tasks necessary for corporate human rights responsibilities, as well as cooperation, consultation, test operations and courses with large companies.

The Danish Institute for Human Rights has developed an interactive database that companies can use anywhere abroad. The HRCA online tools contain around 350 questions and an extensive collection of over 1,000 human rights indicators which have been developed using the provisions outlined in the Universal Declaration of Human Rights, 80 other major human rights treaties and ILO conventions. About 70 companies have participated in the development of the tool, and the database is currently being improved with versions for each area of human rights.[77)]

> In the case of Korea, the National Human Rights Commission has developed the *'Human rights management self-diagnosis tool'* in 2009, based on the UN's human rights management guidelines.

On the other hand, corporate ethical management introduced as an ethical management system in which individual companies voluntarily draft an ethics charter, etc., and the FKI (Federation of Korean Industries) has developed the *'Ethical Management Self-Assessment Index'* to promote ethical management of member companies.[78)]

The guidelines for self-diagnosis of human rights management and ethical management make sense as the companies themselves check their level and fill in the gaps. However, there is a limit to the reluctance to disclose and confirm it to the external stakeholders or even to the internal company. Therefore, it is necessary that the self-diagnostic system related to human rights management, ethical management and ESG management is used in parallel with the following management certification system and social reporting systems.

3 Practice by Certification

Regarding international quality standards, the ISO has led companies to voluntarily obtain certification from an external certification body to prove the practice of ESG management. Accordingly, CSR, that is, norms on corporate social responsibility, is evolving into the form of a social responsibility manage-

77) For the free use and dissemination of human rights compliance assessments, *the "Rapid Human Rights Compliance Assessment Verification"* system has been developed so that companies can verify them easily, quickly, and effectively.

78) Federation of Korean Industries (FKI), *Ethical Management Self-Assessment Index*, 2007.

ment certification system by ISO in addition to international conventions and laws and regulations of each country.

The CSR management certification system includes ISO's *ISO9000* (*Quality management systems,* 1987, 1994, 2000, 2008, 2015), *ISO14000* (*Environmental management systems,* 1996, 2004, 2008, 2015), affiliated with the US Department of Labor, and Establishment of SAI (Social Accountability International),[79] an organization that researches labor issues *OHSAS18001* (*Occupational Health and Safety Assessment Series,* 1999, 2007, 2015)[80] etc.

Among these management certification activities, the most representative work was emerged in November 2010, carried out by the ISO, to integrate various management certification systems for CSR, is highlighted. As such, the corporate social responsibility certification scheme allows a third party to review and certify whether a company is following universal standards of social responsibility, but it also has a limitation in that it does not disclose information on the degree of CSR outward compliance.

In addition, the CSR certification system being a universal guideline for humanity, it requires standards and indicators to which the whole of global society being obliged to comply. As the like, there left critical limits to which companies have no choice but to step up to the evolving standards.

> The social responsibility management assessment system has been integrated into the ISO26000 standards, and it caused a sensation because ISO26000 is applicable to all organizations not only the private sector but also the public sector. However, ISO26000 still has limitations as it needs to be combined with the social reporting system to specifically confirm the performance of socially responsible management to a third party.

1. ISO9000

ISO9000 Quality Management Systems (1987/1994/2000/2008/2015), established by the ISO, is an international standard which stipulate the requirements of the quality management system applicable to all industrial fields and activities. On

79) Formerly the Council of Economic Priorities Accreditation Agency (CEPAA).

80) ISO45001, which replaced OHSAS18001, published in March 2018.

the other hand, ISO9001 certification is a system that objectively certifies whether the product or service complies with regulations and operates efficiently. At the end of 2020, there are 916,842 certificates and a total of 1,299,837 certified sites.[81)]

1) ISO9001 (1987)

- ISO9000 (1987): With the same structure as British standard BS5750, there are 3 models of quality management system, which can be selected according to the scope of activities of the organization.
- ISO9001 (1987): The design, development, production, installation, and service quality assurance model are intended for companies and organizations engaged in activities including the development of new products.
- ISO9002 (1987): The production, installation and service quality assurance model basically use the same material as ISO9001, but can be selected when not applied to R&D.
- ISO9003 (1987): Final inspection and testing quality assurance model can be selected for final inspection of finished products.

2) ISO9001 (1994)

- ISO9000 (1994): Emphasizing quality assurance through precautionary measures instead of checking the final product and continuing to require evidence of compliance with documented procedures is sometimes a burden for companies.

3) ISO9001 (2000)

- ISO9001 (2000): The 2000 version, which replaced the three standards ISO9001, ISO9002 and ISO9003, established in 1994, monitors and optimizes the work and activities of the company instead of inspecting the final product.

4) ISO9001 (2008)

- ISO9001 (2008): It explains the existing requirements of ISO9001 (2000) and introduces only a few changes to improve the consistency of ISO14001 (2004).

---

81) In 1979, BS5750 was announced in UK, ISO9000 series was announced by ISO in March 1987, and Korean industry standard *'KS9000'* series was announced in April 1992 in Korea.

5) ISO9001(2015)

- The 2015 version adopts the "Plan-Do-Check-Act (P-D-C-A)" cycle for all process activities in the organization and applies a more flexible standard than before.

2. ISO14000

ISO14000 Environmental Management Systems (1996/2004/2008/2015), with the *Rio Earth Summit* in 1992 as an opportunity, emerged as a new paradigm of business management as a practical methodology to achieve sustainable and environment-friendly development. ISO 14000 strongly requires organizations to adopt a new corporate business strategy that encompasses not only economic profit but also environmental sustainability. At the end of 2020, ISO14001 displays 348,473 certificates and a total of 568,798 sites.

- 1974: International Chamber of Commerce (ICC) issued 'Environmental Guidelines for Global Industry'
- 1989: 'Environmental audit (Position Paper)'
- July 1991: Business Conference on Sustainable Development (BCSD) called on ISO to standardize environmental management.
- March 1992: BS7750 released in UK
- 1993: European environmental standards
- October 1996: Announcement of the implementation of ISO 14000
- 2004; 2008; 2015: Revised editions issued

ISO14000, aimed to break with the existing management method operated by certain environmental managers, is a systematic approach to upstream management of environmental problems with the participation of all employees. Meanwhile, ISO14001 is an international standard for environmental management systems which can be applied to all industrial fields and activities.

Companies can effectively manage environmental risks by systematically identifying, assessing, managing, and improving environmental aspects through these environmental management systems. In general, companies can enjoy the dual effect of creating economic benefits and improving environmental performance through ISO14001 certification.

3. SA8000

SA8000 (Social Accountability 8000) Labor Management Certification System

(1997/2001/2008/2014), established by the US CEPAA (Council of Economic Priorities Accreditation Agency)[82], is a system for auditing and certification via standards established to enable the activities.

As such, SA8000 encourages organizations to develop, maintain and apply socially acceptable practices themselves. SA8000 was developed in 1989 by the *International Organization for Social Responsibility* (formerly the Economic Priorities Council) and an advisory committee made up of trade unions, NGOs, civil society organizations and businesses. The SA8000 certification is a standard management system modeled according to ISO standards, and companies wishing to be certified must integrate it into management practices and prove that they are constantly complying with the standards.[83]

- Established SAI (Social Accountability International) in the United States in 1997
- Adopted as a standard in 12 countries around the world through the ILO (International Labor Organization) General Assembly
- Accepted as the first certification standard for workers' rights
- Mostly accepted in the 2002 GRI Sustainability Report Revision (G2)
- 2001; 2008; 2014 revised edition issued

As of October 2021, there are 4,608 SA8000 certified facilities, with a total of 2,191,838 workers across 56 countries and 58 industries.

4. ISO45001 (OHSAS18001)

OHSAS18001 Occupational Health and Safety Assessment Series (1999; 2007; 2015) was jointly established by 13 world-class standardization organizations and certification bodies such as the British Standards Institution (BSI). And later ISO45001, replacing OHSAS18001, was published in March 2018.

- 1982: European Federation Regulations (Seveso Directive) enacted
- 1991: HS(G)65 (Occupational Safety and Health Management System) by the British

82) CEPAA later changed to SAI (Social Accountability International), a research institute on labor issues, working under the US Department of Labor.

83) SA8000 is accredited and overseen by Social Accountability Accreditation Services (SAAS) and is based on the principles of international human rights norms set out in the ILO Convention (Convention on the Rights of the Child and the Universal Declaration of Human Rights). It measures company's performance in 8 areas important to social responsibility in the workplace: Child labor, Forced labor, Health and safety, Freedom of association and Collective bargaining, Discrimination, Disciplinary practices, Working hours and Compensation.

Occupational Safety and Health Agency

- 1996: BS8800 (Occupational Safety and Health Management System) in England
- 1996: OSH management system by the Industrial Hygiene Association in the United States
- 1999: 13 standards and certification bodies including BSI established OHSAS18000
- 2001: ILO approved an independent Safety and Health Management System
- 2007; 2015 revised edition issued

ISO45001, established in 2018, is an international standard management system for *'Occupational Safety and Health (OH&S)'*, and the purpose is to reduce occupational accidents and diseases. ISO45001 mainly follows the ISO standards structure such as OHSAS18001, ILO-OSH2001, ISO 9001(2015) and ISO14001(2015).[84)]

5. AA1000

AccountAbility's AA1000 standard series for verification of sustainability reports is a simple and practical standard and analysis framework used to demonstrate the leadership and performance of sustainability-related responsibilities of various organizations, including global companies, private companies, governments, and NGOs.

6. ISO26000

ISO26000 is a representative international standard created by CSR experts around the world voluntarily to integrate various certification systems related to CSR (corporate social responsibility) into one led by ISO.

- September 2001: Resolution of ISO-Committee on Consumer Policy (COPPLCO)
- 2002: Started to promote standardization by resolution of ISO General Assembly
- March 2005: 1st ISO/SR/WG meeting
- September 2005: 2nd ISO/SR/WG meeting

84) As of March 2021, companies and organizations must transition to ISO45001, and ISO has extended the transition period up to 6 months (September 11, 2021) for organizations affected by COVID-19. BSI officially withdrew BS OSHAS 18001 in September 2021 at the end of the extended migration period (adjustment period due to COVID-19).

- June 2006: 3rd ISO/SR/WG meeting, and 2006 Committee Draft published
- 2007: DIS (Draft International Standard)[85] published
- March 2008: Publication of international standards
- 2010: 8th General Assembly and enacted and announced in November 2010

CSR certification systems such as ISO26000 do not recognize differences by region or country as they suggest universal guidelines for mankind and require the global community to follow them in common. Even when each country enacts international standards as national standards, international standards are being converted into national standards as they are.

As soon as ISO26000 was published in 2010, 40 countries around the world, including the United States, France, Germany, England, Denmark, South Africa, and Japan, rushed to introduce it as a national standard. Korea also announced *'KSA-ISO26000'* as of August 30, 2012. KSA-ISO26000 has been disseminating through the Korean Standards Service Network (www.kssn.net).[86]

In response to the growing demands and expectations of stakeholders for transparent management since the 2008 global financial crisis, developed countries have enacted laws and regulations related to CSR to strengthen the effectiveness of ISO26000 as a national standard. In addition, global conglomerates are strengthening their supply chain management (SCM) by requiring suppliers to report social responsibility-related activities and conducting social audits.

> Therefore, *"Compliance with ISO26000"* became essential for exporting companies from Europe and the United States, companies involved in international supply chain management, companies whose products and services have a significant impact on the environment and society, companies receiving funding from socially responsible investing (SRI), and companies in fierce market competition that want to secure a sustainable competitive advantage.

ISO26000 compliance is used as a major indicator of corporate investment and evaluation by financial institutions and credit rating agencies, or as a standard

85) DIS is the result of the work produced by a Working Group and approved by a Technical Committee. A document in the DIS stage is more than 95% technically accurate.

86) KSA (Korean Standards Association), https://www.ksa.or.kr/ksa_kr/875/subview.do

for monitoring activities by stakeholders such as consumer groups and NGOs. ISO26000 is also applied in various ways such as public purchasing standards, tax exemption criteria and preferential interest rates etc.

As such, in CSR (corporate social responsibility) certification systems such as ISO26000, a third-party review to see whether a company complies with universal norms for social responsibility and grants a certification system according to conformance. However, there exists a limitation in that information on the degree of CSR compliance is not officially and transparently disclosed to the outside.

4 Practice by Reporting

The social reporting which reports corporate social responsibility activities, is evolving from the *'Bilan Social'* (social report framework in France) to the environmental report, environment, safety and health report, sustainable development report and now, integrated ESG report.

Social reports covering all areas of CSR are published under different names, such as *social responsibility report, social report,* and *sustainability report etc.*, depending on the choice of company. Reporting on social responsibility is a highly valued management activity insofar as it discloses the social situation of a company to all stakeholders and objectively assesses the performance of its efforts, just like reporting on the financial situation of a company.

The management certification system and the social reporting system have been developing while interacting with each other. In the early days, social reports promoted the establishment of the management certification system, and as the management certification system for social responsibility was established, the Sustainability Reporting Guideline (SRG) of the Global Reporting Initiative (GRI) was born.

Meanwhile, *'GRI-SRG'*, an integrated management certification system for social responsibility, became the basis for the establishment of ISO26000 in 2010. However, due to the delay in the establishment of the ISO26000 integrated management certification system, the social responsibility certification system remained stagnant for a long time, such as not being able to integrate ISO9000 and ISO14000.

Development of management certification and social reporting system

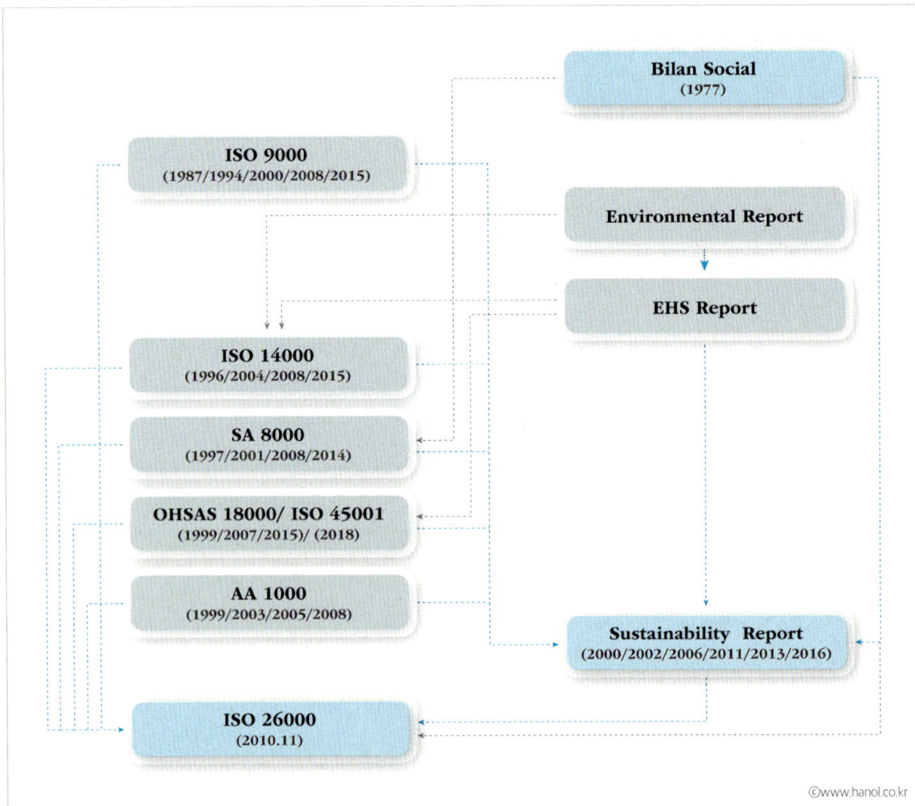

1. Bilan Social (social report): Social reporting system on the internal social performance of companies in France

'Bilan Social', a social reporting system in France, has developed into a social reporting system that only targets internal social performance by limiting employees among stakeholders. In the case of France, the Bilan Social system, a social reporting system, was established by synthesizing research results related to corporate social performance issues that were actively developed in the 1960s and 1970s.

What is interesting is that the Bilan Social legally mandated quantitative information on the seven areas of social performance in the last three years from the beginning. As such, French companies have been developing social audit and human resource management based on Bilan Social platform, which can evaluate social performance within an organization. In addition, this social report stimulates and promotes corporate social policies and realizes information sharing on corporate social information between trade union and management.

In French academics, based on the company's social performance report, that is Bilan Social data, which is provided as quantitative information, the company's social performance by year is comparatively analyzed and policy scenarios are evaluated from a long-term perspective (Park, 1999[87]; 2015[88]).

7 main themes of 'Bilan Social'[89]

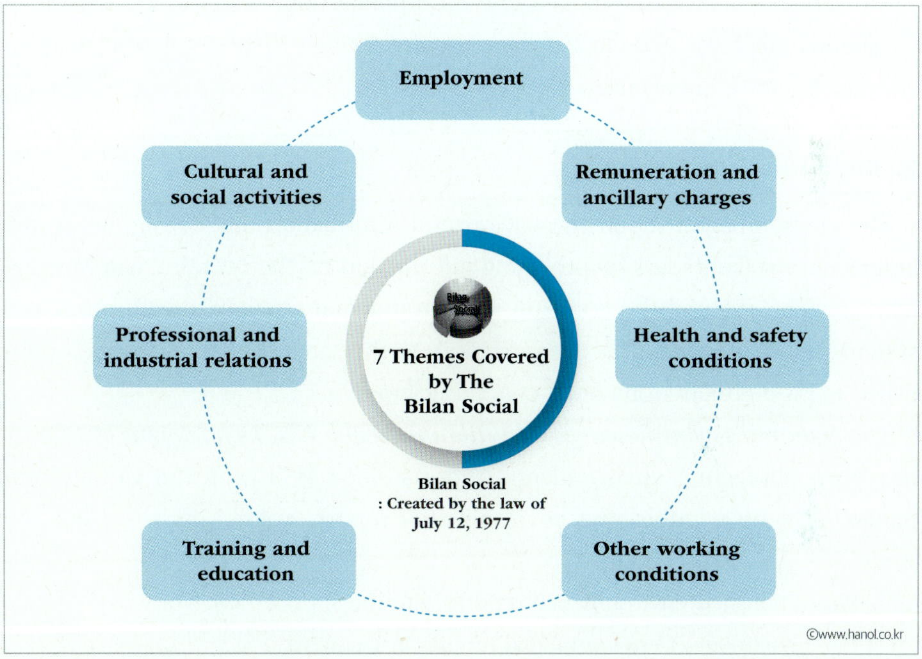

- 1975: Submission of the *'Sudreau Report'* and provision of quantitative information on social performance within the company became mandatory[90]

---

87) Park K. (1999), *Social Audit*, Korea Management Association.

88) Park K. (2015), *Professor Kichan Park on Strategic Management*, Inha University Press.

89) *The Bilan Social* (Social Report) recapitulates in a single document the main figures making it possible to assess the company's situation in the social field, to record the achievements made and to measure the changes that have occurred during the past year and the two precedent years.

90) *The 'Sudreau Report'* emphasized that, *"Like financial and economic performance, to treat social performance as a corporate strategy, it must be provided as quantitative information even if it is conducted through relative*

- 1977: Enacted as a labor law for large corporations with more than 300 employees (public construction, transportation, commercial service, industry, and agriculture). In addition, supplementary evaluation indicators were added for large enterprises with more than 750 employees and more than 2,000 employees.
- 1979: Enactment of the Bilan Social Act enacted on July 12, 1977 (employment, wages, occupational safety and health, working hours, education and training, labor-management relations, welfare, etc. are the main issues). All companies with 300 or more employees must prepare a social report related to working conditions and submit it after consulting with the employee representative and the labor union
- December 20, 1993: Legislation for companies with less than 300 employees to submit annual social reports to the Corporate Committee, which consists of unions, employer, and employee representatives
- June 20, 1994: Enforcement of the 1993 Act

2. Environmental report

The environmental report provides useful information that can influence the judgment of stakeholders by providing information on the overall environmental management, such as the company's environmental strategy, organization and system, and its performance over a period. At the same time, this report is published to promote environmental communication.

The National Fermi Research Institute under the U.S. Department of Energy has been publishing environmental reports since 1971, and the global companies have been publishing environmental reports voluntarily since the late 1980s.

- 1990s: Published environmental reports with the support of UNEP
- 1996: Enactment of environmental reports in Denmark
- 1999: Enactment of environmental reports in the Netherlands
- 2001: Enactment of environmental report legislation in France

In Korea, the Ministry of the Environment initiated research on the development of guidelines for environmental reporting in 1999, and in 2001 the first pilot project was carried out to improve the field applicability of the project.

---

and subjective qualitative evaluation. Especially when the goal is set as a national policy, these efforts are even more important."

guidelines for corporate environmental reports drawn up in 2000.

- In the first pilot project in 2001, electricity/electronics (Samsung Electro-Mechanics, Samsung Electronics, LG Electronics, Samsung Corning), chemicals (LG Chem Yeosu/Cheongju plants, Pacific), automobiles (Hyundai Motors), paper (Yuhan-Kimberly), aviation (Korean Air, Asiana Airlines), and lodging (Hotel Shilla) participated in the preparation of environmental reports by 13 companies
- In May 2002, '2002 Environmental Report Guideline' was released, and from July 2002 to April 2003, the second pilot project for environmental report was promoted for the expanded application of 'Environmental Report Guideline 2002'. Dongbu Steel, Korea Water Resources Corporation, Korea East-West Power Co., Ltd., Samsung SDI, LG Cable, and LG Chem participated and prepared an environmental report
- In 2003, '2003 Environmental Report Guidelines' was developed and published, and the 3rd environmental report pilot project was conducted. Korea Water Resources Corporation, GM Daewoo Auto & Technology Co., Ltd., Korea Midland Power Co., Ltd., LG Petrochemical Co., Ltd., Halla Climate Control, Samsung Techwin, Korean Air, Samyang Corporation, LG Household & Health Care, Toray Saehan Co., Ltd. 10 companies Participate and prepare an environmental report conforming to the guidelines
- Information disclosure areas of '2004 Environmental Report Guidelines' developed in 2004 include (1) overview (2) environmental vision and strategy (3) environmental management system (4) environmental impact and performance (5) stakeholder partnership (6) Sustainable Corporate Strategy (7) consists of 41 items (25 core items and 16 supplementary items) in 7 areas, including annexes
- In February 2005, 'Guidelines for Sustainability Management – Focusing on Environmental Aspects' was released, in November 2006, research service was carried out for the development of sustainable management techniques, and in November 2007, '2007 Environmental Report Guidelines' was released, in 2007 Conducting in-depth interviews with domestic companies that have experience in publishing environmental reports or expected to publish in 2007 to supplement problems and make efforts to meet the GRI's international standard 'Sustainability Report Guideline G3'
- However, as the 2002 World Summit in Johannesburg recommended to publish a sustainability report, along with the policy change, instead of publishing the environmental report led by the Ministry of Environment, most companies in Korea replaced it with a sustainability report

In Japan, Sony first published an environmental report in 1994, and the name of the environmental report was changed to *CSR Report* in 2003 to strengthen information on corporate social responsibility.

- Sony: To keep up-to-date information according to changes in business areas and circumstances, CSR activities have been disclosed on the web since 2014 and changed to a 'Sustainability Report' in 2018 to provide financial and non-financial information related to business performance as well as management policies and business strategies. And announced 'Corporate Report 2019' dealing with mid- to long-term value creation by integrating the business reports
- Fujitsu Group: Published the environmental report (1996-2017, to enhance social responsibility and transparency), a separate CSR report (2003-2017, focused on social activity approaches, initiatives, and results), and now Fujitsu Group publishes a sustainability report (since 2018, by integrating the CSR report and the environmental report into one)
- Suzuki: Prepared and reported the environmental report up to 2003, the environment and social report from 2004-2015, and the CSR and environment report from 2016
- Astellas Pharmaceuticals: CSR report until 2011, environmental report 2012-2018, and EHS report from 2019

On the other hand, unlike Korea and Japan, some companies still prepare and publish environmental reports separately. For example, in France, it is compulsory to draw up an Environmental Report jointly with the *Bilan Social*.

In the United States, Apple, Google, and IBM have been preparing 'Environmental Reports' since 1990, and from 2002 all of these global companies are publishing *'CSR Report'* in parallel with the *'Environmental Report'*. The separate publication of Environmental and Social reports is as important as the two areas, and the analytical views in each area are in fact very different.

3. EHS (Environment, Health and Safety) Report

Historically, safety and health management arose out of the need to protect workers against occupational hazards and to secure the productive workforce led by *"occupational safety and health rules"*. It is mainly limited to problems occurring at work, as in the case of the social report (*Bilan Social*) in France.

However, as regulations on impacts outside the factory increase, many companies are integrating environmental issues with operational issues, that is, they include external environmental issues in their policies and existing occupational safety and health management procedures.

On the other hand, as public interest in environmental degradation increases with tighter regulations, companies are taking their responsibility for EHS (environment, health and safety) seriously, and reporting on EHS and environmental safety management at work are highlighted as mandatory and essential. As a result, companies have started publishing annual EHS reports to inform external stakeholders of their promises, strategies and goals, and some companies have reported environmental issues separately from health and safety related issues.

In developed countries, the *Environmental Report* was converted to an *EHS Report* in the late 1990s, and after 2002 it was changed to a *Sustainability Report* on the recommendation of the *Johannesburg World Summit.* In Korea, Hynix Semiconductor prepared an *Environmental Safety and Health Report* from 2002 to 2004, an *EHS Report* in 2005, and a *Sustainability Report* from 2008.

4. GRI Standards

The GRI is an organization created primarily by the CERES (Coalition for Environmentally Responsible Economics), an American environmental protection organization that established the CERES Principles, and the UNEP (United Nations Environment Program) in 1997.

① In June 2000, the GRI (Global Reporting Initiative) published the first edition (G1) of the GRI Guidelines for Sustainability Reporting, which incorporated *"Environmental, economic, and social performance"*.

② In August 2002, the first edition was revised and published (G2).

③ In November 2006, the third edition (G3) was released to strengthen corporate governance issues.

④ In March 2011, supplementing the sector of human rights, community impact and performance-related indicators, the 3rd edition was revised and published (G3.1).

⑤ In May 2013, the fourth edition (G4) was published.

⑥ In October 2016, the fifth edition, as the global standards for sustainability reporting, the 'GRI Standards' have been published.

The evolution of the GRI Standards (SlidePlayer.com Inc., 2021)

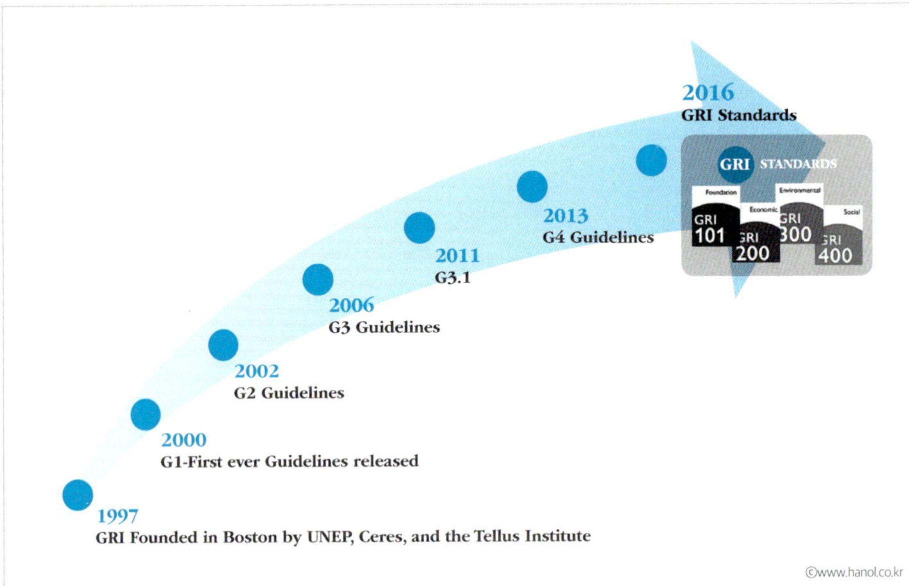

The GRI sustainability reporting guidelines include all environmental (E), social (S) and governance (G) aspects and have become the sustainability reporting guidelines that can best express the corporate ESG management performance.

5 Practice by Technology

1. Carbon Zero technology

To reduce the global temperature, increase to 1.5℃ by 2050, as promised in the Paris Climate Agreement, all businesses, including power generation, steel, cement, and petrochemicals, which are high carbon industries, must actively use zero carbon technology. In other words, the use of renewable energy and hydrogen in the power generation industry, the use of hydrogen-reduced steel technology in the steel industry, the supply of electric and hydrogen vehicles in the automotive industry, the use of zero carbon technology in the shipbuilding industry, the aircraft industry, and the construction industry, it requires active development and use. In this way, ESG management can be directly practiced by actively using zero carbon technology throughout the main process and the value chain where companies are creating value.

2. Carbon Capture technology

Carbon capture, utilization, and storage (CCUS) technology is a technology that literally captures, utilizes, or Storages/Sequestrates carbon, and refers to the 'resourceization' of captured carbon dioxide.[91] As promised in the Paris Climate Agreement, to reduce the increase in global temperature to 1.5°C by 2050, zero carbon scavenger technology is essential, however, since it is not feasible right now, the CCUS technology must also be used effectively. As the like, the active development and utilization of these technologies is an important factor for companies to practice ESG management.

Companies with high carbon emissions, such as power generation, steel, cement, and petrochemicals, directly capture carbon dioxide from air with high carbon dioxide concentration immediately after mass combustion, remove carbon from fuel before combustion, or start from the combustion stage. ESG management can be directly practiced through investment and strategic use of CCUS, a variety of carbon capture, utilization, and storage technology, such as a method of increasing the concentration of carbon dioxide after combustion to facilitate the carbon capturing.

6 Practice by Index

1. ESG management evaluation

When social reporting on CSR activities is promoted, the evaluation of CSR

91) Trends and Leading Companies of Carbon Capture Utilization Storage Technology, Deloitte Insights Editorial Board, 2021 No.19, p. 2.

performance can be also activated. As a typical example, *EIRIS* in the UK and *Innovest* in the US have independently developed CSR performance evaluation models to assess CSR performance and each of them has created a huge database.

The global CSR performance assessment institutions that developed the CSR and the SRI (socially responsible investing) index are disseminating this methodology around the world, which is in the interest of global institutional investors. Global investment institutions compare the CSR and the SRI performance in advanced countries with the emerging markets to determine and verify the level of each social risk of the company.

In Korea, the CSR performance assessment and database systems are operating mainly in the private sector, despite a few listed private companies prepare and publish sustainable development reports.

- Eco-Frontier: Launched in 1995 as an eco-management consulting firm, Eco-Frontier has partnered with Innovest in the US to evaluate social performance of 500 Korean companies.
- Sustinvest: Established in 2006, Sustinvest has established an independent methodology to evaluate ESG-based social performance for 200 Korean companies.
- KOCSR: Korea CSR Evaluation, affiliated with the Center for Corporate Responsibility, evaluates social performance of 100 Korean companies in partnership with EIRIS in the UK and provides data to investment institutions related to FTSE and SRI.
- CGCG: Center for Good Corporate Governance, launched in 2001, built a database with the evaluation of transparent management across Korean listed companies focusing on corporate governance.
- KPC: Since 2009, the Korea Productivity Center has developed and announced DJSI Korea jointly with S&P Dow Jones Indices, a global financial information provider, and S&P Global Switzerland SA, a sustainable management evaluation agency.[92]
- KCGS: The Korea Corporate Governance Service of the Korea Stock Exchange has been carrying out corporate governance assessments with the support of

92) The DJSI is a sustainability assessment / investment index that comprehensively considers economic and environmental, social and governance (ESG: Environmental, Social, Governance) performances. It is made up of the global index and the DJSI Asia Pacific index which assesses the top 600 companies in Asia / Oceania and the DJSI Korea index which assesses the top 200 Korean companies.

Eco-Frontier since 2003. Since 2011, the level of sustainability management of domestic listed companies has been assessed each year, using ESG indicators, including social responsibility and environmental management. In fact, out of 2,200 listed Korean companies, only 100 companies write sustainability reports and collect basic data through corporate disclosure data, media data such as news and public data from supervisory authorities and regulatory authorities such as local governments. ESG assessment after basic assessment and advanced stage assessment, provides feedback on ratings to the listed companies.[93)]

2. ESG management index

Based on the database of ESG performance we can prioritize the performance and develop the ESG index. In Korea, the Korea Stock Exchange, the Korea Productivity Center, and the Hankyoreh Economic Research Institute (HERI) of the Hankyoreh Newspaper, and the Economic Research Institute for a Sustainable Society (ERISS) under the Kyunghyang Newspaper have worked to develop CSR performance indices using ESG indicators. In addition, they have built an independent index system to rank the CSR or ESG performance by synthesizing the data on reputation and performance with a questionnaire.

Countries, where SRI (socially responsible investing) is developed, such as the United Kingdom and the United States, develop various types of SRI index using this database. Representative SRI indices include the UK FTSE4Good Index (developed by FTSE, a joint venture between the UK Stock Exchange and the Financial Times) and the US Dow Jones Sustainability Index (DJSI).

1) FTSE4Good Index Series

The FTSE4Good index is a series of ethical investment stock indices launched in 2001 by the British Group FTSE. It has the advantage of being able to use the stock indexes of several countries, including the United Kingdom, United States, Europe, and Japan, according to various standards of CSR, and index research

93) In October 2021, ESG levels for 2021 were assessed for 950 listed companies, and 7 levels (S, A +, A, B +, B, C, D) were announced for 765 companies. Going forward, it will be mandatory for all companies listed in Korea to prepare a sustainability report and use it to perform an ESG assessment.

is supported by EIRIS. The FTSE4Good index excludes from the assessment companies participating in the tobacco, nuclear weapons, conventional weapons systems or coal-fired power generation industries, and rates them based on environmental sustainability, relationships with stakeholders, attitudes towards human rights, supply chain labor standards and corruption standards. Academic research shows that including indexes has little effect on a company's behavior and performance, but index-focused investors don't have lower average returns than those who don't.

2) MSCI-KLD400 Social Index (US Social Index MSCI-KLD400)

The MSCI-KLD400 Social Index, launched in 1990, is designed to allow socially conscious investors to choose the weighting of their social and environmental factors when investing.[94) The MSCI-KLD400 Social Index is designed to assess the common stocks of companies that KLD deems to have positive ESG (environmental, social and governance) characteristics. KLD400 includes 400 of the 3,000 largest US companies by market capitalization. The KLD400 index is made up of around 90% of large-cap companies, 9% of mid-cap companies selected for sector diversification and 1% of small-cap companies with exemplary social and environmental performance. In 2010, the UK social index FTSE-KLD400 was renamed the *US Social Index MSCI-KLD400.*

3) Calvert Social Index (CSI)

The CSI is a stock market index created by Calvert Impact (renamed *Calvert Social Investments* in 2017) as a benchmark for large companies considering social or ethical responsibility. Currently, the CSI consists of 680 companies based on market capitalization among the 1000 largest listed companies in the United States. The social index criteria include the environment, construction sites, product safety, local communities, weapon contracts, international trade, and human rights. The Calvert Social Index, constructed with the *Domini 400 Social Index* from KLD Research & Analytics, Inc., is currently used as a benchmark for performance in many socially responsible mutual funds.

94) KLD's Amy Domini establishes the Domini 400 Social Index.

4) Dow Jones Sustainability Indices (DJSI)

DJSI is a representative index that evaluates the sustainability of more than 10,000 companies that have been operating since 1999 through a strategic alliance between S&P Dow Jones Indices of the United States and S&P Dow Jones Indices' RobecoSAM (Sustainable Asset Management). DJSI is the world's oldest global sustainability benchmark and has become a key criterion for making sustainable investment decisions for investors and businesses alike. Since 2012, the S&P DJSI has been published as a consolidated index established by the merger between the S&P and Dow Jones Indices. DJSI evaluates issues related to governance, risk management, brand, climate change, supply chain standards and labor practices based on analysis of a company's TBL (economic, social, and environmental) performance. They are strengthening the qualification evaluation that excludes companies that do not operate as a negative screening. It includes industry-specific sustainability criteria for each of the 60 industries defined under the *'Industry Classification Benchmark (ICB)'*.

The DJSI product family includes the DJSI World index and various indices based on regions (Europe, Northern Europe, North America, and Asia Pacific), including for example, an industry-specific index called the *'Blue Chip Index'*. Companies wishing to enter the DJSI are evaluated by submitting long-term TBL (economic, social, and environmental) asset management plans every year.

- September 1999: Launched DJSI in collaboration with Dow Jones Indexes and SAM (Sustainable Asset Management), a global investment company focused on sustainability investment (including the top 10% of 2,500 Dow Jones listed companies)
- 2001: STOXX Ltd. in the DJSI Index. The Dow Jones-STOXX Sustainability Index, including the index, has been expanded and utilized for major European sustainable companies.
- 2005: Created Dow Jones Sustainability North America Index
- 2006: Dow Jones Indexes and SAM jointly launched the Dow Jones Islamic Market Sustainability Index, which combines DJSI's Islamic investment principles and sustainability criteria.
- 2009: Launch of Dow Jones Sustainability Asia Pacific Index and Korea Index
- 2010: SAM and Dow Jones Indexes end cooperation with STOXX: Dow Jones Indexes is responsible for calculating, marketing, and distributing indices, including European indices, while SAM is responsible for component selection

- 2010: SAM and Dow Jones Indexes jointly launch DJSI Nordic Index
- 2012: S&P and Dow Jones Indices merged to form S&P-Dow Jones Indices

Meanwhile, DJSI is divided into several references by region or country across the world as follows:

- **DJSI World Index:** The Dow Jones Global Composite Stock Index (DJGTSMI), launched in September 1999, is based on 2,500 major companies, and is derived from about 300 companies that occupy the top 10% in TBL (economic, environmental, and social) criteria. As a result of DJSI evaluation in 2021, 322 companies, or 12.7%, of 2,544 global companies are included in the DJSI World index, and

21 Korean companies are included. DJSI World is again divided into *'DJSI World 80'* and *'DJSI World ex US 80'*, both of which were launched in August 2008 and analyzes the performance of 80 US companies and 80 overseas companies, respectively.

- **DJSI Europe Index:** DJGTSMI targets the top 20% of 600 European companies in terms of sustainability and announces the Dow Jones Sustainability Eurozone Index (DJSI Eurozone) for small European companies. Both indices have been publishing Dow Jones Sustainability Europe 40 (DJSI Europe 40) and Dow Jones Sustainability Euro Zone 40 indexes, respectively, since August 2010. *DJSI Europe 40* and *DJSI Eurozone 40* are reviewed and analyzed on a quarterly basis to maintain the accuracy of index formation, and DJSI Europe 40 and DJSI Eurozone 40 are reviewed annually.
- **DJSI North America Index:** Like DJSI Europe, it was launched in September 2005 with the Dow Jones Sustainability United States Index (DJSI United States), which includes 20% of the 600 largest companies. Detailed indices are also published as the Dow Jones Sustainability North America 40 Index (*DJSI North America 40*) and the Dow Jones Sustainability United States 40 Index (*DJSI United States 40*).
- **DJSI Asia Pacific Index:** The DJSI Asia Pacific Index was launched in January 2009 concurrently with a single subset, the Dow Jones Sustainability Asia Pacific 40 Index (*DJSI Asia Pacific 40*). In terms of sustainability in 2009, the method including 20% of the top 600 companies in the Asia-Pacific region and the index evaluation method for the sub-set DJSI Asia Pacific 40 leading companies are operated in the same way as in the Americas and Europe. As a result of the DJSI evaluation in 2021, 153 companies, 25.1% of the 609 companies subject to evaluation, were included in the DJSI Asia Pacific index, and 32 domestic companies were included.
- **DJSI Korea Index:** DJSI Korea targets the top 30% of sustainable Korean companies. It started in October 2009 with the Dow Jones Sustainability Korea 20 Index (*DJSI Korea 20*) targeting the top 20 companies. Like other regions, DJSI Korea is reviewed on a quarterly basis and DJSI Korea 20 is evaluated on an annual basis. As a result of the DJSI evaluation in 2021, 43 domestic companies, 21.2% of the 203 companies subject to evaluation, were included in the DJSI Korea Index.

DJSI indicators and evaluations are particularly noteworthy because the top 10%, 20%, 30%, or companies in their 20s, 40s, and 80s that are included in the DJSI can enjoy various benefits such as:

- **Benchmarking feedbacks:** All companies participating in the evaluation provide the *'RobecoSAM Bechmarking Scorecard'* so that the company's sustainability performance for evaluation items can be checked by comparing the industry average score and the global top company score in the industry.
- **Reputation and Brand Value:** Improves the company's reputation and brand value with shareholders, analysts, and the public.
- **Sustainable Management Investment (Responsible Investment):** Stocks of companies included in DJSI are potential investments in DJSI-based portfolios and can directly benefit from the growing demand for Socially Responsible Investing (SRI).
- **Promotional effect:** Companies incorporated into DJSI can use membership logos and qualifications for internal and external marketing and communication purposes.

In the case of Korea, to achieve an integrated level of indicators and assessment activities like DJSI, the overall status of assessment and certification institutions needs to be established. To this end, it is necessary to separate the institutions that analyze the ESG activities of companies and those that publish ESG management indices.

In other words, the institutions that analyze ESG management should focus on building the database, and the ESG management indicator should be developed, analyzed, evaluated, and published by a trusted institution with an independent point of view. In addition, information necessary for the development of ESG management evaluation indicators and maintenance of the evaluation system should be provided by the institution in charge of ESG management analysis through the accumulated database.

Since measurement and analysis are possible only by quantitatively evaluating a company's non-financial information, it is necessary to create an in-house transparent management climate so that the company can disclose its information transparently and assign evaluation indicators and weights to evaluate objectively. It is also required for Korean companies to build a framework initiated by the FKI (Federation of Korean Industries), the KCCI (Korea Chamber of Commerce and Industry), rather than being led or controlled by the government.

Therefore, to establish an ESG management system trusted by all stakeholders, companies, and corporate groups themselves, they must establish 'Self-diagnose system (human rights and ethical management)', 'Management certification system by experts (social responsibility management)', 'ESG management reporting system (sustainability reporting)', 'ESG management evaluation system', 'ESG management index' and SRI (socially responsible investing) more comprehensively and operate accordingly.

7 Practice by PRI and SRI

1. UN PRI (Principles for Responsible Investment)

The UN PRI was established in 2006 as a representative responsible investment principle for financial institutions. UNEP FI (United Nations Environment Program Financial Initiative) is a voluntary gathering of global financial institutions with the participation of 170 financial institutions from 40 countries and it played a pivotal role in establishing the PRI. UNEP FI aims to smoothly collect opinions from the major banks and investment trust companies.

The UNEP FI established PRI for financial institutions based on the discovery of ESG issues by industrial sector through its Asset Management Working Group (AMWG) and evidence of the correlation between ESG performance and value of the company through various studies.

PRI encourages financial institutions to take ESG issues into account in investing and management when making investment decisions, and as of 2021, more than 4,000 financial institutions are participating. PRI has two major partner organizations, UNEP FI and UNGC:

- **UNEP FI:** In close cooperation with more than 200 financial institutions, UNEP FI seeks to link sustainability and financial performance and joint development, and to create a desirable operating environment for financial institutions and enhance sustainability through peer-to-peer networks, research, and training.
- **UNGC:** As a policy platform launched in 2000, it is a practical framework for enhancing corporate sustainability and practicing responsible management and contains ten universally required principles in the fields of human rights, labor, environment, and anti-corruption. As of 2021, UNGC, with over 7,000 companies from 135 countries, is recognized as the world's largest voluntary corporate sustainability initiative.

2. SRI (Socially Responsible Investing)

In the United States and Europe, SRI has been developed mainly by the religious institutions and pension funds. According to the Global Sustainable Investment Association (GSIA), ESG related SRI amounted to $35.3 trillion at the end of 2020, and Deutsche Bank reported that it will grow to more than $160 trillion by 2035 if ESG obligations are maintained. And according to Bloomberg, the size of sustainable bonds also surged from $565.9 billion in 2019 to $732 billion in 2020.

Trend of global ESG investment (Unit: 1 billion dollars)

Region / Year	2016	2018	2020
Europe	12,040	14,075	12,017
United States	8,723	11,995	17,081
Japan	474	2,180	2,874
Canada	1,086	1,699	2,423
Oceania	516	734	906
Total	22,890	30,683	35,301

Source: Lee J. O. (Korea Social Forum, October 03, 2021), *"Why ESG Now?"*.

3. History of SRI in Korea

SRI in Korea started with the launch of *'Eco-funds'* in 2001 and has since expanded in earnest in 2005. In 2006, the Korean Corporate Governance Fund

(KCGF) was launched, and the National Pension Service started to implement SRI consignment operation. Dr. Yang Chun-seung, executive director of the Korea Social Responsibility Forum (KOSIF), said that, for domestic SRI to be activated, first, disclosure of corporate social responsibility-related information, second, expansion of SRI by pension funds, third, establishment and application of guidelines for socially responsible investment fund, fourth, the development of indicators related to SRI should be presented.[95)]

Therefore, a global perspective is required in which domestic institutional investors actively participate in the UN PRI and ESG issues in investment decision-making. Recently, Korea's ESG investment has grown rapidly from $27 billion in 2019 to $88 billion in 2020. The SRI bonds also exceeded $120 billion as of September 2021 after being listed for the first time in 2018. As an example, the National Pension Service, which manages more than $750 billion in funds, plans to expand investment based on ESG ratings to 50% of total assets under management from 2022. In this case, it is expected that more than $330 billion will flow into the investment directly linked to ESG.[96)]

SRI bonds are issued for projects to create eco-friendly social benefits. They are used as green bonds, social bonds, sustainable bonds, ESG bonds, thematic bonds, and social contribution bonds. International standards for SRI bonds include Green Bond Principles (GBP), Social Bond Principles (SBP), Sustainability Bond Guidelines (SBG) published by the International Capital Markets Association (ICMA), and The Climate Bond Standards (CBS) of the Climate Bond Initiative (CBI), etc.

In Korea, they are collectively referred to as *'ESG bonds'*, and there is a recent issuance boom. In addition to the general bond issuance procedure, the issuance of ESG bonds is carried out through a process of review and certification by an external professional organization on whether the purpose of the raised funds and the management system meet the standards for applying ESG bonds.[97)]

95) Yang Chun-seung, *"Status and Challenges of SRI in Korea"*, KOSIF, 2009.

96) Lee Jong-oh, *"Why ESG Now"*, KOSIF, October 3, 2021.

97) Information on ESG bond issuance is provided by the Korea Exchange website for SRI bonds (https://sribond.krx.co.kr/).

8 Practice by Reporting Standards

The *'GRI Standards'*, which are most widely used as reporting standards for ESG management, were completely revised in 2016 by the GRI (Global Reporting Initiative) and partially revised again in 2018. The GRI Standards contain indicators related to the TBL performance in the environmental, social, and economic areas.

1. Changes in GRI's sustainability reporting standards

GRI was established in 1997 led by CERES, an American NGO, and UNEP. GRI announced the first edition (G1) of the Sustainability Report Guidelines in June 2000, and then the revised version (G2) in August 2002, and the third edition (G3) in November 2006. In March 2011, the supplementary edition of the 3rd edition (G3.1) with human rights, community impact and performance-related indicators added, the 4th edition (G4) in May 2013, and the international standard established in October 2016 the 5th edition (GRI Standards) was published.

Version	Year	Main Content
GRI G1	2000	The first publication after the draft published in 1999: consists of summary, general indicators, detailed indicators
GRI G2	2002	Emphasize stakeholder engagement, environment, labor, and human rights: industry guide, core and additional indicators, total of 142 indicators
GRI G3	2006	Reinforce external verification, reporting boundary setting, management disclosure: industry/indicator/technical code provision for a total of 121 indicators
GRI G3.1	2011	Reinforce negative issue reporting, complementation of human rights, local communities, and diversity: 126 indicators in total with 5 additional performance indicators
GRI G4	2013	Introduce reporting system focusing on material issues. Reinforce stakeholder participation, abolition of application level, confirmation of materiality: Implemented in 2016
GRI Standards	2016/ 2018	Published as an international standard for the preparation of sustainability report in October 2016, and partially supplemented and expanded in 2018

The environmental and social performance indicators of the GRI repository published in 2016 are consistent with the environmental (E) and social (S) indicators of ESG standards. And by using the ethical management indicators, the board of directors, risk management and ethics and integrity indicators among the economic performance indicators of the GRI repository, a new and more practical repository for drafting ESG management reports can be developed applying the *'GRI Standards'* as follows.

ESG management report indicators applying GRI Standards

Area	INPUT indicators	OUTPUT indicators	OUTCOME indicators
Environment	GRI 302 *Energy* GRI 301 *Raw Material* GRI 303 *Water* GRI 307 *Environmental Compliance* GRI 308 *Supplier Environmental Assessment*	GRI 305 *Emissions* GRI 306 *Waste* GRI 303 *Wastewater*	GRI 304 *Biodiversity*
Social	GRI 401 *Employment* GRI 405 *Diversity and Equal Opportunity* GRI 406 *Non-discrimination* GRI 407 *Freedom of Association and Right to Collective Bargaining* GRI 408 *Child Labor* GRI 409 *Forced Labor* GRI 410 *Security Practice* GRI 412 *Human Rights Assessment* GRI 413 *Supplier Social Assessment* GRI 419 *Social and Economic Compliance*	GRI 402 *Industrial Relations* GRI 403 *Occupational Safety and Health* GRI 404 *Education and Training*	GRI 416 *Customer Safety and Health* GRI 417 *Marketing, Labeling* GRI 418 *Customer Privacy* GRI 415 *Public Policy* GRI 411 *Rights of Indigenous Peoples* GRI 413 *Community*
Economic	GRI 202 *Market Position* GRI 204 *Purchasing Practice*	GRI 205 *Anti-corruption* GRI 206 *Anti-competition behavior*	GRI 201 *Economic Performance* GRI 203 *Indirect economic impact*
Governance	GRI 102-18 *Governance* GRI 102-20 *Management Responsibilities* GRI 102-21 *Advisory Stakeholders* GRI 102-22 *Composition of organization and subcommittees* GRI 102-23 *Chairman of the organization*	GRI 102-19 *Empowerment* GRI 102-25 *Conflicts of Interest* GRI 102-28 *Performance evaluation of the organization*	GRI 102-30 *Effectiveness of risk management and processes*

Area	INPUT indicators	OUTPUT indicators	OUTCOME indicators
Governance	GRI 102-24 *Organization Nomination and Selection* GRI 102-26 *The role of the organization* GRI 102-27 *Organization collective knowledge* GRI 102-32 *The role of bodies in reporting* GRI 102-35 *Remuneration Policy* GRI 102-36 *Remuneration Decision Process* GRI 102-37 *Stakeholder Engagement in Remuneration* GRI 102-16 *Values/Principles/ Standards/Code of Conduct* GRI 102-17 *Ethics Advice and Concern Mechanisms*	GRI 102-29 *Impact identification & management* GRI 102-31 *Topic Review* GRI 102-33 *Serious problem communication* GRI 102-34 *Serious problem nature and total number* GRI 102-38 *Total annual remuneration rate* GRI 102-39 *Annual Total Compensation Increase Percentage*	

2. GRI 300 Environmental Performance Reporting Standards

If the eight GRI Standards environmental performance indicators are classified in a logic model; [Input indicators] include energy, raw material, water, supplier environmental assessment, compliance with environmental legislation, [Output indicators] are emission, waste, sewage, and [Outcome performance indicator] comes from the keeping biodiversity.

GRI Environmental Performance Reporting Indicator by Logic Model

INPUT indicator	OUTPUT indicator	OUTCOME indicator
GRI 302 Energy GRI 301 Raw Material GRI 303 Water GRI 307 Environmental Compliance GRI 308 Assess Supplier Environment	GRI 305 Emission GRI 306 Waste GRI 303 Wastewater	GRI 304 Biodiversity

In terms of responding to the climate crisis, greenhouse gas emissions are the most serious among environmental indicators. Therefore, we must first look at how much energy we use and how much we convert into new and renewable energy. And it is necessary to understand the biodiversity index as a symbolic expression not to repeat the experience of the extinction of life on earth, including humans. The Earth has experienced five massive extinctions: 86% extinction 450 million years ago, 75% extinction 380 million years ago, 96% species extinction 255 million years ago and 80% of species extinction 205 million years ago. It is said that 75% of species became extinct 70 million years ago.[98)]

This implies that humanity must recognize responsibility for all living things on the planet and respond to climate change to avoid another mass extinction event due to climate change caused by greenhouse gases. Therefore, the practice and reporting of ESG management should focus on environmental indicators, especially greenhouse gas emission indicators for responding to climate disasters. In other words, it is necessary to report the amount of greenhouse gas emitted from all buildings and production activities and the reduction results.[99)]

3. GRI 400 Social Performance Reporting Standards

If 19 GRI Standards social performance indicators are categorized into a logic model, the [Input indicators] are employment, freedom of association and collective bargaining rights, child labor, forced labor, safety practices, human rights assessment, social assessment of suppliers. Meanwhile, [Output indicator] can be the labor-management relations, occupational safety and health, education and training, diversity and equality in matters employment, non-discrimination, socio-economic compliance, and [Outcome performance indicators] include aboriginal management, community, public policy, customer safety and health, marketing and labeling, and customer privacy for social ecology.

Human rights management is the most important aspect of social performance. In other words, the creation of fair and diversity-respected employment, freedom of association and collective bargaining rights, the prevention of child labor and forced labor throughout the supply chain, the implementation of social evaluation for suppliers and compliance with all economic laws and regu-

---

98) Wallace-Wells D. (2019), *The Unhabitable Earth: Life After Warming*, Tim Duggan Books.

99) Gates B. (2021), *How to Avoid Climate Disaster*. Human activity share of greenhouse gas emissions: heating and cooling 7%, electricity generation 27%, livestock production 16%, manufacturing (cement, iron, plastic) 31%, transport 16%.

GRI Social Performance Reporting Indicator by Logic Model

INPUT indicator	OUTPUT indicator	OUTCOME indicator
GRI 401 Employment GRI 405 Diversity, Equality in Employment GRI 406 Non-discrimination GRI 407 Freedom of Association/ Right to Collective Bargaining GRI 408 Child Labor GRI 409 Forced Labor GRI 410 Security Practice GRI 412 Human Rights Assessment GRI 413 Supplier Social Assessment GRI 419 Socio-Economic Compliance	GRI 402 Industrial Relations GRI 403 Industrial Safety & Health GRI 404 Training	GRI 416 Customer Health and Safety GRI 417 Marketing and Labeling GRI 418 Customer Privacy GRI 415 Public Policy GRI 411 Indigenous Rights GRI 413 Community

lations and education for security must be followed. Based on this awareness, sound industrial relations, health and safety for employees and suppliers, and regular education and training on obsolete knowledge should be implemented. This consideration for the employees and suppliers is reflected in its contributions to customers, governments, natives, and local communities. Ultimately, prevent the extinction of mankind and all species on the planet by reducing GHG emissions.

4. GRI 200 Economic Performance and Governance Reporting Standards

If the six economic performance indicators of the GRI Standards are classified into a logic model, [Input indicators] include market position and purchasing

GRI Economic Performance Reporting Indicator by Logic Model

INPUT indicator	OUTPUT indicator	OUTCOME indicator
GRI 202 Market Position GRI 204 Purchasing Practice	GRI 205 Anti-Corruption GRI 206 Anti-Competitive Behavior	GRI 201 Economic Performance GRI 203 Indirect Economic Impacts

practice, [Output indicators] imply anti-corruption and anti-competitive behavior, and [Outcome performance indicators] are classified as economic performance and indirect economic impacts.

The economic performance of the GRI standards express an organization's economic contribution as distinct from its financial performance. Thus, it would be desirable to report it by including in each ESG sector.

Governance sector reports on the board of directors, ethical management, and risk management, etc. Among the economic indicators, anti-corruption (GRI 205) and anti-competitive behavior (GRI 206) can be reported as ethical management items. On the other hand, in the case of economic performance (GRI 201), climate change as environmental performance, pension system as employee-related social performance, government financial support and indirect economic impact (GRI 203) can also be included in public policy. In addition, market status (GRI 202) including employee diversity and employment equality and purchasing practice (GRI 204) can be reported as social performance.

In the environment (E) part, the board's efforts to respond to climate change, and in the governance (G) part, the impact of climate change on financial impact and other risks and opportunities (GRI Disclosure 201-2) in economic performance (GRI 201) and how to deal with it.

In the case of GRI Standards, separate chapters and indicators are not presented for governance. Accordingly, in the outline part of the report, the governance structure (G) should be prepared as a separate item to explain the operation of the board of directors, practice of ethical management, and risk management.

9 Practice by Corporate Initiatives

A company's financial performance is reported so that external stakeholders can rigorously evaluate it according to the following process for each company:

- A company prepares its own accounting report
- A certified public accountant outside the company verifies the prepared accounting report and submits an audit report
- Corporate business reports, including audit reports, are acknowledged by the general meeting of shareholders after going through the BOD
- Report to the Securities Supervisory Service and disclose the reports

On the other hand, the preparation of ESG management performance reports, which mainly deals with the non-financial performance of companies, and required information disclosure activities, has limitations and problems in various aspects as follows:

- Companies prepare their own ESG management reports, but lack of experts
- The reporting standards for ESG management reports are not standardized
- The ESG management report is not submitted as an ESG management audit report after having been verified by an approved external professional body
- The decision procedure for the ESG management report and the ESG management audit report through the BOD (board of directors) and the general meeting of shareholders is not fixed either
- The process by which external stakeholders can rigorously assess a company's ESG management performance by reporting and disclosing the ESG management report to public agencies has also not been established

In such a state where the confidence of external stakeholders is low, the activity itself to assess the level of ESG management practice is inevitably poor. Therefore, assessing the level of ESG management practice without an integrated ESG reporting standard will only increase the additional burden on the company, and it will never become a coordination towards SRI or carbon neutrality. In the EU, where a social agreement has been founded, since 2018, ESG management reports (sustainable development reports) are mandatory for companies with more than 500 employees. And they plan to make it mandatory for all businesses in the EU in stages.

The practice of ESG management begins with the work of closely examining the GRI Standards. In the case of Korea, if the private and public sectors are considered based on 500 employees, at least 3,000 organizations should be the target for ESG management and reporting.[100)]

100) (1) 54 Ministries of the central government (*Ministry of Knowledge Economy reported in 2011; 2013*) (2) 340 Public institutions under the central government (*currently about 34 reports*) (3) 17 Metropolitan and local governments (*Incheon Metropolitan City 2014; 2018 reports*) (4) 52 Public institutions under metropolitan and local governments (*excluding water supply and sewerage: before the merger with Seoul Metro in 2008; 2009; prepared in 2010*) (5) 192 Basic local governments (*2 Non-administrative cities and autonomous districts, excluding 34 cities and 32 districts: 4th report in Bupyeong-gu in 2020, Gangdong-gu in 2010; 2011; 2012; 2013-2014*) (6) 130 Public institutions under Basic local governments (*No reported case*) (7) 339 Universities (*Wonkwang University 2015; 2017 reports*) (8) 110 University hospitals (*no reported case*) (9) 2,268 Listed corporations (*2020: 80 reports*), etc. Institutionalization is required to report ESG management reports (sus-

- Environmental (E) Performance: To achieve *'Net Zero by 2050'*, it is necessary to account for greenhouse gas emissions and reduction efforts, energy consumption and reduction efforts, and the ratio of consumption and use of new and renewable energies by head office and business sites. In the case of ESG management reports of large Korean conglomerates, the sector's environmental indicators include greenhouse gas emissions, energy, raw materials, water, wastewater and waste, and biodiversity are required to assess the reporting.
- Social (S) Performance: In the social field, according to the GRI Standards, human rights, employees (employment, labor relations, safety and health, training and education, diversity, non-discrimination, freedom of association and collective bargaining rights, child labor, forced labor, security practices), evaluation and reporting of supply chain, shared growth, customers, public policy, taxation, social contribution, etc. are required to report.
- Governance (G) Performance: Corporate governance is of particular interest in Korean society requesting transparent report on BOD (organization and operation method), risk management, and ethical management (anti-corruption and anti-competition behavior). To respond to 2050 Carbon Neutrality, the BOD should take the lead in identifying economic, environmental, and social impacts and managing strategic goals to deal with the issues in detail in a way that meets global standards, agreements, and government policies.

In fact, all the reports (sustainability report, sustainable management report, environmental report, social report, CSR report, corporate citizenship report, social value report, ESG report, integrated report, etc.) are required to be carefully reviewed. In other words, it is necessary to establish an integrated system that identifies what is missing in content, considering ways to achieve unification in writing, and discovers best practices in each field. As the like, companies preparing an ESG management report or sustainability report now should design an evaluation framework according to the characteristics of each company based on the suggested checklist for each ESG field as is shown below:

---

tainability reports, integrated reports) at the level of business reports of a total of 3,502 governments, public institutions, universities, university hospitals, and private companies.

GRI Standards-based Environmental (E) Sector Reporting Checklist

Item	No	Indicator	O/X	Score
Raw Materials	301-1	Weight or volume of raw materials used		
	301-2	Recycled input raw materials		
	301-3	Recovered products and packaging materials		
Energy	302-1	Energy consumption within the organization		
	302-2	Energy consumption outside the organization		
	302-3	Energy intensity		
	302-4	Energy consumption reduction		
	302-5	Reduce the energy requirements of products and services		
Water	303-1	Interaction with water as a shared resource		
	303-2	Wastewater release-related impact management		
	303-3	Water intake		
	303-4	Water discharge		
	303-5	Water consumption		
Biodiversity	304-1	Businesses owned, leased, or managed in or near protected areas and areas of high biodiversity value outside protected areas		
	304-2	Significant impacts of activities, products, and services on biodiversity		
	304-3	Habitat protection or restoration		
	304-4	The International Union for Conservation of Nature (IUCN) for Habitat in Areas Affected by Businesses, Number of Endangered Species and Number of National Conserved Species		
Emissions	305-1	Direct (Scope 1) Greenhouse Gas (GHG) Emissions		
	305-2	Energy Indirect (Scope 2) Greenhouse Gas Emissions		
	305-3	Other Indirect (Scope 3) Greenhouse Gas Emissions		
	305-4	Greenhouse Gas Emission Intensity		
	305-5	Reduction of Greenhouse Gas Emissions		
	305-6	Ozone-depleting substances (ODS) emissions		
	305-7	Nitrogen oxides (NOX), sulfur oxides (SOX) and other important air emissions		

Item	No	Indicator	O/X	Score
Wastewater and waste	306-1	Discharge by water quality and destination		
	306-2	Waste by type and treatment method		
	306-3	Significant spill		
	306-4	Hazardous Waste Transport		
	306-5	Water bodies affected by drainage and/or surface runoff		
Compliance	307-1	Violation of environmental laws and regulations		
Supplier environmental assessment	308-1	New suppliers screened for environmental standards		
	308-2	Negative environmental impacts in the supply chain and actions taken		

GRI Standards-based Social (S) Sector Reporting Checklist

Item	No	Indicator	O/X	Score
Employment	401-1	New hires and employee turnover		
	401-2	Welfare benefits provided to full-time employees that are not provided to temporary or part-time employees		
	401-3	Parental leave		
Industrial Relations	402-1	Minimum notice period for business changes		
Occupational Hygiene and Safety (OHS)	403-1	Occupational safety and health management system		
	403-2	Risk identification, risk assessment and incident investigation		
	403-3	Occupational Health Services		
	403-4	Worker participation, consultation and communication on occupational health and safety		
	403-5	Worker training on occupational health and safety		
	403-6	Promoting worker health		
	403-7	Prevention and mitigation of occupational health and safety impacts directly linked to business relationships		
	403-8	Workers subject to the OSH management system		
	403-9	Industrial accident		
	403-10	Occupational disease		

Item	No	Indicator	O/X	Score
Education and Training	404-1	Average annual training hours per employee		
	404-2	Employee competency improvement program and transition support program		
	404-3	Percentage of employees receiving regular performance and career development evaluations		
Diversity and Equal opportunity	405-1	Governance and employee diversity		
	405-2	Ratio of basic wages and remuneration of women to men		
Anti-discrimination	406-1	Discrimination Incidents and Corrective actions		
Freedom of Association and the Right to Collective bargaining	407-1	Businesses and suppliers where freedom of association and the right to collective bargaining may be at risk		
Child labor	408-1	Businesses and suppliers at significant risk for child labor incidents		
Forced labor	409-1	Businesses and suppliers at significant risk of forced labor incidents		
Security practices	410-1	Security personnel trained in human rights policies or procedures		
Indigenous rights	411-1	Indigenous Rights Violation Cases		
Human rights assessment	412-1	Workplaces that have undergone human rights screening or impact assessment		
	412-2	Employee training on human rights policies or procedures		
	412-3	Significant investment agreements and contracts that contain human rights clauses or have undergone human rights screening		
Community	413-1	Businesses with community engagement, impact assessment and development programs		
	413-2	Businesses that have a significant actual or potential negative impact on the local community		
Supplier social evaluation	414-1	New suppliers screened using social criteria		
	414-2	Negative social impacts on the value chain and actions taken		
Public policy	415-1	Political contribution		

Item	No	Indicator	O/X	Score
Customer health and safety	416-1	Assessment of health and safety impacts by product and service category		
	416-2	Non-compliance incidents regarding health and safety impacts of products and services		
Marketing and Labeling	417-1	Information and labeling requirements for products and services		
	417-2	Incidents of non-compliance with information and labeling of products and services		
	417-3	Non-compliance incidents regarding marketing communications		
Information protection	418-1	Proven complaints of breaches of customer privacy and loss of customer data		
Compliance	419-1	Non-compliance with laws and regulations in the social and economic sphere		

GRI Standards-based Economic (Ec) Sector Reporting Checklist

Item	No	Indicator	O/X	Score
Economic performance	201-1	Direct economic value creation and distribution → ESG management overview		
	201-2	Financial Impacts and Other risks and opportunities from Climate change → Risk management among the governance structures (E) of ESG management		
	201-3	Defined benefit pension plans and other retirement plans Employment (GRI 401)		
	201-4	Government financial support → Public policy (GRI 415)		
Market Position	202-1	Ratio of standard entry-level wages by gender to the provincial minimum wage → Diversity and Equal opportunity (GRI 405)		
	202-2	Percentage of senior management employed in the community Employment (GRI 401)		
Indirect economic effect	203-1	Infrastructure investment and support services → ESG management overview		
	203-2	Significant Indirect Economic Impacts → ESG management overview		
Procurement practices	204-1	Expenditure ratio paid to local suppliers → Supplier social evaluation (GRI 414)		

Item	No	Indicator	O/X	Score
Anti-corruption	205-1	Businesses that have assessed risks related to corruption → Ethical management among the governance structures (E) of ESG management		
	205-2	Communication and training on anti-corruption policies and procedure → Ethical management among the governance structures (E) of ESG management		
	205-3	Identified corruption cases and measures → Ethical management among the governance structures (E) of ESG management		
Anti-competition behavior	206-1	Legal action against unfair competition, antitrust and monopoly practices → Ethical management among the governance structures (E) of ESG management		

GRI Standards-based Governance (G) Sector Reporting Checklist

Item	No	Indicator	O/X	Score
Board of Directors	102-18	Governance		
	102-19	Delegation of authority		
	102-20	Management's Responsibilities for Economic, Environmental and Social Topics		
	102-21	Stakeholders advising on economic, environmental, and social topics		
	102-22	Composition of the supreme governance body and sub-committees		
	102-23	Chairman of the highest governance body		
	102-24	Nomination and selection of the highest governance body		
	102-25	Conflict of interest		
	102-26	The role of the highest governance body in establishing purpose, values and strategy		
	102-27	Collective knowledge of the highest governance body		
	102-28	Performance evaluation by the highest governance body		
	102-29	Identify and manage economic, environmental, and social impacts		
	102-30	The effectiveness of the risk management process		

Item	No	Indicator	O/X	Score
Board of Directors	102-31	Review of economic, environmental, and social topics		
	102-32	The role of the highest governance body on sustainability reporting		
	102-33	Serious problem communication		
	102-34	The nature and total number of serious problems		
	102-35	Remuneration policy		
	102-36	Remuneration decision process		
	102-37	Stakeholder engagement in remuneration		
	102-38	Annual total remuneration rate		
	102-39	Annual total remuneration ratio increase ratio		
Risk management	201-2	Financial Impacts and Other Risks and Opportunities from Climate Change		
Ethical management	102-16	Values, Principles, Standards and Code of Conduct		
	102-17	Ethical advice and concern mechanisms		
	205-1	Business assessed for Corruption-related Risks		
	205-2	Communication and training on anti-corruption policies and procedures		
	205-3	Identified Corruption incidents and Actions		
	206-1	Legal action against unfair competition, antitrust and monopoly practices		

As a measure of socially responsible investing (SRI) and evaluation of ESG performance, GRI Standards are highlighted as international standards. And now even universities, hospitals as well as private and public corporations are all invited to prepare ESG or sustainability reports strategically according to GRI Standards considering national characteristics and attributes by sector and size. On the other hand, the Korean government has declared guidelines for ESG reporting on December 1, 2021, however, this is also only a kind of draft and will require continuous improvement and periodic revisions as is illustrated with some practical cases in Korea and those of foreign universities.

1. The case of Hyundai Motors

Hyundai Motors Korea has been preparing the "Sustainability Report" from

2003 to 2021. According to the 2021 Sustainability Report, a total of 65 and 6,200 global sales networks including 121,403 employees, 14 production plants, 11 technology research centers, and 40 sales corporations are being established.

Environmental sector: In the main text of the Sustainability Report treats, environmental management, carbon reduction (climate change risks and opportunities, greenhouse gas emissions, product carbon reduction, LCA (Life Cycle Assessment) performance, workplace carbon reduction, hydrogen ecosystem construction), circular economy (product recycling, workplace resource use). The report is classified and reported by strengthening the management of hazardous substances. Meanwhile, greenhouse gas emissions, global EV market share expansion goal, cumulative sales of electrified vehicles, EU average carbon emissions, average fuel efficiency in China, average fuel efficiency in the US, resource recovery when scrapped vehicles, input to business sites and detailed information for 3 to 6 years on the status of environmental emissions. Carbon reduction by business site is reported separately for efforts to realize eco-friendly factories of not only domestic factories (Ulsan, Asan, Jeonju) but also overseas subsidiaries (China, Indonesia, India, Turkey, Czech Republic, Russia, USA, Brazil).

In the indicators and data related to environmental performance in the appendix, energy consumption, energy use intensity, greenhouse gas emission, greenhouse gas emission intensity, raw materials, water resource consumption, refrigerant gas consumption (domestic and overseas), VOC emission (domestic and foreign), air pollutant generation (domestic and foreign), water pollutant generation (domestic and foreign), waste generation (domestic and foreign), treatment status by waste treatment method, hazardous chemical usage (domestic and overseas), environmental investment, etc., are reported on trends over the past three years. However, it is necessary to report all these matters to each domestic and foreign production corporation.

Social sector: In the main text, human rights, employees (workplace safety and health, establishment of a flexible organizational culture, recruitment and nurturing of talent), partners (support for shared growth, ESG management of supply chain), quality (quality and safety, new car safety evaluation, quality management and assurance), customers (customer experience programs, customer service, protection of customer rights) and local communities (CSV promotion strategy, CSV activity area, global CSV activity) are reported separately. The social performance-related indicators and data in the appendix show the current status of manpower by region (domestic, North America, Europe, China, India, etc.) and occupational group (domestic), manpower status by region/sex (domestic and overseas), and female employee status by region (domestic, North America, Europe) , China, India, etc.), female managers (domestic and foreign), employment of the disabled (domestic), employee status by age group (domestic), union membership (domestic), education status (domestic), parental leave status (domestic), New employment status (domestic), internal recruitment ratio, youth interns employment, turnover status (domestic), organizational culture diagnosis, investment by social contribution field (domestic), amount by social contribution type (domestic), employee volunteer performance (domestic), region Social contribution amount (America, Asia, Europe, China), association donations, major sponsoring groups, quality index, quality management system, customer satisfaction, industrial accidents (domestic and foreign), work-loss accident rate (domestic and foreign), occupational disease incidence (domestic and foreign), Auto Parts Industry Promotion Foundation support status, partner companies' shared entry status, shared growth and fair trade agreements are reported in detail, but it should be specified as a reporting system for each business site.

Governance sector: The main body reports on the board of directors (committees under the board of directors, operation of the board of directors, protection of shareholders' rights), risk management (global risk management system, tax strategy), ethical and compliance management (ethical management, voluntary compliance with fair trade, compliance management), etc. The Transparent Management Committee under the Board of Directors was expanded and reorganized into the 'Sustainability Management Committee' in March 2021 to deal with the practice of sustainable management, transparency in internal transactions, ethical management and ESG management, and protection of shareholder rights. The economic and governance-related indicators and data items in the appendix report the status of compliance management education (domestic and overseas) and violations of laws/voluntary rules, but it is necessary to consistently report for each domestic and foreign production corporation.

> Hyundai Motors 2021 Sustainability Report can be appreciated as the most clearly divided E-S-G report. In the main text, if the indicators and data in the appendix for each ESG item are classified by domestic and foreign production companies, and trends and meanings are analyzed and reported for three years, it will be a more desirable report that serves as a model for other companies.

Reshaping ESG Reporting of Hyundai Motors

AS IS	TO BE
Introduction	**Introduction**
003 CEO Message	003 CEO Message
004 Company overview and major performance	004 Company overview and major performance
005 2025 Strategy	075 Global Network
006 Electric Vehicle	005 2025 Strategy
007 Autonomous Driving	006 Electric Vehicle
008 Connected Car	007 Autonomous Driving
009 Robot	008 Connected Car
010 Mobility	009 Robot
012 Hydrogen	010 Mobility
014 Open Innovation	012 Hydrogen
015 Smart Factory	014 Open Innovation
016 ESG Management	015 Smart Factory
016 ESG Promotion Direction	**016 ESG Management**
017 ESG Key Performance	016 ESG Promotion Direction
018 Environmental	017 ESG Key Performance
019 Environmental Management	098 Stakeholder Engagement
020 Carbon Reduction	099 Materiality Assessment
029 Circular Economy	**018 Environmental**
032 Reinforcement of Hazardous Substance Management	019 Environmental Management
033 Social	020 Carbon Reduction
034 Human Rights	029 Circular Economy
035 Employees	032 Reinforcement of Hazardous Substance Management
044 Partners	**033 Social**
049 Quality	034 Human Rights
051 Customer	035 Employees
055 Community	044 Partners
066 Governance	049 Quality
067 Board of Directors	051 Customer
070 Ethics and Compliance Management	055 Community
072 Risk Management	**066 Governance**
073 ESG Factbook	067 Board of Directors
074 Report Overview	072 Risk Management
075 Global Network	070 Ethics and Compliance Management
076 Summary of Key Business Performance	**073 ESG Factbook**
078 Indicators and Data	074 Report Overview
089 GRI Index	076 Summary of Key Business Performance
093 TCFD Index	078 Indicators and Data
094 SASB Index	089 GRI Index
095 WEF IBC Stakeholder Capitalism Metrics	093 TCFD Index
098 Stakeholder Engagement	094 SASB Index
099 Materiality Assessment	095 WEF IBC Stakeholder Capitalism Metrics
101 Third-Party Assurance Statement	101 Third-Party Assurance Statement
103 Greenhouse Gas Verification Statement	103 Greenhouse Gas Verification Statement

Hyundai Motors 2020 Sustainability Management Performance

Award Institution	Performance
Dow Jones Sustainability Indices (DJSI)	Incorporated into DJSI Korea from 2019
Carbon Disclosure Project (CDP)	Carbon Management Sector Honors Award Award of Excellence in Water Resource Management
Chinese Academy of Social Sciences CSR Assessment (CASS-CSR)	'2020 China CSR Development Index Evaluation' No. 1 in the auto industry for 5 consecutive years
iF Design Award	'2020 Hyundai Motor Company Sustainability Report' received the first '2021 iF Design Award' (Communication Division)

Hyundai Motors Global Production and Sales as of the end of 2020

Market	Production (unit: car)	Sales (unit: car)
Domestic	1,618,411	787,854
Foreign	2,115,011	2,956,883
Total	3,733,422	3,744,737

2. The case of Samsung Electronics

Samsung Electronics has been preparing "Green Management Report" from 2000 to 2001 and 2004 to 2005, "Environmental and Social Report" from 2006 to 2007, and "Sustainability Report" from 2008 to 2021. According to the 2021 Sustainability Report published in 2021, there are 267,937 employees, 2,122 partner companies (primary), 74 countries, 233 business sites, 53 sales bases among business sites, 36 production bases, etc.

Most of Samsung Electronics' sales and production bases are large-scale, and the economic, environmental, and social impacts on each local community are enormous. Therefore, Samsung Electronics' sustainability report is actively requested to develop into a representative company that provides global standards for global society through the ESG management report based on 15 regional managers, 53 sales bases, and 36 production bases.

Environmental sector: In the main body of the report, climate action (governance, risk management, GHG reduction at business sites, product energy efficiency, other GHG reductions, cooperation to respond to climate change), circular economy (enhancement

Samsung Electronics' Global Network

Center	Korea	China	Japan	SEA	SWA	MEA	CSI	EU	Africa	NA	SMA	Total
Regional HQ	1	2	1	2	1	1	1	2	1	2	1	15
Sales Base	1	4	1	8	1	8	3	16	2	2	7	53
Production Base	6	9		7	2	1	1	3	1	3	3	36
R&D Center	4	7	2	3	5	5	2	3		7	1	39
Design Center	1	1	1		1			1		1	1	7
Others	-	5	1	10	7	10	3	15	6	13	13	83
Total	**13**	**28**	**6**	**30**	**17**	**25**	**10**	**40**	**10**	**28**	**26**	**233**

Source: Samsung Electronics 2021 Sustainability Report, page 4.

of resource use, extension of product life span, electronic product recovery and recycling, waste landfill, water resources, and chemical management) are explained separately.

The Facts & Figures environmental performance section of the appendix shows trends for the following three years: greenhouse gas management, energy management, product energy use efficiency, resource use efficiency enhancement, collection and recycling of waste electronic products, waste management, water resource management, chemicals management, pollutant management, business environment management, customer value enhancement level, etc. The amount of recovered waste products is reported by continent (Asia and Oceania, Europe, and the Americas), and the status of water resources is reported by region.

Meanwhile, although GHG emissions, energy consumption, renewable energy usage, waste generation, water usage, and chemical usage are reported by business sector (CE-IM sector, DS sector), as pointed out above, the large scale of the business site is considered. Therefore, it is necessary to report by each region and business site. At the same time, it is required to become a model for ESG management reporting as a global leading company by comprehensively analyzing the Facts & Figures environmental performance information in the appendix in the main text to present the trends and meanings for the past 3 years by item in the environmental field.

Social sector: In the main text, labor rights, diversity and inclusion, safety and health, human resource development, organizational culture, supply chain that grows together, responsible supply chain, environment-friendly supply chain, responsible mineral management transparency, customer communication and customer satisfaction, personal information protection, cyber security, AI ethics, accessibility, digital well-being, support for SMEs and startups, and social contribution are reported systematically.

In the Facts & Figures social performance section of the appendix, labor human rights, diversity and inclusion, safety and health, human resource development, sustainable supply chain, responsible mineral management transparency, third-party verification for suppliers, compliance rate by major items, support for small and medium-sized enterprises, customer value increase, personal information, etc. are attached. It reports on trends over the past three years in terms of protection and social contribution.

Meanwhile, the number of employees by region and the proportion of female workers by region are reported in Korea, Southeast Asia, Southwest Asia, Japan, China, North America, Latin America, Europe, the Middle East, and Africa. However, it is necessary to analyze and report the trends and strategic meanings of the last three years for each item in the social field by using the Facts & Figures social performance-related information in the appendix of the main text.

Governance sector: Reports on Samsung Electronics' governance, compliance and ethical management are well documented. However, there is a governance committee under the board of directors to fulfill social responsibility and enhance shareholder value, but the explanation of the committee's activities is insufficient. On the other hand, it is required to comprehensively explain changes and trends in the contents of the main report using the data on compliance and ethical management in the Appendix Facts & Figures.

Reshaping ESG Reporting of Samsung Electronics

AS IS	TO BE
21 Environment 22 Climate Action 23 Governance 24 Risk Management 25 Reduction of GHG emissions at business sites	**Environmental** 22 Climate Action 23 Governance 24 Risk Management 25 Reduction of GHG emissions at business sites

AS IS	TO BE
26 Product Energy Efficiency 27 Other Greenhouse Gas Reduction 28 Cooperation to respond to climate change 29 GHG Emissions 30 Circular Economies 31 Efficient uses of resources 32 Extend product life 33 Collection and recycling of waste electronic products 34 Waste Landfill 35 Water resources 36 Chemical Management **37 Empowering Communities** 38 Social Contribution 41 Support for SMEs and Startups **42 Digital Responsibility** 43 Privacy 45 Cyber Securities 47 AI Ethics 48 Accessibility 50 Digital Wellness **51 Our Employees** 52 Labor Human Rights 56 Diversity and Inclusion 59 Safety and Health 62 Talent Development 63 Organizational cultures **65 Sustainable Supply Chain** 66 Supply Chain Growing Together 68 Responsible Supply Chain 70 Environmentally Friendly Supply Chain 71 Securing Responsible Mineral Management Transparency 72 Sustainability Foundation 73 Materiality test 74 Activities linked to the UN SDGs 75 Sustainable Management Value Creation **76 Facts & Figures** 77 Economic Performance 78 Social Performance 81 Environmental Performance 84 Performance by Business Division **85 Appendix** 86 Independent Verifier's Verification Report 87 Greenhouse Gas Emission Verification Statement 88 GRI Checklist 91 TCFD Checklist 92 SASB checklist 94 Customer Communication and Customer Satisfaction 95 About This Report	26 Product Energy Efficiency 27 Other Greenhouse Gas Reduction 28 Cooperation to respond to climate change 29 GHG Emissions 30 Circular Economies 31 Efficient uses of resources 32 Extend product life 33 Collection and recycling of waste electronic products 34 Waste Landfill 35 Water resources 36 Chemical Management **Social** 52 Labor Human Rights 56 Diversity and Inclusion 59 Safety and Health 62 Talent Development 63 Organizational cultures 66 Supply Chain Growing Together 68 Responsible Supply Chain 70 Environmentally Friendly Supply Chain 71 Securing Responsible Mineral Management Transparency 94 Customer Communication and Customer Satisfaction 43 Privacy 45 Cyber securities 47 AI Ethics 48 Accessibility 50 Digital Wellness 41 Support for SMEs and Startups 38 Social Contribution **Governance** 05 Governance 07 Compliance and ethical management **76 Facts & Figures** 77 Economic Performance 78 Social Performance 81 Environmental Performance 84 Performance by Business Division **85 Appendix** 86 Independent Verifier's Verification Report 87 Greenhouse Gas Emission Verification Statement 88 GRI Checklist 91 TCFD Checklist 92 SASB checklist 17 External evaluation and Awards About This Report

It should be recognized that the data presented in Fact & Figure and Appendix parts of the Sustainability Report are also important for international comparison of ESG management performance.

3. The case of POSCO

POSCO has been preparing the "Sustainability Report" from 2003 to 2014, the "POSCO Report" from 2015 to 2018, and the "Corporate Citizenship Report" as of 2021 after 2019. In 2021, ESG Factbook is added as an appendix to the Corporate Citizenship Report, dealing with matters that become models for other companies.

Environmental sector: In the main body of the report, response to climate change (carbon management system, POSCO 1.5°C climate change scenario, POSCO Carbon FLOW and reduction technology application status, Green Process, Green Product, Green Partnership), implementation of eco-friendly steelworks (environmental strategy, environmental organization, environmental investment, Environmental management certification, air, by-products, water, chemicals, environmental education, stakeholder communication, biodiversity, and iron life cycle) are covered. And in the appendix, ESG Factbook environmental matters include trends for the last 4 years on air, water resources, waste, resource circulation, management, energy, and greenhouse gas.

Social sector: In the main body of the report, responsible business foundation (human rights management), trust and creativity organization (recruitment, talent cultivation, career development, steel challenge, competency enhancement program, New Collar Level certification system, customized education support, evaluation and compensation, organizational culture, win-win labor-management relationship), safe workplace, sustainable supply chain, responsible business basis (fair trade), business competitiveness, responsible business basis (information protection), economic contribution (tax policy), symbiosis with stakeholders etc. are separately explained. In the appendix section, the ESG Factbook social sector reports four-year trends on safety, HR, education, pension support, diversity, work-life balance, social contribution, and customer satisfaction survey results.

Governance sector: In the main text, transparent governance (governance structure, corporate citizenship advisory meeting), responsible business (ethical management), and ESG bond issuance are presented. It reports the trend over the past four years. It is emphasized that the ESG committee under the Board of Directors specifically presented environmental and low-carbon policy reviews, safety and health plan pre-deliberation, and ESG-related implementation monitoring.

Since POSCO's innovative ESG management activities are being carried out in a situation where negative domestic and foreign public opinion on environmental issues is rising due to the nature of its business, internal and external responses to the promotion results are noteworthy.

Reshaping of POSCO 2020 Corporate Citizenship Report

AS IS	TO BE
OVERVIEW	**OVERVIEW**
07 CFO Message	07 CFO Message
20 Top 5 Brands for Corporate Citizenship	20 Top 5 Brands for Corporate Citizenship
26 ESG materiality assessment	26 ESG materiality assessment
BUSINESS	**Environmental**
36 Response to climate change	36 Response to climate change
43 Implementation of eco-friendly steelworks	43 Implementation of eco-friendly steelworks
49 Business Competitiveness	- Atmosphere
SOCIETY	- Water resources
55 Sustainable Supply Chains	- Waste
61 Coexistence with Stakeholders	- Resource circulation
PEOPLE	- Management
68 Safe Workplace	- Energy
72 Organization of trust and creativity	- Green gas
GOVERNANCE	**Social**
78 Transparent Governance	85 Responsible Business Foundation (Human Rights Management)
82 Responsible Business Foundation (Ethical management, human rights management, fair trade, information protection)	72 Organization of trust and creativity
	68 Safe Workplace
	55 Sustainable Supply Chains
90 Economic Contribution (Tax Policy)	87 Responsible Business Foundation (Fair Trade)
92 ESG Bond Issuance	49 Business Competitiveness
ESG Factbook / ESG DATA	88 Responsible Business Foundation (Information protection)
Environment	90 Economic Contribution (Tax Policy)
- Atmosphere	61 Coexistence with Stakeholders
- Water resources	- Safety
- Waste	- Greetings
- Resource circulation	- Education
- Management	- Pension support
- Energy	- Diversity
- Green gas	- Work-life balance
Social	- Social contribution
- Safety	- Results of customer satisfaction survey
- Greetings	**Governance**
- Education	78 Transparent Governance
- Pension support	
- Diversity	
- Work-life balance	

AS IS	TO BE
- Social contribution - Results of customer satisfaction survey **Governance** - Board composition - Board operation - Board performance evaluation - Stock holding - Compensation SASB Assurance Statement	82 Responsible Business Foundation (Ethical Management) 92 ESG Bond Issuance - Board composition - Board operation - Board performance evaluation - Stock holding - Compensation SASB Assurance Statement

4. The case of Korean Air

Korean Air's ESG management activities, which are sensitive to the international situation due to the nature of their business and are exposed to global competitive information such as ICAO and IATA every day, started even before ESG indicators appeared. The "Environmental Report" prepared in the early 1990s was expanded to the "Environmental Social Report" in 2005, and the "Sustainability Report" was prepared in 2006-2020. From 2021, Korean Air reshaped it in "ESG Report". Korean Air's '2021 ESG Report' is appreciated as the closest to the ESG management prototype. According to the 2021 ESG Report, there are 20,072 employees, 136 passenger planes, 23 cargo planes, 108 passenger service cities, and 47 freight service cities, serving a total of 121 cities. Korean Air is the only airline company in the world to run the aerospace business in parallel.

Environmental sector: The main body of the report covers Korean Air's response to climate change (the aviation industry's climate change response goal, Korean Air's climate change response strategy) and environmental management (environmental management system, energy management, environmental pollution prevention, and upcycling of retired aircraft). As a climate change response strategy, it deals with trends and management processes for the last three years by indicator for climate change-related risk management. Environmental management analyzes and reports trends in energy consumption trends and reductions, environmental cost usage trends, emission levels compared to permissible emission standards for each business site, waste generation rate, waste recycling rate, and water resource recycling rate. In the environmental items of the main performance indicators in the appendix, details of fuel and energy, greenhouse gas emission, water consumption, water resource recycling, water pollutant emission, air pollutant emission, waste generation, waste recycling rate, waste treatment amount, environmental education, etc. for the last 3 years providing information.

Social sector: The main body of the report provides the following information: Talent management, safety management, win-win management, Korean Air's response to COVID-19, customer satisfaction, information protection, sharing management, employee status, female employee status, maternity protection system performance, employees Information security education performance, number of reports of leaks of customer personal information, status of online education contents possession, graduate school scholarship support for employees, volunteer hours per person, social contribution expenses, ratio of local managers at the manager level, human rights education results, employee training results, union membership status, social contribution activities (2003-2020). The social category of the main performance indicators in the appendix provides data on the following items for the past three years: Employee status, new hires, number of employees turnover, turnover rate (domestic), local employment, maternity leave, parental leave, employee education, and social contribution Performance, information security training, customer personal information, pension, and investment status. Nevertheless, there are parts that are frequently changed, such as overseas local manpower, so it is required to add these items and report issues related to manpower management together.

Governance sector: In the main text, reports are classified according to international standards such as corporate governance, risk management, and ethical management. In particular, the recently established 'ESG Committee' under the Board of Directors reviews and decides on internal transactions as stipulated by laws such as the Fair-Trade Act and reviews of major management issues that have a significant impact on ESG-related implementation matters and shareholder value. On the other hand, the ESG standard is applied to the governance structure of the appendix. It would also be desirable to summarize these contents and explain them in the main text.

Reshaping of Korean Air 2021 ESG Report

AS IS	TO BE
COMPANY OVERVIEW 04 CEO Message 06 Management Philosophy	**COMPANY OVERVIEW** 04 CEO Message 06 Management Philosophy

AS IS	TO BE
08 About Korean Air	08 About Korean Air
11 Global Network	11 Global Network
12 Main Business Strategy	12 Main Business Strategy
ISSUE REPORT	68 Stakeholder Engagement
14 Issue 01. Response to COVID-19	71 Materiality Assessment
21 Issue 02. Response to climate change	**Environmental**
ESG PERFORMANCE	21 Issue 02. Response to climate change
Environment	29 Environmental Management
29 Environmental Management	**Social**
Social	43 Talent Management
35 Safety Management	35 Safety Management
38 Customer Impression	50 Win-win Management
42 Information Protection	14 Issue 01. Response to COVID-19
43 Talent Management	38 Customer Impression
50 Win-win Management	42 Information Protection
52 Sharing Management	52 Sharing Management
Governance	**Governance**
54 Corporate Governance	54 Corporate Governance
57 Ethical Management	59 Risk Management
59 Risk Management	57 Ethical Management
60 ESG Key Performance Indicators	**60 ESG Key Performance Indicators**
OTHER INFORMATION	**OTHER INFORMATION**
68 Stakeholder Engagement	74 Third Party Assurance Report
71 Materiality Assessment	76 GRI Index
74 Third Party Assurance Report	80 SASB Index
76 GRI Index	81 Efforts to achieve the UN SDGs
80 SASB Index	82 UN Global Compact
81 Efforts to achieve the UN SDGs	83 Awards and Association Membership
82 UN Global Compact	
83 Awards and Association Membership	

5. The case of universities

As of September 11, 2020, there are 191 universities in Korea, 136 junior colleges, 10 education colleges, and 2 industrial colleges, for a total of 339. Out of a total of 339 universities, none of them are currently preparing a sustainability report, and only Won Kwang University reported cases in 2015 and 2017. On the other hand, in the case of overseas, there are various exemplary cases that Korean universities should benchmark.

- **Harvard:** Harvard University has prepared a 'climate action plan' to create a fossil fuel-free future by 2050 and presented the long-term goal of not using fossil fuels by 2050 as follows:
  ① The electricity Harvard buys comes from clean, renewable energy sources that do not burn fossil fuels such as solar or offshore wind.
  ② Harvard's regional energy system operates without fossil fuels.

③ Harvard-owned vehicles operate without fossil fuels.

④ Set purchase goals for externally provided services or activities to minimize dependence on fossil fuels.

Installed Solar PV Capacity at Harvard

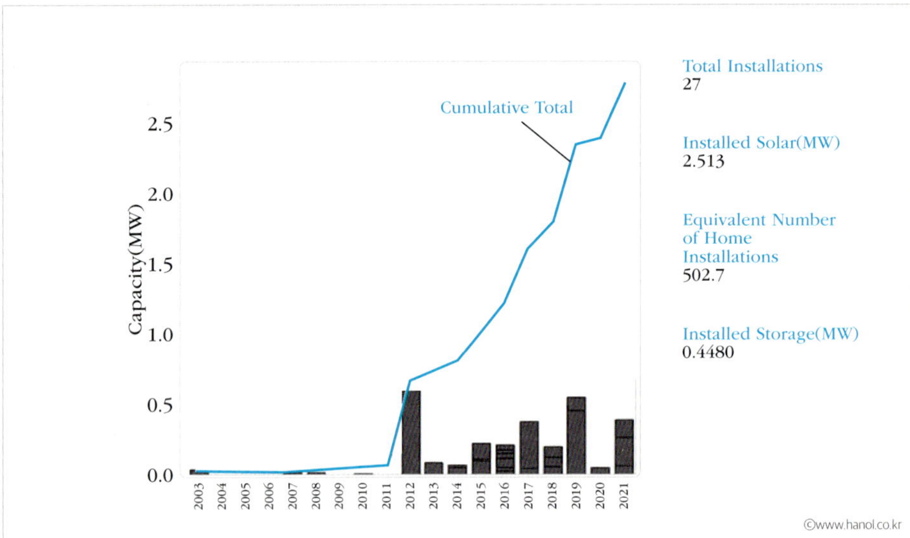

Harvard Greenhouse Gas Emissions [MTCED(GreenHarvard, 2021)]

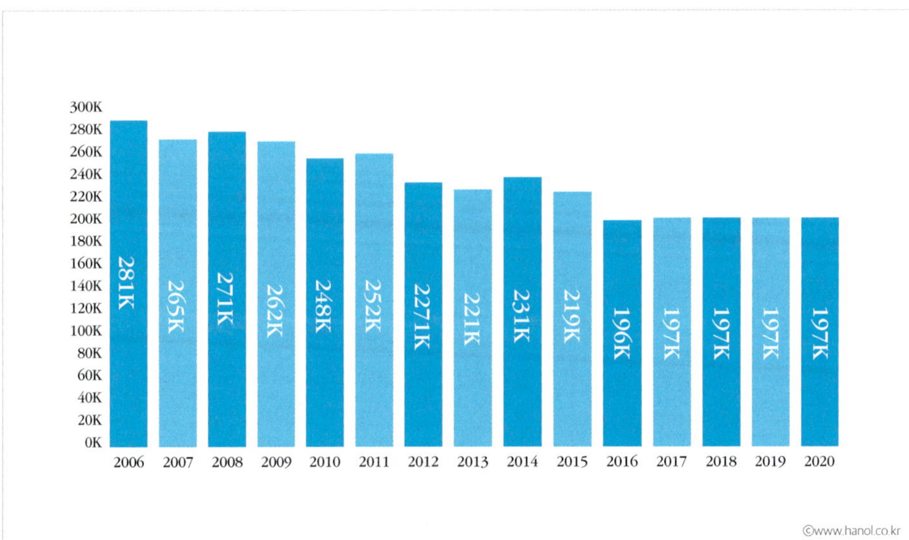

Meanwhile, Harvard University has also proposed a short-term goal for being fossil fuel neutral by 2026.

① Prioritize the active reduction of campus energy use.

② Invest in off-campus projects, such as renewable energy, to offset or neutralize remaining greenhouse gas emissions.

③ Engage researchers and industrial climate leaders to identify and, where possible, invest in projects that reliably reduce emissions while providing positive benefits for human health, social equity, and ecosystem health.

- **Yale:** In 2016, Yale University established the 'Sustainability 2025 Plan', which included 38 measurable and time-constrained goals in 9 areas and publishes a sustainability progress report every year.
- **MIT:** MIT reports the Sustainability Initiative Report every year, and in 2016, the Student Leadership Report 'MIT Student Sustainability Recommendation 2016' was prepared and published by the Sustainability Working Group, which serves as a starting point for collective future actions on campus sustainability.
- **US:** Many American universities including Stanford University (Sustainability Report 2020-2021), University of North Carolina Chapel Hill (Sustainability Report 2021), University of California (Annual Sustainability Report 2012-2020), North Carolina State University (Annual Sustainability Report 2020), etc. are publishing sustainability reports.
- **Japan:** Osaka University (Environmental Report 2006-2021), Chiba University (Environmental Report 2004-2018, Sustainability Report 2019), Hokkaido University (Environmental Report 2005-2014, Sustainability Report, 2015-2020), etc. issue the Environmental or Sustainability Report.
- **UK:** Oxford (Environmental Sustainability Report 2012-2013, 2015-2017, 2018-2019, 2019-2020), Cambridge (Environmental Sustainability Report 2019-2020), University of London (Annual Sustainability Report 2018-2019), University of Exeter (Environmental Sustainability Report 2019-2020, Carbon Year-end Report 2019/2020) and the University of Manchester (Annual Sustainability Report, 2018-2019) are publishing sustainability reports that mainly emphasize the environmental sector.
- Other Cases: Free University of Berlin in Germany (Sustainability Report 2020), University of Freiburg (Environment Report 2018/2019-2019/2020), University of Basel in Switzerland (Sustainability Report 2019/2020), University of Gothenburg in Sweden (Sustainability Report 2009-2012, Sustainability Report 2013-2019), University

Suggested ESG Reporting Items for Korean Universities

AS IS	TO BE
No representative examples	**Outline** Stakeholder engagement Materiality assessment Education Research Industry-University cooperation Internationalization **Environmental** Energy consumption Renewable energy production and usage Water consumption Greenhouse gas emissions and reduction results Air pollutant emissions Water recycling capacity Wastewater discharge Waste generation **Social** Human rights management Talent management Occupational safety and health Win-win cooperation with the supply chain Customer satisfaction management Information protection Social contribution Community activities **Governance** Governance (Foundation Board) How to appoint the president, etc. Risk management Ethical management **Appendix** **ESG Factbook**

of Aalto in Finland (Sustainability Report 2019), UBC University in Canada (Annual Sustainability Report 2019-2020), University of Waterloo (Environmental Sustainability Report 2020), University of Melbourne in Australia (Sustainability Report 2020) and the University of Victoria in Wellington, New Zealand (Sustainability Report 2020) are also publishing standardized sustainability reports.

As such, ESG management using the sustainability report can be said to be the area that universities should lead the most through systematic theories and models. However, the fact that universities are not reporting their own sustainability reports is interpreted as showing a serious contradiction while there are many arguments by university professors and researchers who insist on responding to climate disasters like in Korea. To systematically establish ESG management reporting through the sustainability report from universities, rather than relying on external consulting companies, the university's higher education system can be developed through voluntary consultations and practical activities among universities led by the *Korea University Education Council*, in which university professors and experts participate. It should be induced to write in a way that distinguishes their characteristics, location, and scale etc.

The Practice of
ESG Management

Epilogue

ESG as Objective Functions for Strategic Management

Due to the climate changes and the COVID-19 pandemic, the practice of ESG (Environmental, Social, Governance) management with CSR (corporate social responsibility) management is increasingly emphasized. As we mentioned earlier, Bill Gates measured Earth's annual greenhouse gas emissions in tons of carbon dioxide equivalent and suggested 51 billion tons.

> Globally, 31% of greenhouse gas emissions from manufacturing such as cement, iron, and plastics, 27% from electricity production, 19% from plant and animal husbandry, 16% of means of transport such as airplanes, freighters and trucks, and heating and cooling installations. It is said that 7% of cases result from the operation of refrigerators, etc.

Korea's greenhouse gas emissions stood at 73 million tons in 2019, and the government has announced an ambitious target to reduce net greenhouse gas emissions to zero by 2050, according to the 2050 global carbon neutrality policy.

- The reason that the environmental (E) area is highlighted in *the practice of ESG management* is that the target year has been presented as an international standard. In the environmental field GHG (greenhouse gas) emission (direct GHG emission, energy indirect GHG emission, other indirect GHG emission, GHG intensity, GHG emission reduction, ozone layer depleting substances emission, other important air emissions, etc.), energy, raw materials, water, waste, and biodiversity are emphasized as global standard indicators.
- In the social (S) area, human rights, employees (employment, labor relations, occupational safety and health, training and education, diversity, non-discrimination, freedom of association and right to collective bargaining, child labor, forced labor, security

practices), supply chain, shared growth, customers (safety and health, marketing and labeling, information protection), public policy, taxation, and social contribution are required to be reported, and ESG management performance is especially emphasized throughout the supply chain.

- In the area of governance (G), reporting to the BOD, risk management, and ethical management (anti-corruption, anti-competition, etc.), the weights and details of the indicators are required to be strategically restructured. Here, while considering the existing *negative screening* method that judges whether a company is eligible, the *positive screening* focusing on the exemplary companies is strongly required for the desirable practice of ESG management in Korea.

In the case of Korea, the issue of social fairness and equity is emphasized, and interest in transparent governance is growing due to the abuse of power and the decision-making activities such as the scarecrow of the board of directors. Therefore, although ESG may be appeared as a trend, our practical wisdom requires to take advantage of the opportunities of the responsible ESG management, utilizing SDGs and GRI Standards that have come into the business world. In other words, the principle *of "authority comes with responsibility"* should now be engraved as a corporate strategic issue that is faithful to the principle *"the more you take responsibility, the greater your authority"*.

Until now, environmental protection, social contribution, and governance issues have been treated as major variables in the *'constraint function'* in corporate management activities. However, it is now required to utilize all these ESG areas as *'objective functions'* for corporate strategic management to be actively pursued. Thus, through *'the practice of ESG management'*, the corporate stakeholder groups should protect the global environment and support social responsibility in a fairer and more transparent society, so that they can look at the fairness and transparency of governance, and ethical integrity management.

References

- Alderfer C.P. (1972), *Existence, Relatedness, and Growth: Human Needs in Organizational Settings*, Free Press.
- Ali M., and Park K. (2016), "The mediating role of an innovative culture in the relationship between absorptive capacity and technical and non-technical innovation", *Journal of Business Research*, vol.69, no.5, pp.1669~1675.
- Allen D.G. (2018), "Rethinking Impact", *Journal of Management*, vol 44, issue 7.
- Ann S.A. (2012), "Sustainability report, transition from G3.1 system to G4 system", *CGS Report* No.19, pp.12-15 (*Korean*).
- Barney J. (1991), "Firm Resources and Sustained Competitive Advantage", *Journal of Management*, vol.17, issue 1.
- Bell D. (1973), *The Coming of Post-industrial Society: A Venture in Social Forecasting*, Basic Books, N.Y.
- Berg F., Kölbel J.F., Rigobon R. (2019), "Aggregate Confusion: The Divergence of ESG Ratings", *SSRN*: https://ssrn.com/abstract=3438533 (revised 21 Jan 2022).
- Bird F.E., and Germain G.L. (1996), *Loss Control Management: Practical Loss Control Leadership*, Revised Edition, Det Norske Veritas.
- Bowen H.R. (1953), *Social Responsibility of the Businessman*, University of Iowa Press.
- Carroll A.B. (1979), "A Three-Dimensional Conceptual Model of Corporate Social Performance", *Academy of Management Review, 4*(4), 497–505.
- __________ (1991), "The Pyramid of Corporate Social Responsibility: Toward the Moral Management of Organizational Stakeholders", *Business Horizon* 34(4):39-48.
- __________ (1999), "Corporate Social Responsibility: Evolution of a Definitional Construct", *Business and Society, 38*(3), 268–295.
- __________ (2004), "Managing ethically with global stakeholders: A present and future challenge", *Academy of Management Executive, 18*(2), 114–120.
- __________ (2008), *A history of corporate social responsibility: Concepts and practices,* The Oxford handbook of corporate social responsibility.
- __________ (2015), "Corporate social responsibility", *Organizational Dynamics*, 44(2).
- Chang A. (2021), "Patagonia shows corporate activism is simpler than it looks", *Los Angeles Times*: https://www.latimes.com/business/story/2021-05-09/patagonia (9 May 2021).
- Cheng B., Ioannou I., and Serafeim G. (2014), "Corporate Social Responsibility and Access to Finance", *Strategic Management*, vol 35, issue 1.

- Chevalier F. & Dejoux C. (2021), "Intelligence artificielle et Management des ressources humaines: pratiques d'entreprises, *Enjeux Numériques*, No 15, Annales des Mines.
- Choi J.C. (2006), "Social Responsibility Management and Sustainability Reporting: Focusing on the analysis of domestic companies' introduction of sustainability reports", *Business Ethics Research*, vol 11, Korea Academy of Business Ethics (*Korean*).
- Choi Y.C. (2011), "Applicability of performance management of logic model", *Policy Analysis and Evaluation Journal*, 21(3), 13-38 (*Korean*).
- Christensen D.M., Serafeim G., and Sikochi A. (2021), "Why is Corporate Virtue in the Eye of the Beholder? The Case of ESG Ratings". *The Accounting Review*, https://doi.org/10.2308/TAR-2019-0506.SSRN:https://ssrn.com/abstract=3793804.
- Cookson A. & Niessner M. (2020), "Why Don't We Agree? Evidence from a Social Network of Investors", *The Journal of Finance*, vol 75, issue 1, pp.173-228.
- Crozier M. (1982), *"On ne change pas la société par décret"*, Collection Pluriel.
- Davis K. (1960), "Can Business Afford to Ignore Social Responsibilities?", *California Management Review*, vol 2, issue 3.
- Dawar N. (2013), "When Marketing is Strategy", *Harvard Business Review* (Dec 2013).
- Deloitte (2021), "Trends and Leading Companies of Carbon Capture Utilization Storage Technology", *Deloitte Insights Editorial Board*, No.19.
- Delta Air Lines (2021), "Delta named the World's Most Admires Airline by Fortune Magazine for the 10th time", *Delta News Hub* (1 Feb 2021).
- Drucker P.F. (1954), *The Practice of Management*, Harper & Row
- __________, (1973), *Management: Task, Responsibility, Practices*, Harper & Row
- __________, (2008), *The Essential Drucker: The Best of Sixty Years of Peter Drucker's Essential Writings on Management*, Harper Business.
- Drucker P.F., and Frances Hesselbein Leadership Institute (Editor, 2008), *The Five Most Important Questions You Will Ever Ask About Your Organization*, Jossey-Bass.
- Eccles R.G., Ioannou I., and Serafeim G. (2014), "The Impact of Corporate Sustainability on Organizational Processes and Performance", *Management Science*, 60(11), pp.2381-2617.
- Elkington J. (1997), *Cannibals with Forks: The Triple Bottom Line of 21st Century Business*, Capstone.
- __________ (1998), "Accounting for the Triple Bottom Line: Measuring Business Excellence", *Journal of Enterprise Information Management*, vol 2, no 3, pp. 18-22.
- __________ (2007), "Partnerships from cannibals with forks: The triple bottom line of 21st-century business", *Journal of Environmental Quality*, vol 8, issue 1, pp.37-51.
- Euronext (2020), *Exchange in Focus: Euronext ESG Guidelines for listed compa-*

nies, Sustainable Stock Exchanges Initiatives.
- European Commission (2020), *Circular Economy Action Plan*, European Union.
- FKI (2007), *Ethical Management Self-Assessment Index*, Federation of Korean Industries (*Korean*).
- ____ (2021), *ESG Readiness and Perception Survey for the 500 largest domestic companies*, Federation of Korean Industries (*Korean*).
- Fortune (2022), "World's Most Admired Companies", *Fortune Magazine* (Feb 2, 2022)
- Frederick W.C. (1960), "The Growing Concern Over Business Responsibility", *California Management Review*, vol 2, issue 4.
- Freibott B. (2013), *Sustainable safety management: incident management as a cornerstone for a successful safety culture*, Safety and Security Engineering V, WIT Press.
- Freshfields Report (2005), *ESG-A Legal Framework for the Integration of Environmental, Social and Governance Issues into Institutional Investment*, Freshfields Bruckhaus Deringer.
- ____________ (2009), *Fiduciary Responsibility: legal and practical aspects of integrating environmental, social and governance issues into institutional investment*, Freshfields Bruckhaus Deringer.
- Friedman M. (1970), *The social responsibility of business is to increase its profits*, New York Times Magazine.
- Friedman M. (2020), *Capitalism and Freedom*, University of Chicago Press.
- Gates B. (2021), *How to Avoid a Climate Catastrophe: The Solutions We Have and the Breakthroughs We Need*, Penguin Random House.
- GRI (2000), *Sustainability Reporting Guidelines: Reporting of economic, environmental, and social performance.*
- ____ (2002), *Sustainability Reporting Guidelines.*
- ____ (2006), *Sustainability Reporting Guidelines G3.*
- ____ (2011), *Sustainability Reporting Guidelines G3.1.*
- ____ (2013), *Sustainability Reporting Guidelines G4.*
- ____ (2018), *Consolidated Set of GRI Sustainability Reporting Standards.*
- GRI News Center (2021), "GRI and SASB reporting complement each other" (8 April 2021).
- Guenster N, Derwall J, Bauer. R, and Koedijk K. (2011), "The Economic Value of Corporate Eco-Efficiency", *European Financial Management*, vol 17, issue 4, pp.679-704.
- Ha H.J. (2011), "Main contents of GRI G3.1 guideline revision", *Eco-Frontier Sustainability Issue Papers*, No.122, ECO201105 (*Korean*).
- Hammer M., and Champy J.A. (1993), *Reengineering the Corporation: A Manifesto for Business Revolution*, Harper Business Books.

- Harrison S. (2020), *ERG Theory, Maslow's Need Hierarchy, And How Alderfer's ERG Explanation of Motivations Differs from Maslow's Hierarchy of Needs, Needs*, Independently published.
- Harvard University (2021), "Harvard Greenhouse Gas Emission (MTCDE)", *Green Harvard.*
- Heald M. (1970), *The Social Responsibilities of Business, Company, and Community, 1900-1960*, Routledge (2018).
- Heinrich W.H. (1931), *Industrial Accident Prevention: A Scientific Approach*, 4th Edition (1959), McGraw-Hill Book Company, Inc.
- HERI, "The appearance is world-class, but the practice of social responsibility appears in various ways.", *HERI Review* No. 10 (24 June 2011).
- Hoang L. (2017), "Patagonia's circular economy strategy", *Business of Fashion* (16 Jan 2017). Available at: https://www.businessoffashion.com/articles/news-analysis/how-patagonia-transformed-the-circular-economy.
- Hofstede G. (1983), "National cultures in four dimensions: A research-based theory of cultural differences among nations", *International Studies of Management and Organization, 13*(1/2), 46–74.
- Hubbard T.D., Christensen D.M., and Graffin S.D. (2017), "Higher Highs and Lower Lows: The Role of Corporate Social Responsibility in CEO Dismissal", *Strategic Management Journal*, 38(11).
- Hyundai Motors (2022), *2021 Hyundai Motor Company Sustainability Report.*
- Jensen M.C (2002), "Value Maximization, Stakeholder Theory, and the Corporate Objective Function", *Business Ethics Quarterly*, vol 12, no 2, pp.235-256.
- Johnson H.L. (1971), *Business in contemporary society: Framework and issues*, Belmont, CA: Wadsworth.
- Jones T.M. (1980), "Corporate Social Responsibility Revisited, Redefined", *California Management Review*, vol 22, pp.59-67.
- Kaplan D.P., and Norton R.S. (1996), *The Balanced Scorecard: Translating Strategy into Action*, Harvard Business School Press.
- Khan M., Serafeim G., and Yoon A. (2016), "Corporate Sustainability: First Evidence on Materiality", *The Accounting Review*, vol 91, no 6.
- Korean Air (2022), *2021 Korean Air ESG Report.*
- Lee J.O (2021), "Why ESG Now", *KOSIF*, (3 Oct. 2021, *Korean*).
- Lewin K. (1939), "Field Theory and Experiment in Social Psychology: Concept and Methods", *American Journal of Sociology*, vol 44, no 6.
- Markovits D. (2019), *The Meritocracy Trap: How America's Foundational Myth Feeds Inequality, Dismantles the Middle Class, and Devours the Elite*, Penguin Books.
- McGuire J.W. (1963), *Business and Society*, McGraw-Hill.

- Mckinsey & Company (2020), "The ESG premium: New perspectives on value and performance".
- Morgan J. (2018), "The North Face channel issues SWOT analysis", *Case 48* (15 Feb 2018). Available at: https://www.case48.com/swot-case/38161-The-North-Face-Channel-Issues.
- Nonaka I., and Takeuchi K. (1995), *The Knowledge Creating Company,* Oxford University Press.
- Park K. (1997), *Team Performance Appraisal,* Korea Management Association (*Korean*).
- ______ (1999), *Social Audit,* Korea Management Association (*Korean*).
- ______ (2015), *Professor Kichan PARK on Strategic Management,* Inha University Press.
- ______ (2020), *Team Activity Value Analysis Report,* Inha Vision Committee (*Korean*).
- ______ (2021), *ESG and Sustainable Society,* https://youtu.be/mpvi_6F1c84 (*Korean*).
- Park K., Ali M., and Chevalier F. (2012), "Desirable ethical climates on Organizational effectiveness", *African Journal of Business Management,* 6(14).
- Park K., and Chevalier F. (2010), "The Winning Strategy of the Late-comer: How Korea was awarded the UAE Nuclear Power Contract", *International Review of Business Research papers,* 6(2), pp.221-238.
- Park K., and Cho B.S. (2009), "Business Ethics Practice Mechanism and Business Ethics Index Development", *Korean Journal of Business Ethics,* vol.11, no 1. The Korea Academy of Business Ethics (*Korean*).
- Park K., and Choi J.C. (1999), "Establishment of the Korean-style social reporting system – Focused on Bilan Social", *Industrial Relations Research,* volv10 (Nov. 1999), Center for Industrial Relations, Seoul National University (*Korean*).
- Park K., and Woo K.H. (2021), "Korean Air's Moment of Truth Realized through the Management Philosophy 'SAFER'", in *K-Management from Incheon,* Knowledge Platform.
- Park K., Cho J.R., and Park J.H. (2015), "Competence-Evaluation Modeling for Positive Safety Culture: In and Around of Nuclear Power Industry", *Creativity and Innovation,* Peter Drucker Society of Korea, 8(2), pp.197-235.
- Park K., Lee Y.C., Lee D.H. (2005), *Management Gurus* (*Readings on Management Culture*), Denan Publishing (*Korean*).
- Porter M.E., and Kramer M.R. (2011), "Creating Shared Value: How to reinvent capitalism and unleash a wave of innovation and growth", *Harvard Business Review* (Jan-Feb 2011).
- POSCO (2021), *POSCO Corporate Citizenship Report 2021.*

- Ray R., Toler D., Canales M., and Nyfeler M. (2015), "Siemens Scandal" (21 Sep 2015).
- Ricardo D. (1817), *On the Principles of Political Economy and Taxation*, Batoche Books (2001).
- Samsung Electronics (2022), *Samsung Electronics Sustainability Report 2021.*
- Seo J.Y. (2017), "GRI social reporting standards change from G4 to Standard", *Sustainability Journal* (4 June 2017, *Korean*).
- Shine E.H. (2010), *Organizational Culture & Leadership,* 4th Edition, Jossey-Bass
- Simon H. (1955), "A Behavioral Model of Rational Choice", *The Quarterly Journal of Economics*, 69(1), pp.99-118.
- Sinek S. (2009). *Start With Why: How Great Leaders Inspire Everyone to Take Action*, Penguin.
- Smith A. (1759), *Theory of Moral Sentiment: To which is added a dissertation on the origin of language*, Gutenberg Publishers (26 March 2011).
- _______ (1776), *The Wealth of Nations,* CreateSpace Independent Publishing Platform (1 Nov 2018).
- Song E.H. (2018), "EU companies to disclose non-financial information starting this year", *News Tomato* (15 Jan 2018, *Korean*).
- Spreckley F. (1981), *Social Audit-A Management Tool for Cooperative Working*, Beechwood College.
- Taylor F.W. (1911), *The Principle of Scientific Management*, Dove Publications (1997).
- Toffler A. and Toffler H. (2007), *Revolutionary Wealth: How it will be created and how it will change our lives,* Currency; Reprint edition (12 June 2007).
- Trépo G., and de Geuser (2003), "Managing the unmanageable: How can SEAM give back to employees and work situations their anthropological original substance?", *Journal of Organizational Change Management*, vol 16, issue 1, pp.99-106.
- UNEP (1987), *The Brundtland Commission Report 'Our Common Future'*, United Nations Environment Program.
- UNEP FI (2005, 2009), *The 'Freshfields Report'*, United Nations Environment Program Finance Initiative.
- UNGC (2005), *Who Cares Wins-Connecting Financial Markets to a Changing World,* United Nations Global Compact.
- Visser W. (2011), *The Age of Responsibility-CSR 2.0 and the New DNA of Business,* University of Cambridge Programme for Sustainability Leadership.
- Wallace-Wells D. (2019), *The Unhabitable Earth: Life After Warming*, Tim Duggan Books.
- WSJ (2021), "BlackRock at Odds with Warren Buffett's Berkshire Hathaway over Disclosures", *The Wall Street Journal* (6 May 2021).

Index

S

T

U

V

The Practice of
ESG Management

About Authors

Kichan PARK is a leading researcher in Organizational Behavior and Strategic Management, currently serving as, president of the Institute for Industrial Policy Studies (IPS), chair professor at Seoul Business School (aSSIST), director of the Jungseok-Inha Education Foundation, Consultant Committee member of Zhejiang University International Business School in China, and president of Korea Society for Sustainability Management (KSSM). Academic experiences in France; Sciences-Po IEP Paris for a DEA in sociology, HEC Paris Business School for PhD in management, researcher at INSEAD, professor at UBC in Vancouver Canada and PSU in Phuket Thailand, pushed him to think more about global sustainability management. Doctor Park introduced *Team Performance Appraisal System* (1997) and *Social Audit* (1999) in Korea with the same titled books, followed by *Management Gurus* (2005), *Strategic Management* (2015, 2017), *Organizational Behavior* (2015, 2017, 2021), *K-Management from Incheon* (2021), with awarded academic papers on leadership, business ethics, and knowledge management. His professional experiences include the chairman of the BOD of Korea Airports Corporation, senior vice-president of Korean Air in addition to active intervention and consulting for Incheon International Airport Corporation, PwC-Samil, Deloitte, Samsung Electronics, SK, and LG Group in management innovation.

Jeongchul CHOI is a researcher in Strategic Management, Organizational Development and HRM, currently serving as professor of Inha University, and executive vice president of Incheon Port Authority (IPA) as well as vice president of Korean Academic Society of Business Administration (KASBA). He received a doctorate in business administration with Social Performance Appraisal Framework for Korean companies. He served as an outside director of Incheon International Airport Corporation (IIAC) and as the chief secretary of the mayor of Incheon Metropolitan City. His major books include *Ask the Way to People and*

the President: 100 key performance indicators that the President should take care of (2014), and *Best practices for corporate human rights management and development of Self-diagnosis tools* (2009).

Françoise CHEVALIER holds a PhD from HEC Paris Business School and the French HDR qualification as a supervisor of doctoral research. She is associate professor in the Management and Human Resources department at HEC. Françoise teaches Master, Doctorate and Executive Education courses and has been a visiting scholar at UC Berkeley. Her research concerns Management Innovation, Organizational Change, Leadership and Human Resources Management, Creativity and Pedagogy. She specializes in qualitative, comparative, longitudinal research methods, and several of the HEC PhD dissertations supervised by Françoise have won national and international prizes. Her most recent publications include: *Gestion du changement: vers un management polyphonique* (2021), *La recherche enracinée en management: contextes nouveaux et perspectives nouvelles en Afrique* (2020), *Research Methods for the DBA* (2019). Currently Françoise is a member of the editorial board of *Gérer et Comprendre* and writes for academic and professional journals.

The Practice of ESG Management

first edition January 30, 2023

author	Kichan PARK · Jeongchul CHOI · Françoise CHEVALIER
publisher	Im Soonjae
place of publication	**Hanol Publishing Co., Ltd.**
registration	No. 11-403
address	83, Sandaenae-ro, Mapo-gu, Seoul
telephone	82-2-376-4298
fax	82-2-302-8073
website	www.hanol.co.kr
e-mail	hanol@hanol.co.kr
ISBN	**979-11-6647-314-2**

• Acknowledgment omitted in consultation with the author.
• Book prices are on the back cover.

The Practice of
ESG Management

The Practice of
ESG Management

The Practice of
ESG Management